C H O O S I N G

S I M P L I C I T Y

Best wishes,

Lynda Breen Pierce

CHOOSING SIMPLICITY

Real People Finding Peace and Fulfillment
in a Complex World

Linda Breen Pierce

Gallagher Press

Attention Organizations, Corporations, Universities and Community Groups:

Quantity discounts are available on bulk purchases of this book for educational, promotional, or fund raising purposes. For information, contact Gallagher Press at PO Box 4136, Carmel, CA 93921 or via E-mail: info@gallagherpress.com.

The individual experiences recounted in this book are true, as reported to the author. However, in some instances, the names and other identifying details have been changed to protect the privacy of the individuals involved.

Grateful acknowledgment is given for permission to reprint excerpts from *Biogenic Dwelling* by Edmond Bordeaux Szekely. Copyright © International Biogenic Society, 1988. By permission of the International Biogenic Society.

PUBLISHER'S CATALOGING-IN-PUBLICATION DATA

Pierce, Linda Breen.
    Choosing simplicity : real people finding peace and fulfillment in a complex world / Linda Breen Pierce. – 1st ed.
        p.   cm.
    Includes bibliographical references and index.
    LCCN: 99-63503
    ISBN: 0-9672067-1-5

    1. Simplicity.   2. Conduct of life.   I. Title.
    BJ1496.P54   2000   178

First edition

Cover design: Mayapriya Long, Bookwrights
Cover photograph: John Foster/Masterfile

Printed and bound in the United States of America
This book is printed on acid free 20% post consumer waste recycled paper.

10 9 8 7 6 5 4 3 2 1

I dedicate this book to my parents,
Tom and Elaine Breen,
who taught me to embrace life with gusto,
without fear or limitation, and to
Jim Pierce,
my husband and best friend.

Contents

Acknowledgments

Researching and writing this book has been an incredible four–year journey. So many people helped me along the way. I want to express my deepest appreciation and gratitude to the following people:

♦ To Duane Elgin, Timothy Miller, Vicki Robin, Marsha Sinetar, and to the memory of Joe Dominguez. Reading your books inspired and moved me, giving me the personal conviction to embark on this project.

♦ To Jacque Blix and David Heitmiller. I will always remember your generous assistance throughout this project, especially in the early phases when I was new to the simplicity movement.

♦ To Vicki Robin for writing the best Foreword I have ever read. Your writing talent inspires me to continue to develop my craft.

♦ To Janis Waldrop Fields, my first writing teacher and coach. Your encouragement gave me the confidence to dare to write this book. Your critique of the early drafts of the book was invaluable.

♦ To Hal Zina Bennett, the editor of this book. You are the editor of every writer's dream. Brilliant, funny, honest, to the point, and hopeful. What more could a writer ask for?

♦ To Colleen Russell, my "Irish sister." I have been blessed with your generosity and support. Thank you for your conscientious review of the manuscript and your enthusiasm.

♦ To my dear friends, Elizabeth Smith, Max Firstman and Sharon Miller. You were there from beginning to end, sharing the thrills and disappointments along the way, and patiently listening to my constantly changing ideas for book titles. Thank you for your unwavering support.

♦ To my parents, Tom and Elaine Breen, and to my seven brothers and sisters and their spouses, all of whom provided ongoing support.

♦ To my dearest husband, Jim. I never would have made it without your constant and unequivocal support. Thank you for supporting us financially for the four years it took me to do the research and writing for this book.

♦ And finally, to the 211 people who responded to the simplicity survey and my endless questions. Thank you for opening up your hearts and souls in sharing your experiences of simplicity. Your stories inspired and enriched me. Without you, this book would not exist.

Foreword

by Vicki Robin

You are in for a treat. The stories in this book are rich in texture and color, the warp on which you will find yourself weaving reflections about your own life. Some people here may have made choices just like the ones you have found, affirming decisions that seemed obvious to you but odd to others. You might be inspired by details in these stories to take the next steps towards reclaiming your life. Since the participants in The Pierce Simplicity Study were delightfully candid about their mistakes, there might be a story here that saves you from setting off down an ill-conceived path. Linda weaves her own experiences and insights throughout and brings a great deal of joy and respect to the telling of each story. The characters are very different from one another, and she molds words around the framework of each life that highlight their unique courage and goodness. I can just imagine her pleasure at sitting with these 200 or so interviews, jewels every one, sifting for meaning and pattern.

I was personally struck with the radical sanity of these people. They are subversively ordinary. They have the uncommon virtue of common sense. Most still live in houses, drive cars and have jobs. The sanity comes from the fact that they have pruned out the dead matter from their lives. This cutting out of excess, like having the huge elm tree in our back yard trimmed, actually makes the living being more handsome, more itself. At first blush, most folks here seem so wholesome that you could wonder if you'd hit a minor speed bump in the space-time continuum and ended up in the Midwest in the 50's. They enjoy such innocent luxuries as time for family and leisure and evening walks in the park. This very ordinariness is extraordinary in a world coming rapidly unglued.

Their common sense reminds me of the story of two novice Zen monks arguing about whose master was more evolved. One claimed that his teacher was so powerful that he could stand on one bank of a river and write his name in the sand on the other shore. "That's nothing," the second one said (thus winning the debate), "When my master is hungry he eats and when he is tired he sleeps." Modern life, with all its overload, stress and clutter, has become a form of senseless torture, and the genius of the people profiled here is that they have figured out how to stop hurting themselves.

But don't mistake the simple life for the sedate life. While these people are embracing a more measured pace and shunning the fast lane, there's plenty of high drama in these pages. There's nothing like facing divorce, disease or death (as no small number here did) to quicken the blood and bring priorities into exquisite relief. And, while most of these folks spend way less on stuff, they often indulge in travel, philanthropy and (for me the grandest quest of all) finding ways that their gifts match the needs of the world. For them, "simplicity" means being more alive than they've ever been.

As Linda says again and again, the simple life isn't the easy life. Each soul here is enormously courageous. The conflicts in their lives have not been trivial. It's taken most of them a great deal of time, introspection and explanation to arrive at their chosen sanity. They are intrepid explorers, leaving the security of the known for the hoped-for brighter tomorrow. Quite a few have fallen down and taken wrong turns along the way—and kept on keeping on. They have inherited the American predilection for individualism and autonomy (but rarely lose that balancing American virtue of neighborliness). Some are "off the grid" in terms of self sufficiency, but even those who are plugged into urban culture are stitching together a unique quilt of life-pieces that makes them truly one-of-a-kind. Once you've read Donna's essay on *The Tao of Nobody* or met Q or Holli-Anne or Blake or the Brophy's or, well…all of them, you will see what I mean.

I detect a thin note of loneliness weaving through many of these stories as well. Having gotten off the work-and-spend treadmill, people often feel out of step with their social context. A few of those profiled lost some of their old friends; several became more reclusive and solitary (though many use their freed-up life energy to engage with their community and service projects more vigorously).

People often write to authors like me asking for guidance on how to connect with others who share their new values and practices. So often their friendships were based on going to restaurants, theater, sports events and other activities that entailed spending money. Do they demur or just order a salad or suggest a cheaper thrill? Gift giving becomes tense. How do you celebrate Christmas and birthdays and baby showers without buying expensive gifts? The homey joys of common, ordinary events can wear thin as they buck, again and again, the commodification of every aspect of daily life. Sanity and simplicity become a source of private pride but public shame. The frugal don't flaunt their choices, nor do they see them reflected in the media. Instead of being celebrated for a breakthrough into maturity, people who've come to their senses about living in balance sometimes feel subtly shunned. The pathetic irony of this dilemma, however, is that Americans are still basically thrifty people—my years of interacting with audiences across the country about *Your Money or Your Life* has taught me that. It's as though the ordinary, humble folks are all playing hide and seek in this big forest of advertising and malls. Someone just needs to end the game and say, "Olly Olly in come free." While the pervasiveness of thrift in America makes this loneliness unnecessary, the pain of it is still very real. So I doubly applaud these people for the changes they've made and Linda Pierce for celebrating them in print.

I find my own journey reflected in the progression of these chapters. Disillusioned and discouraged with the "career ladder to nowhere," I left New York City 30 years ago in search of...I didn't know. Bonding with the natural and authentic way of life I started to develop, I was motivated to minimize my cash needs to liberate my time. Then I was free to learn what Frithjof Bergmann calls "high tech self-providing"—a blend of skills from food production to auto mechanics, from small-town neighborliness to spiritual practice. Having found and grounded myself, I naturally came to a passion for service. What is needed in the world? How can I provide it using my unique set of skills and abilities? That was 20 years ago and the journey has led me through planting and weeding other people's gardens, helping build others' homes and listening to others' problems. Eventually I arrived at my passion for thinking, writing and speaking about one of the burning issues of our times: how to wean Americans (and the world) from the destructive addiction to economic growth.

Linda's book and my own experiences have led me to wonder about the place in our culture of this phenomenon of simple (sane, common sense) living. Are the people in these pages and the estimated tens of millions more who are making lifestyle changes merely a sidebar to the ever increasing tempo of consumerism in our world? Or are they the forerunners of a more sustainable way of living that will originate right here in the heart of Babylon and fan out across the earth in the wake of a global disillusionment with the high-buck high-life? Have we done the world a favor by running the affluence experiment and finding it wanting? Will we then have the courage to admit our errors and help the rest of the world acquire the best of the West while avoiding our worst mistakes? I for one hope that The Pierce Simplicity Study is a harbinger of a large (and largely leaderless) personal, social and political revolution. The possibilities for such a gradual grassroots shift in the tenor of our culture are truly exciting. A slow shedding of the unnecessary, an increasing attunement to the gift of being alive, a strengthening of human bonds, a tenderness and protectiveness towards the earth, an unearthing of all our quirky capacities for humor, art, innovation and caring. With luck siestas and spontaneous singing might eventually be acceptable! Or maybe the change will happen with great gusto, with a third political party thundering to center stage sporting a kind of Populist vigor and a well-thought out agenda for sweeping reforms. Or maybe this book is a testimony to the fact that the future guise of the simplicity impulse may not matter. What matters is that the people in these pages, a relatively small portion of a very large cultural cohort, demonstrate beyond a shadow of a doubt that living more simply, soulfully and servicefully is an idea whose time is now.

So, drink deep. But before you do, how about a walk around the block, a look at the birds, a chat with your mate, a letter to the editor, or a dreamy few minutes just staring out the window and not thinking about anything much at all…. See?

Vicki Robin
Coauthor of *Your Money or Your Life*

Preface

The inspiration for this book originated in 1968 in a small rural village in Senegal, West Africa. I was twenty years old at the time. For three months I lived in this village of 400 people who had no running water, electricity, plumbing, dishwashers, TV's, calculators, or cameras. People lived in simple mud huts clustered along a few dirt paths. There was one car for the entire village. It was the first year of a seven-year drought. I lost 20 pounds from my already thin frame. Nothing that had happened before or since has affected me more. Everything I had learned from my relatively sheltered, middle-class upbringing was brought into question.

In some ways, this book is my attempt to make some sense of that experience. What I found in Senegal was a group of people who were more joyful, vibrant, fulfilled, and loving than 95 percent of the American people I have known, including myself. In that small bush village, it was difficult to distinguish work from play. We were always laughing, singing, and playing games while we ground up grains with pestles and mortars, carried water from the well, and worked in the fields. Humor was ever present and overflowing. You could not go for more than 15 minutes in that village without bursting out in a big belly laugh. Anger was expressed immediately, then released, followed by laughter. Sensuous music and dancing kept us up late every night.

However, life in an African bush village was not some sort of utopia; it was real life. I saw people suffer from malnutrition, skin ulcers and other medical problems. I held dying babies in my arms. There was not enough food. There were tears, yes, and plenty of worry about whether it would ever rain. But somehow, in spite of all of life's challenges and disappointments, these people had a greater sense of well-being, a more intimate and rewarding community life, a deeper spiritual awareness and more joy and fun in their lives than any other people I've come to know.

I returned from Senegal and fell into step with the times, living the life of a typical American "yuppie" baby boomer. I graduated from college, married, and then divorced five years later. I then obtained my admission ticket to a professional life (a law degree), married a second time, and worked as a lawyer for ten years. Mixed into these marker events of my life were years spent working in clerical jobs and time spent traveling in foreign countries.

Then in September of 1995, I stumbled upon the concepts of *voluntary simplicity* and *simple living* when I read an article in *Worth* magazine entitled "Downshifters," by John Brant. I was delighted to discover that the thoughts and feelings that I had been ruminating on for years had been discussed, written about, and critiqued by others. Reading this article would change my life.

I immediately proceeded to read everything I could find on this topic. There was and continues to be a myriad of articles and books published about simple living and all its facets. Most of the simplicity books I read told me *why* or *how* to simplify my life, but I found little written about real people who had actually tried it. I became curious about what had happened in the lives of these people. What did simple living actually look like in the lives of real people? How did it translate into our modern day-to-day world? Could people who embrace this lifestyle sustain it over time? What were the downsides? Was it worth it? Did they miss their former lifestyles?

And so this book was born. In 1996, I started a research project known as *The Pierce Simplicity Study*. I designed a survey and set up a web site on the Internet for the project (http://www.mbay.net/ ~pierce). Between 1996 and 1998, I received 211 detailed survey responses from people living in 40 states and eight other countries. Over a period of several years, I corresponded with the study participants via e-mail to further clarify and understand their experiences. Additionally, I conducted in-depth telephone or person-to-person interviews with 40 participants in the study.

In calculating the total number of participants, I did not include their spouses and significant others, unless those people responded to the survey themselves. While many of the stories in this book relate to family life, the stories are presented from the point of view

of the person in the family who responded to the survey and participated in the interview.

I feel blessed and grateful to receive the gifts of these stories. People
opened up their hearts and souls, revealing impressive creativity and
diversity in the ways they choose to live. I see my role as a midwife,
bringing to life the stories of those who have the courage to walk
their own paths. Their stories are inspiring and humbling.

The events and experiences related in this book are true, to the
best of my knowledge, and as they have been related to me. In some
instances, I changed the names and other identifying characteristics
(primarily geographic locations or occupations) of the participants
to protect their privacy. The stories in this book relate to the experiences of the participants at the time they responded to the simplicity
survey (sometime between 1996 and 1998). Some of them have
made major changes in their lives since that time. While a few have
moved more in the direction of mainstream America, others have
further refined their lifestyle of simplicity.

I encourage you to read the chapters in the order of your interest
and curiosity. This is not a "how to" book, and you do not need to
read the chapters sequentially. There will be no final examination.
Depending on the time you have for reading, you might want to
read one story each day. You will find the people you meet in these
stories will stay with you for a while. You will think about them
from time to time as you work, do your errands, or take a walk.
They may occasionally show up in your conversations with friends
and family. It's best not to invite too many of them into your mental
home at once—they may overwhelm you!

In the chapters that follow, from time to time I step back from
the actual stories to reflect on the lessons to be gleaned from
the experiences of the person being profiled. To distinguish
my reflections from the flow of the person's story, I place my
commentary into a box, as is done in this paragraph.

I have discovered through my own experience that simplifying can greatly improve the quality of your life. Through the choices and decisions I've made, I have learned more about what is truly important to me than I learned in all my years of formal education. The experiences of the simplicity study participants as well as my own have convinced me that it is possible to reclaim the joy of life I discovered in that small village in Senegal.

Chapter One

Why Simplicity?

Joe and Cindy Pfender had it made. They owned a beautiful, brand new 2,200-square-foot home set on one-half acre outside of Houston. Their home was located in a lovely neighborhood brimming with Southern hospitality and seven community pools for those hot Texas summers. They were the proud parents of three children— Chelsea, six, Shane, two, and Quinn, the baby in the family.

Joe worked hard to provide this lifestyle for his family. Every morning he left for work at 7:00 A.M. and returned 12 or more hours later. His commute took 45 minutes each way. He spent his evenings reading and responding to over 200 e-mail messages related to his job as a regional sales manager for a major steamship line. Pressure from senior management and customers was constant, but Joe handled it quite well—at least that's how it appeared from the outside. He entertained his customers frequently with drinks and dinners in fine restaurants. Many weekends he was away on business trips. Joe had the feeling that his work week never really began or ended.

Not surprisingly, Cindy began to feel like a single parent. On those frequent evenings when Joe did not make it home for dinner, she hauled the kids off to a fast food restaurant for dinner, a distraction—something of a treat to compensate for their missing father and husband.

One day Chelsea came to her dad with a drawing and proudly announced, "Daddy, look what I did." Joe pointed to each person in the picture and asked Chelsea to tell him about each one. Chelsea responded, "That's Quinn. He's crying. That's Shane. He just hit

Quinn. I am reading a book and Mommy is cooking dinner." Chelsea then pointed to the one remaining figure, saying, "That's you, Daddy." "But why is my face all colored in?" Joe asked his daughter. "That's not your face, Daddy, that's the back of your head. You're working on your computer."

Chelsea's drawing was a stunning revelation to Joe. He envisioned his daughter all grown up and remembering her dad as a person who was always working, a person who was not there for her. At that moment, Joe understood what was most important to him. It was not the status and stimulation of his job, his house, the swimming pools, or the health club. It was his wife and his three children. As Joe reflected, "No amount of money or position or home or belongings can replace supporting one another and going through the process of raising our children together."

Joe and Cindy's story is representative of millions of people in the world today. As we move into the next millennium, people everywhere, but especially in North America, are questioning what it really means to have the "good life" we have worked so hard to achieve.

It has been a fifty-year odyssey to get where we are today. Shortly after World War II, we entered a period of great prosperity and material abundance—a prosperity that continues to grow unabated, except for minor fluctuations from time to time. But here we are, fifty years later, with many of us finding that our hearts and souls are hurting. The prosperity we have enjoyed—our larger and more luxurious homes that house our increasing cadre of furniture, clothes, gadgets and toys, in addition to our fancier cars, second homes, and lavish vacations—is just not enough. These things do not bring us the happiness and peace we hoped for and expected. According to the National Opinion Research Center at the University of Chicago, we Americans earn twice as much money at the close of the twentieth century than we did in 1957; yet, the percentage of people who report that they are "very happy" has declined during the same period.

In fact, we are struggling to make sense of the spiritual and emotional wasteland we call modern life. We feel trapped in an almost compulsive drive to amass more wealth, status, and power. There is an addictive quality to this consumer-driven lifestyle. No doubt about it, each additional boost of wealth, status, and power gives us a high that feels so good. But like any addiction, the high is fleeting, often leaving us feeling worse than ever and convinced that the solution is to get more.

If materialism is addictive, so is our desire for productivity and efficiency. We are constantly trying to milk the most out of each minute of the day—on the phone while doing something else (like driving), driving instead of walking, reading the newspaper while eating breakfast, watching TV while helping our kids with their homework. Our love affair with productivity and efficiency generates busy, chattering minds. We are like the lead robot character in the movie "Short Circuit," always clamoring for more input. Often we have trouble relaxing when we finally get some leisure time; we cannot easily escape the habit of working, thinking, and above all, saving time.

And we have plenty of company. When an addiction is the cultural norm, it is hard to realize we need help. After all, isn't everybody doing it? Gaining perspective on our condition is a real challenge when our society depends on our staying this way to continue its economic growth.

The 1995 report, *Yearning for Balance*, prepared by The Harwood Group and commissioned by the Merck Family Fund, concluded that we Americans feel our priorities are "out of whack, that materialism, greed, and selfishness increasingly dominate American life, crowding out a more meaningful set of values centered on family, responsibility, and community." However, the report also indicates that we are ambivalent about what to do. We are attached to our material comforts and do not want to give them up. At the same time, we are aware that our deepest aspirations are nonmaterial ones.

And what exactly are our deepest aspirations? What do we seek out of this experience called life on earth? These questions have engaged writers, thinkers, philosophers, and spiritual teachers since time began. I could not possibly address the full scope of these life questions. However, I suggest that most of what we want in life are aspects or manifestations of two overriding desires: inner peace and fulfillment. It is no secret that the pace of life and the organizational structure of work in America do not facilitate inner peace. Rather, they are fertile breeding grounds for agitation, fear, frustration, and anxiety. The corporate world spends millions of dollars a year hiring outside consultants to help them create less stressful and, incidentally, more productive environments. Yet, the problem continues to escalate.

We know, of course, that removing all sources of stress in our lives will not by itself make us happy. We also seek fulfillment; we seek to serve some purpose in this life, to feel that our lives have meaning. We seem to be genetically programmed to learn, to grow, and to make a contribution. And so, our individual life paths become yin and yang affairs. For example, we may try working in a certain job that is challenging and rewarding, bringing us fulfillment. At the same time, however, the job may not be congruent with our values, or the work activity or hours may be too intense, depriving us of inner peace. Peace and fulfillment do not always lead to one another; sometimes they lie at opposite poles. We are continually balancing the desire for inner peace—facilitated by a quiet, inner life—with the desire to go out into the world, interact with others, create, and contribute.

And it is in this respect that the practice of voluntary simplicity can help. Living simply can facilitate a life of balance, purpose, and joy. It allows us to gain perspective on our material needs and desires, which in turn gives us the opportunity to satisfy our nonmaterial drives for inner peace and fulfillment.

Getting Clear About What Simple Living Really Means

Throughout this book I use the terms "voluntary simplicity" and "simple living" interchangeably. We should pause to consider what we mean by these terms. The concept of simple living carries with it numerous myths and misconceptions. Perhaps the biggest misconception is that simple living is the same thing as easy living. Often, it is far from easy. Another common misconception is that simple living involves depriving oneself of the material benefits of modern life. Deprivation is not a part of the true meaning of simplicity. Voluntary is a key element of the philosophy of simple living. Living without adequate food, shelter, clothing, and medical care is not simple living. Nor is it voluntary simplicity; it is involuntary poverty.

The term simple living truly is a misnomer. More descriptive terms might include "mindful living" or "intentional living," terms that are neutral on the issue of whether more is better or less is more. In truth, sometimes more is better, depending on the person and the issue being considered. My best shot at a definition of simple living would go something like this: *Simple living or voluntary simplicity are lifelong processes in which we turn loose of the quest for more wealth, status, and power in favor of an authentic life of inner peace and fulfillment.*

When we view simple living or voluntary simplicity in this way, it becomes clear that there are no rigid rules to this approach to life. When thinking about simple living, some people envision moving to the country, growing their own food, chopping wood for fuel, and living in isolation. Others might picture a life in the city, living in a small, sparsely furnished apartment with no job. You may be surprised to know that only a small percentage of people who simplify their lives choose these lifestyles, which are more the exception than the rule. Many others who simplify live much more conventional lives, often continuing to work for a living, raise their families, explore their religious or spiritual interests, connect with their communities, and enjoy their leisure time.

Living simply is not about rejecting the material comforts in life. However, it does involve unburdening our lives, living more lightly with fewer distractions—whether they are material things, activities, or relationships. It means letting go of anything that interferes with a high quality life.

Many of us are attracted to simple living because our lives are stressful and complicated. Sometimes, we get to a point where we have all the outward appearances of success but feel a vague, unsettling emptiness inside. So, what can we do about this? How exactly do we simplify our lives? The answer is not merely to read a variety of how-to-simplify-your-life books and then select some tips and tricks to incorporate into your life. It involves a much more creative, complex, deep, and soul-searching process.

Simplicity requires a two-step process. First, we must invest the time and energy to discover what stirs us as human beings, what makes our hearts sing, and what brings us joy. Then, we must proceed to create the life that reflects the unique people we truly are. This is the heart and soul of simplicity and is what this book is all about.

Finding out who we really are and what we truly want is perhaps best discovered by learning about others who are in the process of doing the same. To those ends, we will look into the hearts and souls of those who have traveled this path and have been so generous to share their stories. We will experience their doubts, fears, false starts, "aha" moments, and their successes. We will learn what motivated them to start on their journey and what worked and did not work for them. Perhaps their experiences will give us the courage, inspiration, and confidence to embark on our own paths to simplicity.

For many of us, this process necessarily requires us to slow down a bit. It is nearly impossible to discover who we truly are inside if we are rushing through our mornings to get ready for work, squeezing in errands during our lunch hours or on our way home, collapsing in an emotional stupor in front of the TV in the evenings, and filling our weekends with chores and activities that numb us to the inner pain we are feeling. We have to slow down. We will learn from the stories in this book how slowing down and taking regular time for reflection enabled others to champion their authentic selves and how it can do the same for us.

For some people, the primary focus of voluntary simplicity is to enhance the quality of their lives. Often they talk about the joys of personal freedom, precious moments living in the present, relief from stressful or unsatisfactory work, deeper spirituality, and greater intimacy with family and friends. They have found that living simply brings them inner peace.

Others view voluntary simplicity as a means to experience a deeper connection with all other life on the planet. They emphasize taking action to preserve the earth's resources, working towards the realization of global, social and economic equality, and building strong, local communities of interdependence by sharing resources. Their personal sense of fulfillment is wedded to the goal of contributing some of themselves to make this a better world.

There have been some stimulating exchanges and debates in various Internet and other discussion forums about whether the true meaning of simple living is or should be more of the former (personal satisfaction) or more of the latter view (other-directed concerns). What I have learned from the participants in *The Pierce Simplicity Study* is that some people resonate with the former point of view, others favor the latter, but the vast majority of people find meaning in a balance between the personal and the other-directed aspects of simple living.

Another controversial issue debated in discussions on simple living is whether this lifestyle trend pertains primarily to those who are fairly well off, such as the group of professional baby boomers who are now middle-aged and have some savings, or whether simple living has something to offer those in the lower income brackets who have nothing that resembles a nest egg.

It is important to distinguish between people with low incomes and those who have insufficient means to obtain the basics of food, clothing and shelter. If we are struggling to provide the basic necessities for survival, in contrast to acquiring fancier cars, houses, TVs, and all the other accessories of modern life, we are less likely to focus on nonmaterial aspirations, such as inner peace and fulfillment. We are inclined to view the purpose of life as survival and little more. On the other hand, my experience of living in a Senegalese village taught me that even the lack of physical essentials does not negate the possibility of fulfillment and joy.

In any event—and this is especially true in our North American culture—once basic material needs are met and appear not to be threatened for the immediate future, we experience life on a different level. We experience different stresses and types of fulfillment. Our expectations change. For example, once getting a job, any job, is no longer an issue, we then expect our work to be satisfying on a deeper level. We look for further meaning and purpose beyond basic survival.

As you will see in the chapters that follow, the majority of the study participants do not come from high-income backgrounds. Nor do they have the benefit of substantial savings and investments. The principles of voluntary simplicity appear to work for all income levels, at least for those people who have the basic necessities in life.

The issues are different, of course, for the person who is struggling to get unburdened from mountains of debt and the person who is seeking to reinvent his or her life with sufficient financial resources. Even so, the process—the discovery of who you really are and the act of taking steps to create a life that reflects the real you—are the same for both.

Living simply is not an end in itself. It is a way to create lives filled with peace and fulfillment for ourselves and for others.

Chapter Two

My Story:
True Confessions of a Yuppie Lawyer

Most of us don't simply wake up one morning and decide to change the way we live. As a friend of mine reflected, "Coming to simplicity sometimes takes 20 years." In my own life, I know this to be true. Being the second of eight children born to Catholic parents who were neither rich nor poor, I am probably not that much different than most Americans born in the last five decades. My beginnings were modest and my quest for happiness covered a wide range. In the years between entering the convent at the age of sixteen, through becoming an attorney at age thirty, my life took many turns.

I earned a degree in African Studies and went on extended trips to Africa, the Galapagos Islands, and the South Pacific. Except for a five-year period in my early twenties when I was married, I lived on very little, alternating periods of work and college. That all changed when I married at age twenty-two. My husband's parents showered us with generous gifts, buying us beautiful clothes and treating us to lavish vacations in Hawaii, Puerto Rico, and Indonesia. As wonderful as it was to enjoy such material abundance, I felt a puzzling emptiness. After five years, my marriage ended—a simple case of two people who were too young to form a mature relationship.

After my divorce, I returned to my frugal ways while attending law school. A few years later, I obtained my law degree—my ticket to earn the *big bucks*—and came into my material own. I could afford a car, some nice clothes, and frequent ski trips. While I still needed to manage my money carefully, I didn't need to count every cent.

Within a few years I had doubled my income. Now, I had enough money to indulge all my material urgings. I bought silk suits for $500 each, not because I really desired such nice clothes, but for the sake of convenience. I met a designer and manufacturer of high-quality women's clothing who turned my shopping experience into a real pleasure. Loretta invited me to lunch in her office where we would dine on delicious seafood salads and white wine while I tried on clothes for several hours. Typically, we would meet for lunch two or three times each year, and I would always come home with $2,000 to $3,000 worth of clothes.

I married Jim, my second husband, in my early thirties. Jim was earning good money in the corporate world. We spent freely and thoughtlessly on expensive vacations, frequent restaurant meals, and regular household help. For a while, we hired a woman to come in every afternoon for four hours to clean our house, run our errands, launder our clothes, and prepare an elaborate dinner for us. We referred to Martha as "our wife." We would arrive home from work in the early evening, sit down with cocktails for our daily debriefing session, and eventually meander into the dining room where Martha would serve us dinner and then quietly slip out the door.

The Work Thing

The amount of money I earned as an attorney was not important to me for what it could buy, but it was vital to my self-image. My self-esteem seemed to rise in direct proportion to my salary increases. I could feel myself puffing up as I shared with close friends and family the successive annual salary increases I received in my corporate attorney position. When I surpassed the $100,000 mark and gained a Vice President title, a company car, stock options, and pension benefits, I figured I was a *success*. I was *somebody*.

I truly loved much of my work as an attorney. I thrived on the intellectual challenge and satisfaction. I am blessed with a logical, linear mind—but of course would prefer to have a poet's talent—and I took to legal analysis like a fish to water. I discovered I had abilities to organize and lead groups of people in major projects, such

as mergers and acquisitions. It was an unbelievable ego trip to perform well and to do so easily and naturally. I basked in the positive
strokes I received from my superiors and colleagues.

Although my experience as an attorney did wonders for my pocketbook and my ego, it did little for my soul. With few exceptions,
attorneys are, by definition, working with the breakdown of a relationship (litigation), or with the anticipation of a breakdown of a
relationship. I am not a person who thrives on conflict. I also found
a striking lack of courtesy, respect, and cooperation in the legal profession. Working as an attorney was draining the spirit out of me, bit
by bit, year by year.

Similarly, I found that working in a corporate environment was
enormously draining. While I could and did excel at playing corporate games, I did so at a great personal cost. I did not sleep well and
was often sick during those years. I became a tense, uptight person
who was only half-jokingly referred to by one of my colleagues as
"Colonel Breen." I had lost a part of my humanity.

I pushed myself to my limits in my work as an attorney. Sometimes I think I pushed myself beyond my limits. I would pour out
my feelings regularly in my journal. Eventually, there came a time
when I knew I had to leave. On the day I received a very positive
annual review and hefty salary increase, I came home and wrote
this poem:

Not for Sale

That was the surprise,
not the news,
not what was said,
or wasn't said,
but the discovery,
the bitter discovery,
that what I had given,
was not for sale.

My heart feels stolen,
my soul feels robbed,

they say, "We were taken,
unknowingly,
without a say,
no voice in the matter."

My soul asks, "Why?
why did you do this?
didn't you hear me,
crying out, no?"

My heart cries out,
"Of course you knew,
or should have known,
there was nothing left,
nothing left to give."

It was a gift,
not a sale,
and now I know,
the last to know.

So, I take my heart,
I take my soul,
come home now,
"I can hear you."

When I reached the highest point of success, my soul began to rebel and forced me to look at the values in my life.

Nature and Beauty

I had moved from the San Francisco Bay Area to Los Angeles in the early 1980's initially for romance, but stayed there for ten years primarily because of work opportunities. Jim and I lived in the Hollywood hills. While our neighborhood of older, Spanish homes and lush landscaping was beautiful, only two blocks away lay unattractive commercial streets, devoid of any appealing architectural style or other redeeming qualities—a perfect setting for drugs and violence accompanied by the obnoxious sound of patrolling police helicopters in the night.

Living in Los Angeles for many people, and certainly for us, involved working in, playing in, and driving through densely populated areas with little greenery. This environment ate away at me inside. As a teenager, I had enjoyed many summer camping experiences in the High Sierras of Northern California where I fell in love with the mountains, the trees, the dirt and rocks on the hiking paths, the rivers, and the fresh air. Clearly, I am not a "big city" person. Rather, I thrive in small towns surrounded by abundant natural beauty. Inside of me is the sensitive soul of an artist—I soaked up the stresses of Los Angeles like a dry sponge. The population density, the ubiquitous cement buildings and hard surfaces, and the speed of the Los Angeles freeways were all very disruptive to my sense of inner peace. It is true that there are beautiful, less populated areas in the Los Angeles area, but I didn't live or work in those places.

Jumping off the High Dive

I was suffocating in Los Angeles (literally and figuratively) while *becoming someone*. My incessant journal writing became an effective tool for me to connect with my inner self. Gradually, I saw that the price I paid for *becoming someone* was steep indeed. I started to question the value of what I was getting compared to what I was paying. I realized that once I became *someone*, the question would arise, "What next?" Indeed, what was next? I had achieved what I had set out to do professionally.

What I learned in my journey to my inner self was that *becoming someone* was simply not enough. It did not have lasting value. So, having been raised to have few fears, I jumped off the high dive. I quit my job as a corporate attorney in December of 1989, much to the astonishment of friends and family. Jim was fully supportive of this move, even though our only other income—from his computer consulting business—was irregular.

False Starts and Other Detours

When I left the legal profession, I joined Jim's computer consulting firm, which specialized in the legal market. Living in Los Angeles, however, still grated on me, and Jim started to tire of the stress and pressure involved in the computer consulting business. Having survived the loss of income from my attorney job, we were emboldened to go farther toward creating a more satisfying life for ourselves.

We roamed up and down the California coast looking for a small town that we would feel at home in. In 1991, we moved to the Monterey Peninsula. We continued to do computer consulting for the first year after our move and then decided to let that go, also. Bit by bit, we changed all the essentials of our lives—our home, the city in which we lived, and the work that each of us did.

Jim came up with the idea of our selling real estate together. My experience as a real estate attorney and Jim's computer expertise would be assets in the business. So we tried it—first with a small, local firm and then we opened our own firm, with just the two of us.

Real estate sales turned out to be a *false start* for me. In addition to dealing with a depressed real estate market, making it difficult to make a decent living, I discovered that the intense people involvement and the conflicts inherent in buying and selling homes drained me emotionally. There are few things more stressful for people than buying or selling a home, and I absorbed the stress my clients were experiencing.

In addition to discovering that real estate was not a good fit for me, we were losing money. The darkest night of our experience came the year we spent $10,000 more than we brought in, paying ourselves nothing in salaries. Our lack of financial success was a shock to us. Jim and I had always been successful professionals. We somehow believed that we could do anything we wanted to do.

That belief in our invincibility led us to buy a single family home and then invest a bundle of money, time, and energy into a major remodel, all based on the assumption that we could certainly make the kind of money we made in Los Angeles. We believed that income was just around the corner. We both scratch our heads now at how presumptuous we were. We learned the difficult lessons that we are not in total control of our lives and we are not infallible.

Rebuilding our Lives

Fast forward to the fall of 1995. Here we were living in our home worth nearly $500,000, with almost all of our savings invested in that home, and with grossly inadequate income to pay the mortgage and other living expenses. We would sit together in our lovely solarium, looking at each other, wondering what to do. Neither one of us wanted to go back to traditional, salaried positions in order to keep our home. Our freedom was more precious to us.

About this time, I read an article in *Worth* magazine on the voluntary simplicity trend. I started to read everything I could get my hands on about simple living. The lights went on, the bells chimed, and everything became clear. This life we were living didn't make any sense!

We put our home on the market and sold it in about six months. At the same time, some good friends moved to London and did not want to bring their two large Bouvier dogs with them because of England's six-month quarantine rule. They were looking for someone to housesit their Carmel home (with free rent) and take care of their dogs for a few years. The timing of this opportunity was incredible. We volunteered, even though we had no experience with dogs, let alone large dogs, including a three-month-old, not-quite-trained puppy named Murphy. After a difficult first few months of adjusting to being parents of dogs, we became quite attached to our new charges and settled down to a very enjoyable lifestyle in the village of Carmel, walking to town and the beach daily.

With no housing expenses except for utilities, we were able to reverse the rapid deterioration of our savings. I dropped out of real estate sales and decided to write a book about simple living. Jim joined a local Carmel real estate firm. The real estate market improved somewhat and he started to make some money. I was able to earn some income writing for a legal publisher on a contract basis. We were no longer in the red.

During 1996, I continued my research on the simplicity movement. I set up a web site and started collecting surveys of people who had experimented with simplifying their lives. I had discovered my passion, my right livelihood. I loved my work and still do even as I write these words at the close of 1998. I also enjoy the legal writing that I continue to do on a part-time, freelance contract basis. Jim enjoys the real estate business and is now earning a good income.

One more major change occurred in 1997. The owners of the home we were housesitting decided to sell their home. We thought long and hard about whether to rent or buy our next residence. We loved the natural and architectural beauty of Carmel, not to mention the fabulous lifestyle of walking everywhere, including one of the most spectacular coastal walks in the world. We finally decided to buy instead of rent. Our decision was based primarily on the fact that we had moved so many times in the last 15 years we didn't want to face another move if the landlord wanted the property back or decided to sell.

We bought a two-bedroom, two-bath condominium (1,100 square feet) within walking distance of the village and the ocean. It does not have the charm or the privacy of the small quaint cottages in our town, but it's only half the price. We traded in charm and long lists of maintenance chores for our freedom.

Our goal is to pay off our mortgage as soon as possible. Once we do that, we will be close to financial independence. Who knows how long it will take us? Meanwhile, we enjoy our work and our lives very much. We are not waiting until some point in the future to start living the lives we dream of. We are doing it now.

A Spiritual Transformation

Following the path of simplicity has led to more personal satisfaction in my world of work and in my daily life generally. My new, slower-paced lifestyle gives me time to reflect on just about anything and everything. My frequent walks and runs along the spectacular coast of the Monterey Peninsula and my hikes in the Big Sur mountains bring me closer to my spiritual self. I feel a sense of oneness with nature and with all life on the planet. Journal writing, meditation, walking to town to do errands, and the occasional leisurely lunch all contribute to a different way of living for me—a slower, more relaxed way of being. This new way of life has led to a spiritual transformation within me.

When I started reading everything I could find on simple living in the fall of 1995, I discovered that many advocates of simplicity had a strong interest in preserving the earth's resources. I saw in these writings an almost religious respect for nature, plants, and animals. At first, I didn't really see the connection between simple living and caring for the earth. After all, a person might have plenty of good reasons to simplify her life without considering the earth. Even though I had always been passionate about nature, I had never been an environmentalist. To the contrary, I often reacted negatively to what I perceived as extreme stances taken by environmental activists.

Then, over the course of about a year, my feelings about environmental issues changed radically. I started to see a connection between simple living and caring about the earth. For me, this was a spiritual experience, not an intellectual exercise. It was not the reading of simplicity tomes that changed me. It was the time spent by myself in nature and the slower pace of my life that did it. It was also my journal writing and thinking quietly by myself.

The changes I've experienced seem to be spiritually based. They stem from my core belief that we are all connected in some way that our rational, human minds cannot comprehend. I believe that there is some form of a higher level of experience that we share, whether we are consciously aware of it or not. As I see it, when we connect with our inner selves, we touch the part of ourselves that is connected to all other forms of life. When that happens, we naturally start caring about those other life forms, including the earth, plants, animals, other humans, and people who will be born after we are gone.

Living simply has also sharpened my feelings about social injustices. I view the global human population as one world. I don't understand why Americans should have so much more wealth than four-fifths of the remaining world population. I am disheartened to think that our priorities as a global society allow millions of people to go without sufficient food, shelter, and health care. I wonder why so many of us take more than what we truly need to live fulfilling, satisfying lives. Why don't more of us share our abundance with others less fortunate?

When I look at my own life, I see that I have a long way to go before I can truly *walk my talk*. Even though I have reduced my dependence on material possessions and cut back on my utilization of the earth's resources, I still consume more resources than four-fifths of the world's population. Perhaps, if I were a perfect human being, I would not be living a life of comfort in America, but instead would be residing in a third world country trying to help others less fortunate than I.

However, I don't beat myself up about not *walking my talk*. I see my personal growth on these matters as a process. Before a child runs, she learns to walk. Before she walks, she must crawl. I am at the crawling stage. I don't think any of us make a valuable contribution by forcing ourselves to "do the right thing." It must come from within and it must be authentic to make a difference.

What Simple Living Means to Me

When I think about simplifying my life, I see it as a process, rather than a thing or a destination. There is no point in time when I will say to myself, "Ah, I have arrived. Isn't this grand?" It is not something that I have accomplished. It is not even anything I can really define. For me, simplicity is a process, a way of looking at the world and myself. There is nothing static or fixed about living simply. In fact, for me a better term to describe this approach to living would be *soulful living*. By *soulful living*, I mean the process in which a person invests the time and energy to develop her inner self, to connect with whatever higher being or spiritual presence she believes in. In my view, this is all that is required. Once a person does that, everything else falls into place. All of the answers to life's difficult challenges become evident, not necessarily easy, nor without anxieties and fear, but clarity and courage will usually prevail.

My experience illustrates that simplifying often takes years, not weeks or months, and usually consists of small, serial steps rather than a wholesale makeover. I find it to be an exciting and tremendously rewarding adventure.

Chapter Three

Turning Points:
What Motivates Us To Start the Journey?

W ho are these people who simplify their lives, and why do they do it? What motivates them? Why does simplicity appeal to some and not to others? These are some of the threshold questions that informed the research of *The Pierce Simplicity Study*. We are all such complex beings. It is nearly impossible to isolate specific reasons or influences that explain why we behave as we do. For some, a single transformational experience leads a person to pursue simplicity. For others, it is more gradual—a slow building process over a period of years.

Childhood experiences often play a factor. People who were raised to value nonmaterial pleasures often carry those values into adulthood. Living simply is a learned skill. If you learned as a child that happiness is not directly related to material consumption, you are more likely to live simply as an adult.

Cancer: a Hidden Gift—Carolyn Thomas

If the weather is nice and her calendar is clear, you just might find Carolyn Thomas walking home for lunch along the seawall oceanside path that runs between her home and her job in Victoria, British Columbia. Arriving at her small two-bedroom townhouse, she is likely to eat her lunch on the balcony where she can soak in the ocean vista and enjoy the view of the courtyard garden below.

Four years ago, a leisurely midday stroll would have been an unlikely event in Carolyn's day. Back then, she held a high-profile public relations position for the state lottery corporation. Work was a real high for Carolyn. She thrived on the energy and adrenaline that accompanied the frequent media interviews and brainstorming sessions with her colleagues. In fact, Carolyn's co-workers were also her friends—a welcome environment for this divorced, forty-some-thing single mother of two teenagers.

Carolyn's social life was equally full and rewarding. She entertained often in her rambling four-bedroom home, a home enhanced by its magnificent English garden designed by a famous landscape architect and lovingly maintained by Carolyn. Hosting a sit-down Saturday night dinner for ten, followed by her regular Sunday morning run with a group of women friends, was her idea of a perfect weekend. She believed her life was nearly perfect.

Then in the fall of 1995, Carolyn was diagnosed with cancer. With a favorable prognosis for a full recovery, she elected to have surgery. The weeks of recovery gave Carolyn something that was rare in her life—long stretches of unbroken quiet time to reflect. She found herself thinking about what was important to her. She realized that while her fun-filled social life was wonderfully entertaining, sometimes it was too much: "I let other people fill in my calendar for me. If someone called to suggest a get-together, I would check my calendar, and if the page was blank, I automatically said yes." It was almost as if Carolyn herself didn't get a vote. During her recuperation, she came to understand that she wanted to set some boundaries in her life; she wanted to take a more proactive role in structuring her leisure time.

Figuring out who we really are inside is a key component of living simply. But that is not enough. Even when we do get a clue about what we want in life, we then need to live that truth. Learning to say "no" can be a difficult life lesson, especially for women who have assimilated our traditional cultural mandate to please others at all costs. Many of us are not even conscious that we say "yes" to social engagements or other

> commitments we would prefer to skip. Had it not been for
> Carolyn's cancer, she might never have taken the time to com-
> plete the first step—figuring out what she wanted in life.

Carolyn's exploration of her inner self led to another, even more
profound insight. She started to question the value of her work.
While her job provided a generous salary, ego-boosting accolades,
and the camaraderie of a well-functioning team, she sensed a glimmer of protest within. She felt that her work was not making the
world a better place. Her career was not congruent with her values;
she wanted to do something more socially meaningful.

Carolyn's insights were reinforced by other experiences in her
life at that time. For example, while recuperating from her surgery,
she listened to an interview with Janet Luhrs [editor of *Simple Living: The Journal of Voluntary Simplicity*] on the local NPR (National
Public Radio) station. Carolyn's response to this interview was unequivocal: "It was so powerful and inspiring, I almost fell out of bed."
She was mesmerized by Janet's story. She figured that, "If Janet could
give up her law career and lavish lifestyle, then my own downsizing
efforts would be a piece of cake." Carolyn's view of the world changed.
She started to view common everyday events in a different way:

*My girlfriend's hubby bought a $3,000 big screen TV. When I asked if
a $3,000 TV is that much better than a $2,000 TV or a $1,000 TV, she
replied, "Well, John says that in a couple years when he's ready to up-
grade, he will get a much better trade-in price." I asked, "Do you mean to
tell me that in a couple short years he will no longer be satisfied with
$3,000 TV?" It just hit me that there is something seriously wrong with a
society in which people are going to bed hungry and sick, yet some of us
are buying $3,000 TV's and planning to be dissatisfied with them very
soon.*

> It is interesting how serendipity works in our lives. If Carolyn
> had not been recovering from cancer, she would not have been

home listening to the NPR station when the interview with Janet Luhrs came on. But it was not simply the opportunity to hear the interview that transformed Carolyn's life. It was also the inner growth that resulted from her taking time to reflect and ponder the meaning of her life. Without that inner work, Janet Luhrs' comments would have made no impact on her. As many have said, "When the student is ready, the teacher will appear."

Carolyn started to rebuild her life to reflect her true values—values that had been buried under the material and professional successes in her life. Within six months of recovering from cancer, she sold her large, four-bedroom home in an affluent neighborhood and paid cash for a small townhouse in a less expensive area. She did not want the financial burden of a mortgage to tie her down or limit her work choices. Carolyn is thrilled with "my cute little townhouse, an end unit, with a fantastic cottage garden that wraps around the entire side of the complex." Her townhouse maintenance expenses are $110 a month (Canadian currency), a trifling amount compared to the bottomless pit that was the maintenance budget for her single-family home. Even though she does not have room to host sit-down dinners, that doesn't stop Carolyn from entertaining. To the contrary. Recently she hosted an informal party with 35 guests. Potluck dinners, neighborhood barbecues, and coffeehouse gatherings with a few friends have replaced the more elaborate, formal entertaining of her past. And living on a lot less money does not translate into deprivation for Carolyn:

I think this is less about money than about choosing to live consciously. It's not about deprivation. I live very simply, but very well. I still spend over four dollars a jar for Claussen's garlic dill pickles—because they're the ones I like, even though I buy everything I wear (except underwear and shoes) at flea markets, garage sales, and thrift shops. Nothing excites me more than finding a Stielmann blouse (regularly $300) at the thrift shop for six dollars!

Once Carolyn reduced her living expenses, she was then ready to make a career change. She searched for something that would give her a feeling "that in some small way I was leaving the world in better shape today than it was yesterday." She accepted a position with the Salvation Army as manager of a project that offers direct, immediate physical assistance to people in need—homeless people, and those who are temporarily without basic physical necessities due to disasters, such as floods, fires, and earthquakes. She now earns one third of her former salary.

When I first heard from Carolyn, she was just four weeks into her new job. She felt overwhelmed with how much she had to learn and was working extra hours to try to get on top of it. True, she was using her public relations skills in meetings with community groups and in relations with the media. But she was also learning an entirely new field—how to mobilize people and resources to provide food, shelter, and clothing for those in need. That included learning how to drive a thirty-two-foot bus used for disaster relief. This was all quite an adjustment after spending the prior eight years in a corporate public relations position.

Eighteen months later I checked back with Carolyn, and she had nothing but positive reports about her job. She had found what she was looking for; she knew she was making a positive impact. She had even been able to negotiate a four-day work week. Her work benefits her personally as well. Perspective and gratitude enrich her life:

Last Christmas was very special. I was working that night, helping to provide food and warm clothing to the homeless. It was a very busy night and through it all, people had such a positive spirit. They were upbeat and happy. It was so inspiring. When I came home that night, I thought about how much I had and how fortunate I was.

Simplicity breeds gratitude. Slowing down to pay attention to what is happening in our lives seems to lead us naturally to be more grateful for what we do have. We become aware that many people truly do not have enough. That awareness brings perspective to our own lives. The result is that we enjoy what we have so much more than when we were focusing on wanting more.

Carolyn has also reclaimed personal time for herself. Her calendar no longer rules:

I've started baking bread on the weekends again—something I used to do when my babies were tiny (20 years ago) but got too busy to do for the past 17 years! I also schedule naps on weekend afternoons—first time ever! I live one half block from the ocean and seaside path so I take long walks along the shore many nights after dinner. I don't answer my phone just because it's ringing. I write "NO" on the top of each weekly page in my calendar to remind myself to schedule only things I really want to do with people I really want to spend time with. (Them: "Are you free for dinner on Friday?" Me: "Just a sec, I'll check my calendar - ooops, it says NOT!").

Carolyn is clear about the role that cancer has had in her life: "Without the cancer, I never would have made the changes in my home and career." It was the turning point in her life. Her cancer facilitated her inner journey—it gave her the unstructured time to be with herself. Carolyn's values—her true purpose in life—were already there, just waiting to be revealed.

A serious illness is often a transformational experience. Even if the illness is not life threatening, it often forces a person to slow down, and to just *be*, immersed in her own thoughts. The power of this quiet time to reflect is awesome—we gain insight, clarity, and inner peace. The experience supports my theory that the answers to the questions in life are all inside of us. We just need to listen.

A Painful Liberation—Tara Millette

Seven years ago, at age thirty-six, Tara Millette's thirteen-year marriage ended. The divorce was painful, to say the least. Tara had spent
the prior 13 years of her life trying to be the perfect wife and mother
to her two stepchildren. She also worked full-time as a nurse, taking
on many double shifts and night shifts. Tara suspects that her work
ethic derived in part from being raised by hard-working farmers in a
culture of rigid Midwestern Christian fundamentalism. She was attracted to intensive care nursing, believing that if she could work
with the "sickest of sick," she could do anything. She was a very
determined woman:

> I wanted to make as much money as possible to help my husband and
> to educate my stepchildren, who lived with us and attended a church-run
> school. I thought I could work all night and be the perfect wife and mother
> during the day, if I could just squeeze my sleep into precise little time slots.
> I raised a garden, canned vegetables, baked bread, chauffeured the chil-
> dren, and even jogged and exercised. I was my husband's second wife,
> and I was determined to be the perfect wife.

With so much invested in being the perfect wife and mother, Tara's
divorce devastated her. She describes this event as "the turning point
in my life…simultaneously a time of intense grief and slow awakening:"

> With the divorce, almost everything in my life took on a completely
> different appearance than it ever had before. It was like I had been fran-
> tically running around with a blindfold on, and then someone had taken
> the blindfold off. Everything seemed so clear. Material possessions lost all
> importance. Everything looked so fragile and impermanent, so tempo-
> rary. I saw the importance of cherishing the present moment. What were
> goals, anyway? Was there really anything worth working for? I lost some
> of my passion for nursing. I began to question many things about West-
> ern medicine. I was turned off by the narrow interpretations of so-called
> Christians in the Bible Belt. I began thinking about life in a more global
> way. After all, I reasoned, I could have just as easily been born in China,

Russia, or Uganda. Being born in the U.S. does not represent some kind of spiritual superiority.

Tara's divorce was the triggering event that led her to question many of the belief systems she grew up with. For the first time in her life, she started to listen to *herself*, rather than automatically adopting the beliefs and values of her family, the church, and her husband. Her divorce represented not only the loss of a marriage, but also the loss of the identity she had assumed for most of her adult years.

> The effect of Tara's loss reminds me of what happens to a person who has a close call of almost losing a loved one. Such a loss often results in an awakening, an awakening to the present moment, to what is important in life. It's as if the universe grabs you by the shoulders, gently shakes you and says, "Hey, wake up, wake up to what is happening right now, wake up to the beauty of the present moment, be here now. After all, it's all you have—the present moment." During this period of awakening, it is nearly impossible to live a life of role-playing, as Tara did during her marriage.

Tara proceeded to make sweeping changes in her life. Her disillusionment with Christian fundamental religions led her to study other religions. She found support and validation in Buddhism:

It did not take long for me to find that Buddhism made much more sense than anything I had ever been taught in the past. The practice of non-attachment seemed so perfectly sensible to me; after all, I really was no longer attached to anything. I no longer had a home or a family. Actually, the idea of non-attachment and not-desiring was incredibly freeing. I no longer felt pressured. There was nothing to frantically struggle for. Now I could just live with a peaceful mind.

Three years after Tara's divorce, she left the Christian church she had attended for forty years. She has also has made other significant changes in her life. She discovered that she doesn't really need very much money to live, and that time is more important to her than money. She cut back her nursing work to half time. In addition to wanting more time in her life, Tara's disillusionment with America's health care system prompted her to reevaluate the strong devotion she had for nursing. That has led her to enter a program to become certified in therapeutic massage. She finds the massage work to be "sort of a crazy, fun thing to do, something I never would have done in my past."

Tara's friendships have become far more important since her divorce. She has little contact with her birth family; her friends have become her family. She now has the time and energy to enjoy these relationships, including a close and special relationship with her goddaughter. Tara also helps out a few overworked, stressed-out friends with their housecleaning. It is not entirely clear who gets the better deal out of these arrangements:

I clean one friend's house for her every two weeks. Her life is so rushed and harried, what with working as an industry nurse ten hours a day and meeting the needs of her husband. It seems to be a huge help to her. But I find that it does something for me as well. I can't explain it, but I find that it calms me. I don't do it in a rushed manner; I'm kind of methodical about it. Sometimes I listen to tapes on spirituality while I'm working. I call it my "consciousness cleaning." I get more out of four hours of cleaning at her house that I used to out of two hours of church.

There is something very satisfying about manual labor. Oh, we all have different preferences and talents. Not all of us enjoy housecleaning, especially cleaning other people's homes. But one thing is true about manual labor. It keeps you centered in your body. Even if you are daydreaming or listening to music, your body is moving in a functional way, towards a purpose. In our information-obsessed society, we have lost touch with a primal need—using our entire beings, including our bodies, to meet basic life needs.

My husband and I have to discipline ourselves to clean our condo. We both procrastinate until the dust bunnies take over the place. Sometimes I am tempted to hire household help, especially during those times when we are both engrossed in our work. But a little voice inside reminds me that there are intangible benefits to cleaning my own home. Cleaning the house gives me a sense of meeting my own needs, of accomplishing something that I can actually see. It is a reminder that on a spiritual level, all tasks, all efforts, are of equal value. It helps keep me humble, a worthwhile task in itself!

Tara's friends have been very supportive of her, offering her comfort and companionship after her divorce and accepting her choices to work less and simplify her life. They can see the positive changes in Tara. She is so much more relaxed, happy, and at peace. Even though her close friends are supportive of her lifestyle, Tara reports that, "None of them are willing to slow down with me." As you will see from the stories in this book, living simply can sometimes be a lonely path. But at least for Tara, she does not have to contend with judgmental attitudes from her friends and colleagues.

After her divorce, Tara rented a small home for seven years, furnishing it with second-hand furniture and making her own curtains. Recently she bought a modest, older home with her savings. She lives simply when it comes to material possessions, making greeting cards and gifts by hand, for example. Her half-time nursing work produces sufficient income to meet her needs and to put some money away for retirement. Living in a small, Midwestern community with a relatively low cost of living makes it possible for Tara to live as she does.

So many of us (myself included) choose to live in areas with outrageously high costs of living, especially housing costs. When we think of downscaling or simplifying our lives, we often neglect to consider the option of moving to a less expensive area. Of course, if you have established roots and made a commitment to the community you live in, moving is not ideal. The point of simplicity is not to see how inexpensively we can live, but rather how well we can live. For most people, feeling connected to friends, family, and community is an essential ingredient of a high-quality life. However, if you are not already strongly attached to the community you live in, consider relocating to a less expensive area. It will provide you with greater financial freedom over the years.

Tara's divorce was truly a turning point. She has since let go of the beliefs and values that do not reflect her authentic self and has restructured her life—a life of simplicity—that brings her true peace of mind.

A Triple-Whammy Turning Point—Kent Honneger

Kent Honneger's lifestyle resembles that of a young person just starting out rather than the middle-aged, accomplished Ph.D. professional that he is. He rents a 700-square-foot apartment with his twenty-five-year-old son in a densely populated area of Kansas City, Missouri. At this point in his life, he struggles to earn enough for food and rent while exploring various business opportunities, trying to find a new niche. It is not exactly a hand-to-mouth existence since he has the security of savings from the profit he made on the recent sale of the family home. But those funds are limited, and he is trying to stretch them as far as possible. For now, he chooses to live frugally in a style far from his ideal. Still he maintains a positive attitude:

You know, there are lots of parallels to my life 30 years ago. When I was feeling down at the beginning of this process, I remembered that 30 years ago I had little money or possessions and was just starting a career and a family. A year ago I had $40,000 in the bank, enough stuff to keep

*me happy for years, three degrees, and had honed some talents and 30
years of experience. So I should have a great second start ahead.*

It is fair to say that a part of Kent's lifestyle represents involuntary simplicity. The turning points in his life arrived in a triple dose—a
job layoff, a divorce, and a back injury—all within a three-year period. Five years ago, Kent was laid off from his job as a project manager
in an engineering firm after the project lost its government funding.
He had worked as a systems engineer for 24 years. Shortly after Kent
was laid off, his wife quit her job. Within a year the strained marriage had ended. They sold their family home, Kent sold his car, and
Kent and his adult son moved into an apartment together.

Kent has struggled to build a consulting business while living primarily off the profits from his house sale. His son is going back to
college, and Kent has offered to support him with rent and food. The
transition from living in a home in a semi-rural environment to sharing a small, city apartment has not been easy for Kent:

*I hate the noise and lack of full views from the apartment, and since
the living room/dining room is also our office, it is hard to get away for
some quiet time. Since I no longer have the house, I cannot garden vegetables like I did in the past. I find apartment living less conducive to
exercise. For example, getting out on my bicycle is more of a problem than
it was living in a house. I think I spend too much time watching TV
because it drowns out the sounds of others in the building and the street
noise, and because there is no good place to go to get away when my son
wants to watch TV. Although I like my new lifestyle in general, the living
accommodations part I heartily dislike. I would prefer a small cottage in
a more rural area or a quieter part of town.*

When I checked back with Kent two years later, he was still living
in the same apartment with his son. However, his perspective had
changed somewhat. His negative feelings about his living situation
had lessened. While acknowledging that his current housing is far
from ideal, he no longer feels deprived: "I am warm, well fed, have

no bugs or rodents, much entertainment, love, and can come and go as I please. How many in the world wish they were so deprived?"

The concept of deprivation is often mentioned in discussions about simple living. "No Deprivation" is the choral refrain of the simplicity movement. As we can see from Kent's experience, whether a person feels deprived or not often is a matter of perspective, of clarity about what we do have, of looking at the glass half full instead of half empty. When Kent first moved into the city apartment, he felt the loss of his home keenly. Two years later, he is focusing on other things, recognizing that his physical needs are well taken care of.

A year or so after his divorce, Kent suffered an inflamed sciatic nerve that prevented him from working at his computer. His three to four week recovery period became a retreat of sorts—a time for reflection and meditation. Kent recalls, "I used the time to decide what I wanted to do with the rest of my life." He decided to explore his creative interests, especially creative writing and poetry. He also felt a renewed commitment to work in areas that were congruent with his values. Preserving the earth's resources, living gently on this earth, has always been a high priority for him. He wanted to apply his talents to this objective. Out of his health-imposed spiritual retreat, the idea of an earth-friendly newsletter was born.

Does this sound familiar? Kent's story may remind you of Carolyn Thomas' story discussed earlier in this chapter. An enforced retreat of several weeks or months often triggers a major life transformation. The experience is a testament to the power of solitude and the knowledge we hold inside ourselves. It's all there, folks. But you don't have to wait for the opportunity of an illness or injury to take the time for a lengthy retreat. Do it now, voluntarily, and save the grief of a recovery period!

Kent proceeded to write and publish a newsletter that focuses on the benefits of voluntary simplicity and honoring the earth. He has also included his poetry in the newsletter, giving the artist within a voice. While the newsletter venture has not been profitable, at least it is now breaking even, not to mention providing the satisfaction and creative fulfillment it brings to Kent. His newsletter is a labor of love and an expression of his right livelihood.

Meanwhile, earning a living continues to challenge Kent. He picks up a few consulting projects here and there, but still does not have a stable source of income. When I talked to him two years after he responded to the survey, he had just started to work with a good friend to develop on-line "learning for life" courses. Who knows what the future will hold for Kent? One thing is clear; his days of working long hours in jobs with horrendous commutes, doing work that makes little contribution to the betterment of the earth, are over. He cannot turn back.

Kent's experience is not unusual. As we make changes to simplify our lives, we often go through some tough times. If we are trying out new, more meaningful work options, we may grieve the loss of material comfort that our former salaries provided. The vision of a spiritually more satisfying life may sustain us, but it does not take away the sting of change and the fear of the unknown. Living simply requires courage. It helps to know that there are others out there going through similarly challenging times as we make the difficult choices to transform our lives.

Kent's interest in environmental issues has been a constant in his life. He was involved in organizing the first Earth Day and has participated in environmental organizations on and off for many years. When he first lost his job and gained more discretionary time, his involvement in environmental activities increased. However, he found the confrontational style of some environmentalists distasteful, and gradually his involvement in organizational efforts has decreased. Now he focuses on making a contribution through his writing and by helping people on an individual basis to simplify their lives:

A friend of mine came to visit from another part of the country recently. She jokingly announced on the phone, "Tell the stores I'm coming." She loves to shop. When she was here, we took a long hike and I talked to her about my philosophy of living gently on the earth. She started to see some appeal to all of this and took a copy of my newsletter to read on the plane ride home. When she arrived, she called me to report that the newsletter really made an impression on her. Three days later she sold her larger home for a smaller, less expensive one and is now semi-retired.

Kent is also helping a client declutter her life, sorting through her clothes and furniture with her, prompting her to consider her true needs and wants. He is working on starting a simplicity study group in his area as well.

> Kent's involvement in traditional community organizations has decreased, not increased, as he has simplified his life. I was surprised to see a relatively low level of participation in traditional community organizations in the lives of the simplicity study participants. Their sense of community focused more on immediate family and close friends. This subject is explored more fully in Chapter Twelve, *Community: Are We Our Brothers' Keepers?*

Kent's simple living lifestyle was born of economic necessity, and is, to some extent, an involuntary choice. But only to a limited extent. With greater financial resources, Kent would move to a somewhat larger home in a quieter area of town or in the country, but not much else in his life would change. A large, lavish home and abundant material possessions hold no interest for Kent. In fact, in many ways, he has always lived simply. For example, his reduced income has not made a huge impact in the amount of stuff entering his life:

I have cut down on the number of books and magazines I have purchased. As to other stuff, I have bought little in the last two years except business-related computer hardware/software. However, I have been engaged in a simpler lifestyle for many years. When I do purchase a toy or piece of furniture or car or whatever, I tend to keep them for a long time. For example, I am still using my 30+ year-old Roget's Thesaurus, *which I bought for 35 cents.*

As we have seen, Kent's journey of simplicity has not been without struggle. However, the tradeoffs of his enforced simplicity lifestyle have been worth it. They have opened up opportunities to explore his creative side and work in areas that are more in line with his values.

Lessons and Reflections

Carolyn Thomas, Tara Millette, and Kent Honneger all experienced life-altering events that transformed their lives, leading them to seek the benefits of a simpler path. These events—illness, divorce, loss of a job—have no inherent factors that would direct people to simplify their lives. But they do provide fertile ground, an invitation if you will, to take stock of our lives, to journey inward to discover what is truly important to us. Simplicity is in essence an inside job. Oh, we may want to simplify our lives so we can work in more meaningful ways, or so we can afford to have one parent at home with the children. But these objectives are merely external manifestations of inner callings, of wanting to find fulfillment in meaningful work or in parenting.

While it is true that a transformational life experience can lead a person to simplicity, many people embrace simple living without a lot of drama or change in their lives and without the serious wake up calls that the people profiled in this chapter experienced. For some, living simply is natural, obvious, and a matter of common sense (see, for example, the profiles in Chapter Eight, *Long Timers: People Who Have Always Lived Simply*).

The reasons people develop an affinity for simplicity are varied and numerous. We strive for simplicity because we want a higher quality of life, a life that honors our intellectual, emotional, and spiritual needs. It is our desire for a sense of balance, purpose, and joy that leads us on to the simpler path. We have learned from experience that an obsession with material pleasures, status, and power can interfere with getting that life.

The chart in Figure 3-1 sets forth the events and influences that motivated the study participants to seek a life of simplicity, together with the percentage of the participants who mentioned each factor. Most people were motivated to simplify by several events and influences.

Figure 3-1: Motivating Factors Leading to Simplicity

27%	Process of inner growth and/or spiritual leanings
26%	Stress (generally, or in connection with a job, or due to a pace of life that is much too fast)
23%	Worry about money, or burdened with too much debt
21%	Desire for freedom and autonomy
20%	Desire to spend higher quality time with family
15%	Wanted a higher quality of life, generally. Time and energy to stop and smell the roses

15%	Reading one or more books that made a substantial impact
13%	Concern about the earth
11%	Burdened by too much stuff, wanting to reduce the role of consumption and materialism
8%	Has always lived simply (either because of family upbringing or values developed as a young adult)
7%	Loss of a job
6%	Serious illness or injury
5%	Death of a loved one

While money worries and stress were strong motivators, equally strong were the less tangible aspects of life. For example, inner growth and spiritual leanings, the desire for freedom, autonomy and a higher quality of life in general were mentioned with high frequency.

The people in the simplicity study who lost loved ones reported they unexpectedly found that this experience led them to simplicity. Steve Cullinan, a study participant from Albuquerque, New Mexico, explains how this worked for him:

My father died of a sudden heart attack at age sixty-three, less than one year after retirement. It made me really analyze what was important to me, where I was expending my life energy and to start to think about changes that I might make to live a happier and more fulfilling life. I think the realization of our mortality has had the greatest significance in the process of simplifying my life. We are given a very short time on this earth and so many people waste most if not all of it in pursuit of materialism and just don't even think about the way they are living their lives. Most of us are on automatic pilot.

Some of the simplicity study participants were raised in households that modeled the essence of simple living. Kathleen Tierney, a married mother of three children, lives in a small town in rural North Dakota. When you hear the story of her childhood, it is no surprise to see why she is attracted to a life of simplicity:

I was raised in what would be considered a below poverty level home. My parents rented our house and were sharecroppers. They were very self-reliant, growing all our own vegetables, fruits, eggs, meat, and making our own dairy products. Most of our clothes were handmade on a treadle sewing machine. My great-grandmother, who was blind, lived with us. My father practiced ecologically sound methods of farming when it was popular to use chemical fertilizer and to take the governmental loans so widely available then but later led to the ruination of many family farms. We had very little garbage, recycling everything long before it was fashionable. Our livestock and chickens were free-range.

Although poor, our home was immaculate, and my mother practiced many of Martha Stewart's dictates (before there was a Martha Stewart) of keeping a well-run and organized home. Mom had a wringer washer and used the final wash water to keep the outdoor toilet clean and fresh-smelling. Flowers were planted along the walkway to the "biffy." Bath night was Saturday night, and we pushed the kitchen table back to make room for a galvanized tub for which we heated water and kept adding to the tub after each person finished. If the water was too dirty for the last person, they had to take a sponge bath at the kitchen sink. We wore our clothes until they were dirty, which meant we might wear the same jeans and shirt to school three days in a row. I had two good dresses, and the hems were let out as I grew.

I spent summer vacations at the library and the swimming pool in town. We had few toys, but I had horses to ride, and my brother and I had baby rabbits, chickens, pigs, calves, puppies, and kittens to play with—when we weren't acting out scenes from our imagination based on what we had read—near the corncrib, up in the hayloft, or out in the grove. My parents belonged to neighborhood card clubs that met monthly in alternating homes, and no one got a sitter because they brought the kids along with them. Neighbors would have "bees"—plowing, chicken butchering, whatever—whenever someone was too ill to get his or her work done. Mom belonged to social clubs where she socialized and extension clubs where she learned the latest homemaking techniques. We played games as a family in the evening. I had an old upright piano on which I learned to play music. After watching a neighbor lady, I taught myself to knit. We had no trouble finding things to keep us young people occupied; there were always chores, homework, 4-H projects, etc. There was no debate about morality—it was right or it was wrong.

Social workers today would be aghast that our multi-generational family lived in a two-bedroom house, with no plumbing, a house that was heated with corncobs. But we were healthy, very well fed, extremely clean, busy, and most importantly, happy and content. You might say I have tried the modern consumer-oriented world with all its stress, but have regressed to my roots.

For Kathleen, her childhood appreciation of the simple pleasures stayed with her as an adult.

Others are drawn to simplicity for other reasons. The state of the planet, with its rapidly diminishing resources, is of great concern to many people who live simply. Sometimes it is just this concern which triggers a serious interest in simplifying. Karen Steiner of Arlington, Massachusetts, shares her wake up call:

If I had to point to one motivating event it would have to be the summer of 1988. It was hot. Days and days of 100+ degree weather, all through the East Coast and Midwest. We had a massive drought. Crops were failing. The Mississippi River was running almost dry. That summer scared me. Was this a glimpse into the future environmental catastrophe? Although I didn't make any immediate changes in my lifestyle, it made me realize how trapped I was in a system of drive, earn, and consume.

Perhaps the most compelling motivation for people to simplify their lives is a sense of inner disquietude—a feeling of emptiness. Jennifer Young, a twenty-seven-year-old single woman, says it well:

I would have to say that my main motivation for doing this has been a long-term, deeply felt need for personal change and growth. Being young and single it was easy at first for me to get all caught up in my work; then when that became less satisfying (due to a variety of factors), I found myself with this nagging feeling of dissatisfaction that just wouldn't go away. Sometimes it was just barely there on the surface, other times I hardly noticed it, and then there would be these great long periods where I just felt so miserable and just kept thinking: "Is this it? Is this what I waited to be a grown-up for?— too many hours at a job I no longer love, shallow relationships, and bills for things I shouldn't have bought in the first place?" Even though I felt like I should be happy, and had no easily justifiable reason to not be happy, I just couldn't shake off the feeling that I wasn't going in the right direction with my life.

Sometimes the feelings of unease are less defined for a person. Dana Stanley, a fifty-year-old married woman, spends much of her time maintaining and organizing her family's two large homes and all the stuff in those homes. She has a glimmer that change is on the way, but doesn't know yet what it will look like. As she explains, "I want to change, explore, give more meaning to my life, and spend less time on *stuff* and *putting out fires* and more time on the important things—if I can only figure out what they are."

Most of us have had the experience of reading a particular book that transforms the way we look at the world and ourselves. We then rush out to tell our friends and family that they absolutely *must* read this terrific book, sometimes even buying numerous copies to hand out to them. Inevitably, mixed reports come in. There is no doubt that reading a book can be a magical experience, but the magic is unique to each person at that particular time in his or her life.

Many of the simplicity study participants reported that reading a particular book changed their lives. By far, the book most frequently mentioned in this respect was *Your Money or Your Life: Transforming Your Relationship with Money and Achieving Financial Independence* by Joe Dominguez and Vicki Robin. And, surprisingly, it was not the lure of financial independence per se that had such an impact on these readers. Rather, it was the book's radical approach to viewing life that grabbed their attention. It was the notion of valuing one's life energy and nonmaterial rewards in life that shook up so many people. This book presented an alternative to America's cultural mandate to amass as much material wealth, status, and power as you possibly can. You can read the real life stories of people who followed the program recommended in this bestseller in its sequel, *Getting a Life: Strategies for Simple Living, Based on the Revolutionary Program for Financial Freedom, Your Money or Your Life* by Jacqueline Blix and David Heitmiller.

Other books that were described by the study participants as transforming include *Voluntary Simplicity* by Duane Elgin, the series of simple living books by Elaine St. James, and the nineteenth-century writings of Henry David Thoreau, considered by some to be the *father* of simple living.

It is nearly impossible to isolate one or even a few factors that motivate a person to live simply. Often what initially prompts us to seek simplicity becomes less prominent as we discover other reasons for doing so. Claire Mayer of Morristown, New Jersey, describes how this worked for her:

> *I was drawn to simplicity because of my environmental concerns. Before simplicity, my environmental work was outward directed—lobbying, writing protest letters, organizing, producing programs. But the connection of how much driving a car affects global warming, or how quickly our resources (minerals, oil, top soil, etc.) are being depleted by rampant consumerism, or how much each person wastes per day, was not being made. How could I tell others what to do—what laws to enact or repeal—without looking at how my lifestyle, my day-to-day behavior, impacted the health of the planet? Now that I'm into simplicity, I see this lifestyle is much broader than promoting environmental values. It is about putting joy and meaning back into life through dear and loving relationships and spending more time creating and playing. Buying used or less, I use fewer resources and have more money to donate. My spending is becoming more and more conscious, considering the environment, social, human, communal and justice implications of my purchases. My motto is "enough" not only for me but that all people would have enough to have a good life. "Enough" has an upper as well as a lower threshold.*

Claire was initially drawn to simplicity because of her love for the earth. She then discovered other jewels of the simplicity lifestyle—

more meaningful relationships, expanded creativity, and a hope for social justice in the world. We are complex creatures, ideally always learning and growing. Simplicity does not turn us into simple creatures; rather, it expands our life experiences.

Chapter Four

A Parent's Choice:
Savoring Life with Our Children

A h, the pitter-patter of little feet on an early Saturday morning! There is nothing quite like it, except, of course, if you are exhausted from too much work, never-ending household chores, and a to-do list that refuses to shrink. In that case, you utter a silent, guilty prayer that the kids will turn on TV cartoons so you can squeeze in a little more shut-eye.

Many of us struggle to balance child rearing with career goals, while still leaving room for personal growth and a little pleasure. We keep trying to balance it all, but progress is slow, sometimes nonexistent. Inevitably, we ask ourselves, "What's wrong with this picture?"

For some parents, there comes a time when their experience of family overrides other factors in this juggling act, and major life changes follow. These parents seem to develop a heightened awareness of the fleeting time they have with their children, as children. They approach parenthood with a sense of awe and view time spent with their children as more precious than career advancement or increasing their net worth. Choosing jobs or careers that allow them the time and leisure to enjoy their children, they do not feel deprived. To the contrary! They feel blessed to have found a way to participate so fully in their children's lives while still earning enough to support their families.

Chelsea's Legacy—The Pfender Family

In Chapter One, *Why Simplicity?* we met the Pfender family. This family, which includes three small children, lived in a beautiful new home outside of Houston. Joe Pfender worked long hours to support the family's lifestyle. Cindy Pfender shouldered the parenting and household responsibilities. You may recall that it was a drawing made by their daughter, Chelsea—her view of the back of her dad's head while working on his computer—that influenced Joe to reexamine his life. Here is the rest of their story.

For many years before that, Joe had adjusted to his workload and the rest of the family adjusted to his absence. However, even though Joe was an expert in dealing with the stress inherent in a corporate bureaucracy, the internal pressure was building. It felt like a pressure cooker, and Joe realized that something would have to give. He remembers one day when he drove to work, parked his car in the lot, and reached for his cell phone to call Cindy. "I just can't do this anymore. I just can't stand this one more day," he announced. Cindy's support was immediate and total. She assured Joe that they would and could find another way to make it work. Joe doesn't know what he would have done if Cindy had not supported him at that low point. As he reflects now, "You and your spouse need to be on the same page to make this all work."

It is not uncommon for one person to want to simplify before his or her mate comes to the same conclusion. Joe and Cindy were fortunate in that they both wanted to make changes at the same time. Often, if the person who is ready for change (1) focuses on what he or she can do as an individual, (2) introduces changes affecting the family gradually and in small increments, and (3) practices non-judgmental patience, the other spouse will come around. This seems to happen naturally because the other spouse starts to experience the benefits of simplicity. However, it may take several years for both partners to "get on the same page." If you and your spouse are not there yet, do not despair. Patience and understanding will likely get you there.

When clarity arrives, fear often subsides and courage prevails. Once Joe and Cindy saw clearly what they wanted, they found the inner strength to act on it. But it was far from easy. At first, Joe didn't know how to restructure his career. He sought career counseling and read books, searching for work alternatives. After about six months, the Pfenders were ready to make their move. Joe quit his job and the family moved to a Philadelphia suburb, where Joe joined his brother as a broker of ocean transportation services.

Another motivation for the move to the Philadelphia area was to be closer to Joe and Cindy's extended family—their parents, siblings, nieces, and nephews. The Pfender children would now be able to play with their 15 cousins frequently.

Joe and Cindy bought a two-bedroom *twin home* (also called a "duplex" in some parts of the country) with a small yard. Their house payments are comparable to what they paid in Houston for a lot less house, but as Joe sees it, "We have less to clean, repair, renovate, and maintain."

Joe and his brother are partners in the steamship brokerage business. They rent a two-room office with views of farmland (complete with weathervane) that is only five minutes from home. Joe leaves for work around 8:30 A.M. and is home by 6:00 P.M. Gone are the business suits, the time spent entertaining clients in bars and restaurants, and the daily hour and a half commute. Now he wears jeans to work and brown bags his lunch.

What Joe and Cindy did took a lot of guts. In a very short period of time, they reinvented their lives completely—Joe's work, their home, their neighborhood, and the time they spend together as a family. For the Pfenders, it worked out very well. For many people, making smaller changes over a longer period of time makes sense. It is certainly less risky, and it allows you to test the waters as you go deeper into the pool. Of course, as we have learned from the Pfenders, jumping off the high dive is always an option.

And they lived happily ever after—but, of course, life is not like that. The lives of the Pfender family are dramatically different, and substantially better, but not without some struggle. Joe's income as an entrepreneur is about $7,000 less annually than what he earned at his corporate job. This drop in income is a challenge for Cindy who manages a strict family budget for clothes, house repairs, gifts, car maintenance, and food. She admits it is sometimes painful to have to monitor their expenses constantly but, even so, she feels their lives are much more satisfying and fulfilling today than when they had more money. Joe and Cindy are trying hard to live credit card-debt-free, and in the two years since their move, they have not incurred additional debt.

Sometimes when we contemplate working less and spending less, we feel a twinge of deprivation at the thought of giving up the "treats" in our lives. Maybe we treat ourselves to frequent restaurant meals, or we treat ourselves to shopping sprees, a new piece of furniture, some new clothes, a lavish vacation. But we need to examine these treats carefully. Do they really bring us joy, or do they merely offer a distraction, a compensation, for something missing in our lives? And if they do bring us joy, for how long does this thrill last? How many articles of clothing are in your closet right now that gave you an initial thrill when you bought them, but rarely end up on your body? For Cindy, if she had not been able to take the kids out to fast food dinners when she felt lonely and frustrated, she would have felt deprived. But this treat was not inherently a lasting pleasure; it was simply a compensating distraction. As you can see, once this family restructured their lives, giving up frequent restaurant meals was easy.

Many small adjustments add up to some considerable change. They send Chelsea to their parish Catholic school, rather than an expensive private school. They do not eat out as often as before, preferring to share at-home dinners with friends and family. They exercise at home with videos and weights instead of paying for a health club membership. No more bills for a housecleaner, lawn service, or dry cleaning. And of course they no longer have the expense of flying home to visit family; they *are* home.

Joe confesses that a part of him misses flying first class and eating at five-star restaurants. Cindy misses having a brand new home and a cleaning lady. However, they feel that these luxuries are easy to give up when considering what they are getting in return. Joe now spends time with his family, relaxing, puttering around the house and even does some painting and repairs. He can take his daughter to school and has time and energy to play with his children. Cindy doesn't feel like a single parent anymore.

Joe and Cindy continue to discover additional fringe benefits of a downscaled lifestyle. For example, their physical health has improved. Cooking and eating at home means more fresh produce, fewer high fat foods, and less alcohol. Now they have time to exercise and can do it at home for free. They have the energy to enjoy the outdoors and four seasons to do it in.

Joe's colleagues thought Joe had gone off the deep end when he walked away from a successful position that earned him a substantial income and considerable prestige. However, one of Joe's friends put it succinctly when he told Joe, "You just did what we all have wanted to do but never had the guts."

This comment by Joe's friend is revealing. How much of our lives is dictated by fear? Deep down, do we know what we want but are too afraid to go for it? Or could fear prevent us from even hearing our inner voices to begin with? When I saw the movie, *Defending Your Life* (starring Meryl Streep and Albert Brooks), I was moved by its major theme—life is all about overcoming fear. I am reminded of this truth constantly in my own life and in watching my family and friends on their life journeys.

Joe's focus is clear: "I believe in creating your own life, not letting others control it. Simplifying makes this process that much easier." Amen.

Living a Dream-Come-True—Roslyn and Eric Campbell

Back in 1989, Roslyn Campbell worked as a customer service supervisor for a mail order company, putting in a lot of overtime. At that time, she and her husband, Eric, had one son, four-year-old Brian. They wanted to have a second child but with day care costs they didn't know how they could manage it. Plus, they were less than thrilled with having Brian in day care; having both children in day care was a depressing thought. What to do? They felt frustrated and confused.

One day Roslyn sat down at her kitchen table with her checkbook and her calculator. She decided to figure out what her real hourly wage was. Roslyn earned $15.85 an hour at her job. Or did she? Several hours later, after calculating daycare costs, lunch money, the cost of clothing, and other job-related expenses, she discovered she didn't make $15.85 an hour after all. In fact, she was shocked when she calculated her true hourly wage at less than $5 an hour. What an eye opener!

That moment of enlightenment led Eric and Roslyn to do some serious thinking about their lives. Over the next six years, they made substantial changes. During this transition, they had a second child, Emily. Roslyn wanted to find a way to be at home with her children and earn income at the same time. She started a daycare center, but only one family signed up.

Life can be terribly uncooperative. A daycare center would have been the perfect solution to meet the Campbells' goal of combining parenting with earning income. It takes a lot of fortitude to keep on plugging away at structuring a life of simplicity. Many parents who share the Campbells' desire to provide full-time parenting for their children still believe that both parents must work full-time outside the home, away from their children, just to survive economically. After you read this book, you will know that this is not the case (although if you persist, you can probably convince yourself that your situation is different, and while it's possible for some, it wouldn't work for you). It is not mandatory that both parents work full-time, away from their children. It is a choice, your choice. Read on to find out how the Campbells met this challenge.

Finally, Roslyn landed the perfect job—driving a school bus. She drives a morning and an afternoon shift and can bring her own children with her. Her income is less than what she earned at the mail order company, but her work-related stress has also diminished. And for Roslyn, the real pay-off is being able to be with her children much of the day. The only time she is apart from them is when they are in school.

Eric works as a carpenter. He loves working with his hands and would probably continue to work in his job even if they didn't need the money.

How many of us would want to continue to work in our current jobs if we inherited a bundle of cash from a long-lost relative? Getting paid to do what you love is not essential for a fulfilling life, but it is truly a blessing when it happens. In con-

trast, finding and following your passions is essential for a fulfilling life. In Eric's case, his work as a carpenter combines
both.

When people start taking control of their lives, a certain momen-
tum seems to carry them forward. They go on to create more and
more of their dream life. Eric and Roslyn had always dreamed of
moving to the country. They absolutely love wide, open spaces and
playing in nature. They also cherish their privacy. They always assumed that they would have to wait until the children were grown
to make this dream come true. However, when their neighborhood
started to show an increase in graffiti, drug activity, and burglaries,
they began to explore the possibility of moving to the country. They
were pleasantly surprised to discover they could manage it financially.

A few years ago, when Brian was ten and Emily was four, the
Campbells sold their twin home in the city and moved 35 miles away
to a comfortable, ranch style home on three and a half acres. It means
a lot to this family to be able to walk out their front door and not be
surrounded by people. The Campbells enjoy working in their large
vegetable garden. Even the family dog is thrilled to have so much
room to roam. Brian and Emily delight in watching wild turkeys,
hawks, possum, deer, and pheasants. Recently, they sat on their front
porch, watching a wild turkey lead her new brood of 11 babies across
the front yard.

So, here was a dream, the dream of country living, that appeared to be far away in the future for the Campbells. Many
times, we feel that our dreams are just beyond our reach. We
live our lives in the "if only" mode—if only we would win the
lottery, if only...(fill in the blanks), we could then do all the
things we really want to do. In truth, we can often make our
dreams come true sooner than we think. The people you will
meet in this book are living proof of that. The most difficult

aspect of making our dreams come true is determining what our dreams are. What are your passions? What brings you true joy and contentment? Is it a fancy new car, a larger home, designer furniture, and expensive clothes? How much of our lust for material possessions is the result of living in a culture in which we are constantly bombarded by slick, professional images that persuade us that our true happiness is found in buying more things?

Let's take a closer look at this *dream come true* for the Campbells. Life is not perfect for this family. As we will observe time and again, *simple living* is not the same thing as *easy living*. The downsides of the Campbells' rural lifestyle include the 70-mile daily commute for Roslyn for her school bus job. Some of their expenses are higher than they were in the city. The mortgage on their home in the country is about $200 a month higher than the mortgage for their twin home in the city. With Roslyn's long commute, automobile expenses have increased.

The Campbells' choices—a longer commute for Roslyn and increased expenses for housing and transportation—seem to fly in the face of simplicity principles. In fact, their choices are an excellent illustration of why it doesn't work to equate simplicity with a rigid set of rules. Roslyn's long commute must be viewed in context, that is, she is working part-time and even with the long commute, she has substantial time for herself and her family. That's quite a different situation than what Joe Pfender faced—a long commute on top of a ten-hour work day.

However, now that Roslyn is no longer working full-time, she has the time and energy to reduce household expenses. She cooks from scratch as much as possible, including baking bread and freezing produce. No more junk food or canned soda. She also cuts the children's hair. Eric has always been handy with household repairs, often rigging something up with what they have instead of buying a new part.

Eric works more overtime to pay the bills, but even with his additional work hours, the family still spends more time together than they did in their city life. For one thing, there are fewer distractions in the country. No spur-of-the-moment going out for pizzas and movies. Now that friends and family are not that close, Eric and Roslyn tend to spend whatever free time they have with each other and their children. All this time together has resulted in a much closer family. As Roslyn observes, "A lot of people feel they must always be entertaining or running somewhere to be happy and never have…good quality time with their spouses and children."

Their relationships with friends and family have also improved. Even though they see less of them than they did when they lived in the city, their visits seem to be sweeter, the quality of the relationships enhanced.

Many participants in the simplicity study report that their relationships in general have deepened, becoming more soulful and satisfying. Often, people who embrace simplicity tend to let go of relationships that are not authentic, positive, and nurturing. But those that remain are special. It makes sense. When we are not distracted by unnecessary complications and burdens, we naturally live our lives with more directness, fullness and clarity. We start to communicate with others more directly and honestly. Our minds are less scattered so we can pay more attention to speaking and to listening. As Duane Elgin explains in his seminal book, *Voluntary Simplicity*, "When we simplify our communications by eliminating the irrelevant, we infuse what we do communicate with greater importance, dignity, and intention."

The Campbells continue to make other adjustments. Brian, twelve, is old enough to remember and compare the free-spending old life in the city with the frugality of the new life in the country. At times, he has some difficulty understanding why less is better, but he is willing to listen and try. Recently, he made up a list of things he wants to get for the family's computer, and he broke his list down into needs and wants. Roslyn was impressed, especially when she considers that Brian was bombarded with TV advertising for many years.

Some of the Campbells' expenses have increased; others have decreased. The total package is a better quality of life, which for this family means enjoying life close to nature and spending time together as a family. The tradeoffs they have made are clearly worth giving up the mere $5 an hour Roslyn earned for the pleasure of working like a crazy woman.

Eric and Roslyn also were spurred on to make changes by listening to friends talk about how much they were in debt, and how much they had to work. Their friends still seemed unhappy despite all their material abundance. As Roslyn reflects,

Yes, they may have nice things but is it really worth it? I think these folks are not happy, even though they act like they are. They have no focus...or goals in life and just live for the day and spend, spend, spend. I think it is a very sad reflection of the state this country is currently in. We need to wake up and change our ways or we will leave nothing but a big mess for our children that will be impossible to clean up.

There is much to learn from the Campbells' journey. It took them six years to make the significant changes in their lives, namely, a change to part-time work for Roslyn and a move to the country. It happened in stages, and not without some difficult adjustments and sacrifice. The process of first determining our true priorities, and then creating a life that reflects those values, generally does not happen overnight, or even within a few months. It often takes place in small steps over several years, and it is not unusual for people to make a few, or even many, mistakes along with way. And the journey never really ends. The Campbells see further life changes in their future. Roslyn dreams of quitting her job altogether and homeschooling her children. My bet is that she will make that dream come true.

Part-time Parents, Part-time Workers—Mark and Colette Bryant

Fifty years ago, Dad went off to work each day and Mom stayed home to raise the kids and tend the home fires. Then Women's Liberation came along and Mom went off to work as well. In the beginning, as our society was first adjusting to two-income families, Mom also handled the bulk of the household and childcare chores, sometimes with the aid of a housekeeper and day care. Now, most fathers are at least aware that a cooperative effort is needed to manage the childcare and household responsibilities, and many fathers participate fully.

There is no shortage of creative, diverse lifestyles that parents have devised to achieve their objectives of pursuing careers while raising children. For those parents who want to limit the amount of time their children spend in daycare, atypical arrangements are common. For example, a father staying home to take care of the children while Mom pursues a full-time career is no longer viewed by society as some sort of deviate (see the story of Armando Quintero in Chapter Seven, *On the Road to Simplicity: Travelers in Transition*). Many other families have decided to live on Dad's one income and continue the tradition of Mom staying at home to take care of the children. Sometimes the parent at home also works on one or more freelance or entrepreneurial projects, usually during the time the children are at school.

However, in some cases, both parents want the opportunity to work in more traditional jobs in addition to parenting. Colette Bryant is a Ph.D. graduate student. Her husband, Mark, is an assistant professor at a small college. Colette also plans to teach when she completes her graduate work next year. Even though they find the academic environment "somewhat frustrating and incredibly competitive," Mark and Colette appreciate the flexibility their work provides. Mark stays home with their four-year-old daughter, Lucy, three mornings a week and Colette stays home with Lucy the other two work day mornings. Lucy goes to preschool in the afternoons. Mark and Colette work about 40 hours per week between the two of them.

The Bryants realize that their choice to limit the amount of time Lucy spends in daycare comes at a cost. They are not as productive or successful as their peers, but for Mark and Colette, spending time with Lucy is more important than climbing the academic ladder.

Mark's annual income of $30,000 requires this family to live frugally in the large, southern city they call home. They sold their second car and they rent a modest home. They prefer to spend the little extra money they do have on experiences rather than things. Going to the zoo and the aquarium, traveling, and an occasional restaurant treat are more important to them than buying stuff. Colette acknowledges that it has been difficult to balance the pleasure of living in the present with working toward reducing their huge student loan and credit card debts. They hope to chip away at that debt when Colette starts teaching next year.

Colette feels that becoming parents was the primary factor that led them to live simply and frugally. As she explains,

Priorities shift when the kid arrives. Your life changes dramatically. Suddenly, you don't need things to fill in the places...you have this amazing, time-consuming, fascinating and very needy and demanding creature to teach you what is important: being with people, being responsible for the earth and each other, treading lightly and teaching respect....

Mark and Colette are consciously choosing to forego the recognition and big bucks that come with a tenured position at a Big 10 institution. Instead, they will focus on the smaller, private or community colleges that offer less intense and more flexible work schedules. The Bryants have also given up some material luxuries and expensive entertainment. In exchange, they will enjoy and cherish their experience of raising Lucy.

The Bryants' experience reminds us that having children or developing a career is not an either/or proposition. It is possible for both parents to work less than the typical 40-plus hours a week and still spend time with their children. Women do not have to choose between being a full-time parent or having a full-time career. Many parents who both work full-time go through life really believing that they both must work to pay their bills. They would love to reduce their work hours to spend more time with their children, but they tell themselves that it is impossible. I am writing this book to tell you that it is possible. It may or may not require substantial tradeoffs on the material side of life, a change in jobs, or a move to a less expensive area of the country, but we need to realize that these are our choices. We do have substantial control of our lives. You may not want to make these tradeoffs, in which case you would be wise to realize that. In a perfect world, you might prefer to spend more time parenting your children, but maybe other things are more important to you. Which brings us back to what simple living is all about—a two-step process: first, figuring out who you are and what is truly important to you in your life (not what others tell you is important) and second, creating a life that manifests your true priorities and values.

Homeschooling and Other Adventures—Sara and Randy Hobart

Several of the participants in the simplicity study homeschool their children. For these families, the children's education is a unifying activity for the entire family; it is not a distinct activity separated from the rest of family life.

Four years ago, Sara and Randy Hobart and their three sons lived in California. Sara and Randy felt they were investing too much time and energy worrying about paying the bills. The entire family was busy going places and doing things. They rarely spent time alone as a family. They came to a fork in their lives when Randy's job in a manufacturing plant was slated to be eliminated. They had a choice: Randy could take another job in the same area, or they could do something else. They decided to make a change, a huge change.

Randy quit his job, they filled up a large U-Haul truck, picked up Grandma and Grandpa, and left California forever. This extended family of seven moved to Montana, settling down in a rugged and breathtakingly beautiful area. Their first few years were difficult. Randy had trouble finding work. Sara's dad was a contractor and was able to pick up some construction work. The family succeeded in building and selling one home on speculation, but building homes "on spec" felt a little too risky as a way of life. Finally, Randy was offered a job in a manufacturing plant, starting on the assembly line. Now he works in middle management for the same company.

When the Hobart family first moved to Montana, they bought an older home filled with history, paying cash for one half of it. However, with Randy's difficulty finding employment, they decided to sell that house after two years. They bought a mobile home on five acres that they could pay for entirely with cash. Initially they did feel a sense of loss at leaving that much-loved, older home on 35 acres, but they don't focus on it now. Instead, they delight in the warmth, comfort and open floor plan of their light-filled, spacious, newer home, surrounded by 360 degree mountain views. An added benefit to their new home is that it is much closer to the church they attend. As Sara commented, "We found such a wonderful church family, and being closer to them means more than having a great house and lots of land."

The Hobarts' purchase of that first home is a good illustration of a *false start,* an "oops" of sorts, the kind of decision one looks back on and reflects, "Well, that didn't work out, but we recovered and we survived, and that choice led us to something else that is working out much better." If we are open to change and growth in our lives, the odds are excellent that we will go down some paths that don't work out. The art of living well is determined in part by how we respond to the *false starts* in life, particularly by how we interpret them. We can view them as *mistakes*, or we can view them as detours on our journeys— side trips that are of value for a limited period of time, but not for the long term.

The Hobart family did experience some tough times at first with both employment and housing. As with the Campbell family, we see that *simple living* is not synonymous with *easy living*. One wonders whether the Hobarts ever regretted their move. Did they ever feel like moving back to the security of the California job market? Sara admits that there were times they were nervous and scared, but they never once considered moving back. Clearly, the tradeoffs involved in their move weighed in on the positive side. Let's take a look at what this family gained in exchange for the sacrifices and adjustments they made.

For the Hobarts, their highest priority is enjoying close family relationships. They didn't feel this was possible with their California lifestyle. It was not just the cost of living, with its accompanying bill-paying headaches, that troubled them. It was also the pace of that lifestyle, which left little time for their family. During those first few years in Montana, even as they struggled to earn a living, they had what they wanted—a rich, rewarding family life. They delighted in the natural beauty of their surroundings, enjoying picnic lunches overlooking a pond on their 35 acres. Hunting and fishing with Dad became a favorite activity for the boys. As Sara remarked, "It felt like an extended vacation."

One of the most significant changes in this family's life is homeschooling. Sara has not worked outside the home since they had their boys, now thirteen, eleven, and six. When the Hobarts still lived in California, Sara started to homeschool the two older boys. The initial impetus for taking this path came when one of her sons had trouble concentrating in class. The school authorities wanted to transfer her son to another school, but they also introduced Sara to homeschooling as an option, offering to support her with instructional materials and supplies. She decided to go for it, even though she was nervous about being accountable for something so important. That choice has not been a *false start* for the Hobarts at all. Far from it! It has been a deeply rewarding, satisfying experience. Sara reports that, "The boys are happy, doing well in their education and growing into fine gentlemen." Homeschooling enhances their close family relationships and allows Sara and Randy to impart their deeply held Christian beliefs and values to their sons. Even though it was tough at first, now they wonder how they ever existed without homeschooling. You can read about another successful homeschooling experience in Chapter Five, *Urban or Rural Simplicity: Choosing a Nurturing Milieu* (Jenna Duran's family). For further information on homeschooling, check out the *Growing Without Schooling* web site (www.holtgws.com).

The Hobarts were fortunate to have discovered a lifestyle and an environment that supports their most important values—family, church, and living independent lives. They had the courage to follow their hearts. Their Christian faith was, and continues to be, a guiding force in their lives.

> In many ways, our life task is the same as it is for the Hobarts—no, not to move to the country and homeschool our children (although for some us, it may be just that)—but rather to discover the values we cherish in life and go about the business of creating a life that reflects those values.

Lessons and Reflections

Let's face it—raising children is no simple matter. While life with children can be immensely complex and sometimes quite stressful, parenting can also be one of the most deeply satisfying and rewarding experiences of life. Living simply with children may appear at

first blush to make the already challenging task of parenting bur-
densome. After all, how will my child feel if she doesn't have what
the other kids have? How will I provide for her college education?
How can I provide my child with the best in life, be it piano lessons,
sports opportunities, spending a summer in Mexico, or the summer
camp experience of a lifetime?

The answers to these questions are as varied as are the families
with children. But ask any eight-year-old whether she would rather
be dressed in all the latest name brands or have a parent around
after school. She may give you a different answer when she is fourteen, but by then, even name brand clothing will not relieve her of
the angst accompanying this critical life passage.

I have no children of my own and therefore cannot share my
own successes and failures of living simply with children. But I can
tell you what I have learned from the parents in *The Pierce Simplicity
Study*. First, education seems to be a key ingredient to a rewarding
life of simplicity with children. Parents start talking to their children
early on (as early as three years old) about tradeoffs between having
"things," primarily toys, and the pleasures of spending time together
with Mom and Dad.

Except for the highly seductive advertising in our culture, children would not desire manufactured toys nearly as much as they
do. Test it out. Give a five-year-old a choice between playing with
the latest plastic gadget or creating a make-believe world with a "fort"
of blankets and chairs. Which choice she makes will usually depend
on how much television she watches. If she watches a lot, she will
be exposed to advertisements that advocate a consumer lifestyle,
advertisements that excite her imagination about the latest hot toy.
Without television she will usually be more inventive, depending on
her imagination. Some parents eliminate television from their homes;
others monitor and limit a child's TV time. The TV watching habits
of the study participants are discussed more fully in Chapter Fourteen, *The Pierce Simplicity Study: Reflections and Inspiration*.

Of course, the most effective educational tool is modeling. If parents model a satisfying life of simplicity, their children seem to
internalize this value. If parents feel deprived, frustrated, and always wanting more, a child will take on these feelings. The

participants in the simplicity study are aware of how fortunate they are and feel immense gratitude for what they do have. Children are like sponges, especially in their early years. They soak up these values and beliefs easily.

Creativity can go a long way to provide those things that do cost money and are considered worthwhile. For example, if name brand clothing is important, it can usually be found in good condition at thrift shops and consignment stores. A child might be able to swap piano lessons for helping the teacher with household or garden tasks. There are many ways to obtain a college education (again, if this is a priority) without mortgaging the next 20 years of your life. For example, you can move to a state with inexpensive higher education, work full-time the first year while you establish residency in that state, then find a live-in caretaker position to pay for your room and board. Or live at home or with a relative. Ride a bicycle, take public transportation, skip the car.

And, remember, as we all know, money can't buy the most important things in a child's life. A child who grows up in a loving home, with attentive parents who instill a healthy dose of self-esteem in the child, is much richer than a child who enjoys the fruits of all that money can buy but is lacking love and self-esteem. Simplicity offers nourishment for a child's soul.

Chapter Five

Urban or Rural Simplicity:
Choosing a Nurturing Milieu

There are many myths associated with simple living. One is the notion that to live a simple life, you must move to the country, eat vegetables from your garden, and bake bread from a solar-powered oven. While this is exactly what simplicity means for some people, the vast majority of the study participants live in cities, suburbs, or small towns. Indeed, it is possible to live simply in any location. Simple living is unique and subjective for each person and family. Ideally, the environment in which we live should support our efforts to live simply and should be in tune with our most revered values. In this chapter, you will meet people for whom living in the country or the city is an essential element of their experience of simplicity.

A Homesteading Success Story—Jenna Duran

Jenna Duran was born and raised in New Hampshire. Like her farmer grandmother, living close to the earth is in Jenna's blood—she cannot imagine living any other way. Interestingly, Jenna's affinity for rural living does not stem from her upbringing. City bred, she grew up in a traditional, middle class family—Dad worked as a bank vice president, Mom raised the kids, and each year the family bought a new car. Even so, Jenna perceived early on that her life would be different. One experience in particular made a deep impression on her:

During high school, we took on a project of cleaning up one of the rivers in our city. We actually got into the river to clean it up. I was appalled with the amount of trash that we found, and further shocked to realize I had never noticed the trash even though I walked by this river every day.

In the late 1960's, Jenna read *Living the Good Life*, by Scott and Helen Nearing. This book sparked her interest in homesteading. As a single woman in her twenties, Jenna embarked on several home-steading adventures, quickly discovering that a genetic predisposition for rural living and some gardening skills do not by themselves beget an accomplished homesteader. Jenna had no carpentry skills; she could barely chop wood. She also found it difficult to tackle the challenges of homesteading as a single person. Eventually, Jenna opted for a more conventional life, working as a nurse to support herself.

The life stories in this book are littered with false starts. A *false start* is not a mistake—far from it; rather, it is an excellent vehicle to carry us on our journey to a simpler, more authentic life. For it is only by taking action that we learn what truly works for us. Jenna's initial attempts at homesteading taught her several lessons. She discovered that she did in fact love living in a rural environment, but that she wasn't ready. She was too young emotionally to handle it on her own, and she lacked the requisite skills to make it work.

Some years later, Jenna met Sheldon (who would become her life partner and the father of their two children) at a restaurant she owned. Sheldon had lived in a commune for years. In his work at the commune, Sheldon developed many of the skills required for successful homesteading, including construction skills such as carpentry, wiring, and plumbing. Jenna sold her restaurant and moved into the commune with Sheldon. Here, Jenna gained the competence and confidence that she lacked in her earlier homesteading ventures. A year later, Sheldon and Jenna purchased a 45-acre parcel of land, complete with a hunting camp, described by Jenna as a "funky building where weekend hunters would hang out and drink." The hunting camp became a transitional home for Jenna, Sheldon and their new baby girl, Denise.

During the next 18 months, Jenna and Sheldon built a permanent home using lumber that was sawn from logs on their property. Jenna is clearly proud of their 1,400-square-foot home: "It's a great house—passive solar, attached greenhouse, well-insulated, wood heat, and solar electricity." They paid half the cost of the land with cash, paying the seller the balance over the next four years. The Durans have paid cash for everything else—building materials, tools, equipment, furnishings and vehicles—as they go. They have no debt.

Their second child, Sean, was born at home eight years ago. Sean and Denise, now almost twelve, are very close, perhaps due in part to homeschooling. The Durans' approach to educating their children is intriguing; there are no formal programs, homework assignments, course requirements, or school hours. Sean and Denise learn whatever captivates their interest, on their own schedule. Jenna and Sheldon see themselves less as teachers and more as providers of resources. Jenna explains that, "The children's education comes in fits and starts." For example, recently Denise and Sean became totally fascinated with geography. Maps were placed on the walls and for the next few weeks, much of the family's conversations revolved around distant parts of the world. When public radio news programs come on, the children look at the maps to see where the action is happening.

In many ways, Denise and Sean are self-taught. Jenna notes that her children are hungry to learn, eager to become a part of the world they live in. Both kids use the computer as an educational tool. Denise is responsible for caring for 50 chickens and has established her own little egg business. Sean and Denise are building a cabin in the woods together. Denise loves to read, and often reads to Sean. Sean finds numbers to be a lot of fun. Denise is an expert on world mythology. Homeschooling-a-la-Duran style is a persuasive testament to the innate learning ability of a child.

I asked Jenna if she had any concerns about whether home-schooling offers an adequate environment for her children to develop social skills. "None whatsoever," she replied. Jenna then went on to describe the rich social life enjoyed by her children, including weekly soccer games with other homeschoolers and their parents, and many other shared educational and recreational activities. The Duran children are growing up with children of all ages; birthday parties are often attended by kids from ages three to fifteen.

The Duran homeschooling experience is inspiring. Obviously, homeschooling is not for every family, nor for every child within a particular family. It works best with children who have an innate love of learning and parents who delight in being intimately involved with their children's education. Again, there is no right or wrong, here. If you want to explore homeschooling for your children, check out the *Growing Without Schooling* web site (www.holtgws.com). It provides numerous resources in this area.

The Durans' lifestyle does not resemble the stereotype of the rugged individualist—a self-sufficient life, isolated from community. Jenna and Sheldon have sought to "combine a homesteading, self-reliant, simple life with good works in the world." A few years ago, Jenna returned to graduate school to obtain master's degree in divinity. The Duran family moved to California for two years for this purpose. Now back in New Hampshire, Jenna works part-time as a minister at a local church. Sheldon works part-time as a counselor and also does some administrative work for their church. Physically, they are only 15 minutes from a town with all the city conveniences—grocery stores, the library, and movie theaters. Even though they don't spend much time in town, they like the idea that it's there.

The Durans grow most of the food they consume. A one-acre garden provides berries and the family's vegetables for the year, enjoyed all year long thanks to the wonders of canning and freezing. A small orchard contains apple, crabapple, plum, and apricot trees. The Durans raise pigs and chickens as well. Dairy and grains are just about the only items they purchase. Their maple trees produce all the maple syrup they could ever want with enough leftover to sell to local inns and to use as barter for other goods. For example, the midwife who helped Sean come into this world accepted maple syrup and tomatoes for most of her compensation.

Interest in bartering is expanding. In addition to the obvious economical advantages, bartering allows us to directly give and receive assistance from our neighbors and friends without having a middleman—the almighty dollar—come between us. The direct exchange of services or products reinforces the spiritual truth that we are all connected. To the extent we absorb this knowledge into our hearts and minds, we will see a greater sense of purpose in our lives. A variation of bartering is the growing practice by some communities to implement a local currency system. For further information on local currencies, see the Resource Guide (Web Sites section) at the end of this book.

The homesteading lifestyle is seasonal. The Durans view homesteading tasks as both work and play. Each spring, Sheldon and the kids tap the maple trees in preparation for the annual two to three week period when the sap will run. The family then works together to boil the sap, using 40 gallons of sap to produce one gallon of syrup. It is a time consuming yet exciting event for the family.

Summer is a busy time with chopping wood for the winter and tending to the garden, culminating with the harvest in August and September. Jenna, with the rest of the family's help, works on canning, freezing, and drying food for the winter. By October, work on the land eases up a bit, and the Durans can kick back and enjoy a five to six month period of relative leisure—time to cozy up to the fire, read, and indulge in their favorite winter sport, downhill skiing, at a nearby ski resort.

Travel has always been an important priority for the Durans. When the family lived in California, Sheldon, Denise, and Sean explored Yosemite and other nature spots while Jenna focused on her seminary program. When I interviewed Jenna, she was about to take off to England for ten days to participate in an adult singing camp at a medieval castle. If you think this would be expensive, think again. This trip cost Jenna a mere $350 plus airfare, which is relatively low because it is off-season. Jenna and Sheldon appreciate this fringe benefit to homeschooling—you can travel at non-peak times, resulting in lower costs. Traveling during non-peak times also means fewer crowds. For example, the Duran family recently spent a week in Washington, D.C. when most children were in school.

The Durans feel that they have everything they want, not only in terms of basic necessities, but also their cherished luxuries, such as skiing and travel. And they do all this on a low income. For many years, their income was less than $10,000 a year. Now that they spend more time on "off homestead" work, it has gradually increased, but not substantially. Jenna considers the greatest reward of this way of life is being able just to hang out together as a family:

When we're not doing homestead or our other work, we're playing cards and board games with the kids, reading, hiking, canoeing, skiing, talking, whatever. This is one of the most precious parts of this life. Hanging out together and being able to spontaneously decide to stop what we're doing on a nice day and go skiing or canoeing is great.

For Jenna, there is a strong connection between spirituality and simplicity even though she acknowledges, "It's hard to know which came first." As far back as high school, Jenna thought about becoming a minister. However, as she explained, "It took some years to find a church that spoke to the way I lived. My spiritual expression is very much involved with living on the land, working with the land." Her life and her spirituality are now one and the same. Likewise, Jenna's passionate concern with protecting the earth is a part of her spirituality, indeed her entire life:

It's hard for me to separate homesteading from the rest of my life. My whole life is about living in tune with nature, living lightly on the earth, being in the presence of Mystery, and finding space to hang out with my kids, my partner, and my self. Living this way has brought me closer to realizing that each moment is a spiritual, divine moment. I can't separate it out from anything else I do.

> Jenna's experience of simplicity, spirituality, and living with respect for the earth are all one experience—she does not compartmentalize these different areas of her life. This appears to be a natural progression for many people who embrace simplicity. For an expanded discussion of this process, see Chapter Thirteen, *Environmental Champions: A Passionate Love for the Earth* and Chapter Fourteen, *The Pierce Simplicity Study: Reflections and Inspiration*.

Small is Beautiful—Ellen and Brent Farrow

Ellen and Brent Farrow live and work in the Canadian province of Manitoba. Brent, an extrovert who enjoys a steady diet of social activity, is a physical therapist at the local hospital in town. Ellen shares Brent's interest in the medical field; she works as a nurse at the same hospital, often on the night shift. In contrast to Brent, Ellen enjoys regular time alone—to read, to think, to just be. Brent's son from a prior marriage recently moved on to college, leaving Ellen and Brent with the proverbial empty nest and an opportunity to take a fresh look at their lives.

Working in a hospital has influenced the way Brent and Ellen view life. Ellen explains:

Working in healthcare makes one aware of how short life and health can be. We are determined to make our lives worth more than just an accumulation of assets.

This awareness was a factor in the Farrows' decision to make a radical lifestyle change. Two years ago, Brent and Ellen sold their three-bedroom townhome in a quiet, residential area and moved into a 450-square-foot apartment rental in the center of town. Concerned about job security due to recent changes in the Canadian health care system, they wanted the freedom to relocate if they lost their jobs or just wanted to make a change. They did not want to be stuck with a townhouse they could not sell. Brent confided,

We have friends who are very unhappy with their employment and are ready to relocate to a better situation as soon as they sell their homes. The problem is that there are no buyers. That is a scenario we don't have to be concerned with.

Obviously, the Farrows' move into a 450-square-foot apartment required substantial adjustments and downsizing of material possessions. I first heard from them while they were still unpacking boxes. I asked them about the negative aspects of living in such a small space. Brent responded:

Downsizing possessions is a bit of a headache. There are still several piles of boxes to process. "The less stuff, the more life" is our rallying cry. Sometimes it's easier said than done. Simple living can present complex problems.

However, even though the downsizing process can be tedious, the end result has been very satisfying for the Farrows. Ellen explains:

We have had to get rid of a major portion of our belongings, clothes, and appliances (we now use the laundromat). Our 10-year-old car will

not be replaced when it dies. We have found this very freeing. The more we downsize our stuff the better we feel. But we keep the stuff that's important to us. For example, Brent loves hockey and we still have all his hockey equipment in our apartment.

This feeling of freedom experienced by the Farrows is shared by many of the simplicity study participants. And this is true even when the stuff being eliminated does not require much time, money, or energy to maintain. Is it possible that the mere presence of possessions that are neither needed nor valued is a burden even if we have plenty of room to store or display these goods? Perhaps the act of decluttering our physical environment psychologically opens us up a space inside—a space that invites the enduring satisfaction of authentic experience rather than the ephemeral pleasure of material things.

But what about eliminating those things that do serve a purpose—like a washing machine, for example. Really, how satisfying can washing your clothes in a laundromat be? Isn't a trip to the laundromat one of the most lonely, depressing, and boring activities ever conceived by the architects of twentieth century living? At least that is my recollection of laundromat excursions during college. And for those of us well beyond college age, like Brent and Ellen, what would our friends and acquaintances think should they happen to walk by and see us in there, folding our clothes with a long, sad look on our face? Ah, but there we go again, limiting ourselves to choices inside our cultural box. Read on for a broader view.

It is true that some of the Farrows' friends do not understand their choices: "The fact that we ride the bus and use a laundromat frankly horrifies some in our social circle who tell us they could never do that." As it turns out, the reaction of the Farrows' social circle may be a bit shortsighted. Laundromat duty for the Farrows is all but boring and depressing. Each Saturday morning, Brent and Ellen meet up with a few not-so-horrified friends at the local laundromat, conveniently located near their apartment. They load the washers and then the entire group takes off for breakfast at a nearby restaurant. After breakfast they return to the laundromat and continue visiting as they fold their clothes.

This scene is reminiscent of community activities of earlier times and other cultures—working together while talking and sharing. In our highly mechanized western culture, we spend much more time alone in our separate homes outfitted with so-called labor saving devices. What's wrong with this picture?

Brent and Ellen's sense of home—their spatial experience of home base—extends well beyond their small apartment. For example, they frequent the public library a few blocks away. The widowed, Italian woman who lives downstairs is a close friend; she brings such joy to their lives. As Ellen observes, "We would rather be near pleasant people than live in a larger home." They enjoy walking (often with their miniature poodle), stopping at various points to visit with friends and acquaintances.

For Brent and Ellen, the positive aspects of living in a small, urban apartment far outweigh the adjustments and compromises required of them. Deprivation is not part of the scene. As Ellen reflects,

We love to eat and the small kitchen space is an adjustment but I am happily experimenting. Besides, there are several restaurants within a block or two (Ukrainian, Italian, Chinese, Greek) which have excellent food and casual surroundings. Because we are not doing this out of poverty, we can afford to make mistakes and if we need something we gave away we can always replace it.

I have enough space for myself because I have the entire place to myself while Brent is at work. Sometimes I get up and read during the night.

I am often awake at night due to years of working the night shift. I quite enjoy both the night shift and night reading for this reason. Brent is very social and doesn't seem to need or want time to himself.

The Farrows share a common experience in living simply—the feeling of walking this path alone. I checked in with Ellen and Brent almost two years after their move. Ellen reports that,

We are hanging in there with voluntary simplicity but have not found too many kindred spirits. After all, the dominant culture teaches us that, "You are what you have." Canada is a country of moderates and I fear our lifestyle is seen by many as too radical. I think if we were interested in the rural life there would be more support, but we really like city life.

And Brent elaborates:

We have learned not to comment when people complain about not having enough money and their uncertain futures. How much is enough varies greatly from one individual and one couple to the next. Some of our friends have what we consider to be extravagant lifestyles, yet they can't possibly maximize their RRSPS [retirement savings account] or afford the kind of holiday that they really want. On the other hand, we have received support and encouragement from some friends and acquaintances who have been contemplating a similar change in lifestyle. One work friend reported with great excitement that they are selling their house in the new year and renting something smaller. So, whether our friends agree with us or tolerate us, we don't plan on losing any friendships over this.

Brent and Ellen's frugal lifestyle is paying off financially. In fact, they are able to live on Brent's salary and save all of Ellen's income. Living mindfully with money is second nature for Ellen:

I learned a valuable lesson as a child. When I was about nine years old, I spent 25¢ on some Mexican jumping beans. I was devastated when

they stopped jumping after two days. Ever since then I have been very careful about money. This experience taught me to be a good money manager—frugal, responsible and conservative with my money. Now, when I consider a potential purchase, I ask myself, "Is this a Mexican jumping bean?"

The Farrows are gaining ground on their financial target—living off the interest from their savings. Frequently, one partner in a marriage has a lower risk tolerance than the other when it comes to money. In this case, Brent needs a larger nest egg than Ellen does to feel comfortable. Ellen does not plan on working in the healthcare field once they have that nest egg:

I would not have any trouble filling my time. We would get a small house with a big garden. I would get more involved with dog training. We would volunteer for literacy programs at the library and community programs like Habitat for Humanity. We are avid readers. Perhaps I would work as a credit counselor. I feel that I might be able to help those who struggle with managing their money.

Ellen's fantasies of her future life of financial freedom dispel another myth about simple living—that is, the myth that people who seek simplicity have lost all ambition and goals and are simply looking for a financial means to be lazy. As is evident by the stories in this book, most of us have needs and desires for meaningful work, quite apart from whether that work brings in income. Financial freedom gives us the opportunity to work for non-monetary reasons.

Even though Brent and Ellen have a financial goal for the future, they live in the present. They cherish the freedom and ease of living in a small, urban apartment. They have the courage to follow their own paths.

City Boys Take to the Farm—Mike Warren and Bob Smith

Fifteen years ago, Mike Warren was the quintessential city boy, soaking up the stimulation of urban life in Washington D.C. and working 10 to 12 hours a day as a computer programmer. Mike lived with his life partner, Bob Smith, who also worked with computers. As the years rolled on, Mike and Bob grew increasingly dissatisfied with their careers, not only with the long hours, but also with the frustration of dealing with corporate bureaucracies. Finding other more satisfying work would be a challenge—Mike's self-worth was inextricably tied to what he did for a living. He did not know what else he could do, nor did he have the self-confidence to explore other alternatives.

Then, a series of health problems during the 1980's gave Mike and Bob the impetus and courage to take a hard look at their lives. Bob had a congenital lung condition that required surgeries in 1980 and 1983. In 1988, Mike sustained a serious back injury while lifting a stone basin for a friend. During this period, they lost several close friends to AIDS and cancer. These events led Mike and Bob to appreciate how precious life is and encouraged them to live in the moment. Mike explains the process:

I started to make changes in my life after my back injury. Several weeks staring at the ceiling above my bed forced me to rethink a few things. I credit one book with transforming my thinking on many subjects: Notes on How to Live in the World—And Still Be Happy, *by Hugh Prather. It showed me ways of changing my relationships and career; it helped give me the courage to take risks.*

Bob and Mike made changes in their lives gradually. Six months after Mike's back injury, he quit his job to work as a consultant in the same field. Mike credits his successful recovery (by swimming, bicycling to work, and working shorter hours) with giving him the confidence and guts to take this risk. And the risk paid off, financially and otherwise; he found he could make good money as a consultant while working fewer hours.

Mike and Bob focused on saving money for an early retirement. They fantasized about living in Italy, sipping cappuccino from a sun-drenched patio. They sold both cars and bought one to share, using that one car rarely, preferring to ride their bicycles to work. They ate vegetables from their garden. Bob used his carpentry skills to build some of their furniture.

As they started to take more control of their lives, Mike developed greater self-confidence in designing a life of his choosing. The turning point came two years later. Mike explains:

One evening at dinner we assessed our financial situation and our personal and professional lives. Suddenly we realized we could make the break and start something new. After considering the pros and cons, we came to the conclusion we had to make the move or regret it the rest of our lives.

Mike and Bob sold or gave away all their possessions except for Mike's Macintosh computer and whatever they could fit into four suitcases. They took off for Italy, choosing to settle down in the small town of Orvieto. However, the life of their dreams in a small, romantic Italian village was not to be. After several frustrating weeks of searching for an affordable rental, they were about to give up and return home. Then, the proprietor of the small hotel where they were staying offered to rent them an apartment in a palazzo—a former feudal mansion carved up into apartments—in a small, rural town. Chickens and turkeys make their home behind the palazzo, and a 10 to 15 minute walk along a footpath brings you to the palazzo's gardens, orchards, and vineyards. This wasn't exactly what they had envisioned for their expatriate adventure, but they grabbed it with gratitude and gusto.

The palazzo was managed by Palmira and her husband, Nuccio, who lived downstairs from Mike and Bob. The new tenants from America soon became a part of the family:

Nuccio and Palmira grew most of the food (strictly organic) for three families and offered us a plot of land to plant if we would clean it up (it had been an informal village dumping ground). Nuccio and Palmira are

*childless; they adopted us into their extended family of other childless
siblings, took us under their wings, and gave us the confidence to do it on
our own.*

This experience, aptly described by Mike as "accidental living,"
was a major turning point for Mike and Bob. Even though they enjoyed gardening and preserving food in the city, Mike and Bob never
dreamed that they, in Mike's words, "could hack the isolation of
living in the country." However, in Italy they discovered the tranquillity, solitude, and other rewards of living a life deeply connected
with the earth.

The following year, Mike and Bob returned to the states, bought
a ten-acre farm in North Carolina, and settled into a rural life. They
derive much aesthetic pleasure from their contemporary home, a
home they remodeled with their own labor. Mike talks of other pleasures, including "many walks in the woods and much porch sitting."
Most of their food is home grown—chickens, a vineyard, an orchard,
and large vegetable gardens. Baking bread and brewing beer supplement their organic abundance.

I wondered whether Mike and Bob, at one time so entrenched in
city life, felt lonely or isolated in the country. Apparently not. Mike
says they do enjoy occasional visits with friends in a good-sized town
20 miles away. Mike and Bob are also involved in a local historical
society and help organize an annual benefit concert of classical music.

Isn't it interesting how our lives evolve? Mike's term, "accidental living," is so apropos of the way unanticipated events
alter the course of our lives. Mike and Bob never dreamed of
living off the land; their dream was a small town life with
some cultural amenities. But their experience in Italy changed
all that. Living in harmony with the land brought them a deeper
satisfaction than they ever expected. Had it not been for the
lack of affordable apartment rentals in Orvieto, and for staying in a hotel owned by someone who happened to own a

palazzo in the country, it is doubtful that their paths would have led them to rural living. At least that's their best guess.

Think about some of the truly wonderful things that have happened in your life. Were they products of your conscious vision and actions or did serendipitous events occur that altered the course of your life? Certainly, you can benefit from both approaches. Having a vision and then taking action to realize your dreams can no doubt bring rewards. But so can being open to serendipitous events that you never would have envisioned for yourself. The best in life requires a delicate balance between conscious planning and spontaneity.

For Mike and Bob, work and leisure have merged. As Mike explains, "What we used to do in the city for pleasure is now our work—gardening and preparing food for storage. We also enjoy woodworking, music (recorder), reading, genealogical research, pet birds, and bicycling." Maintaining their health and good physical condition is a top priority. In addition to eating a healthy, organic diet, Mike and Bob bicycle three to five times a week and regularly do specific exercises to strengthen their backs. They are conscious of the physical requirements and risks associated with farm work and take appropriate precautions. Mike is forty-six, Bob is fifty-seven, and they hope to live and work on their farm for many years to come.

Financially, this life is doable for Mike and Bob. They bought their farm outright in 1991 at a cost of $108,000. Their annual expenses run about $15,000 a year. The investment income from their savings is sufficient to cover their expenses. They live frugally. They choose not to carry health insurance, focusing instead on prevention, caution, diet, and exercise. Bob is very handy mechanically and can handle most repairs himself. They need few clothes and buy only clothes that are easy to clean and keep in good repair. They cut each other's hair. They own one used, compact truck and rent larger, more comfortable cars to ferry their out-of-town guests to and from

the airport and on sightseeing tours. They often bicycle to the near-
est town for supplies. They enjoy the challenge of "making do."

Health insurance is a thorny issue for those who live frugally
in the United States—in many ways, for all Americans. Wide-
spread social and political commentary attest to the fact that
our health care system is out of control. Even though Mike
and Bob could easily afford health insurance, they choose not
to carry it. Mike feels that the health insurance industry is a
"good idea run amok." Even those who believe that the American health care system is the best in the world acknowledge
that it is very costly.

People facing the question of whether to carry health insurance should evaluate their tolerance for risk carefully. Even
with the best diet, exemplary exercise routines, and fortuitous
genes, a drunk driver (or some other event outside of your
control) can still do major, permanent damage to your body. If
that happens, you may possibly get medical care through various state and federal programs, but your savings and other
assets are not likely to survive the ordeal. You can protect yourself against that risk with health insurance or you can go
without and minimize your risk of a serious illness or injury
with preventive care. Of course in that case, you also assume
the small but potentially devastating risk of an accident that
results in serious injury or illness. Your choice—nobody can
make this decision for you.

Respecting the earth has always been an important value in Mike
and Bob's lives. Mike shares what that means to them:

*Environmental issues have always been important to us; reducing our
impact on the environment was a major reason for changing our lives.*

The changes have not been dramatic because we instituted them over a 25-year period. Most of the changes were made while we still lived in the city. On our farm we don't use pesticides or herbicides. We share our bounty with the wildlife. We also conserve water in order to feed our habit of raising indoor citrus trees—large potted plants require a lot of water. Toward that end, we save gray water. We are letting some of our cleared land revert to woods. Even though we live in the south, we do not use air conditioning. In the winter we keep the house cold and rely on passive solar gain for heat.

Is there a connection between voluntary simplicity and caring for the earth? Does one necessarily involve or lead to the other? For many people, these interests are inextricably connected (see Chapter Thirteen, *Environmental Champions: A Passionate Love for the Earth* and Chapter Fourteen, *The Pierce Simplicity Study: Reflections and Inspiration*). But they wouldn't have to be. For example, Mike and Bob's career dissatisfaction and health concerns provided abundant motivation to simplify their lives. However, in their case, environmental concerns have always been a priority. The vast majority of simplicity study participants (82 percent) feel strongly about preserving the earth's resources. Some have always felt this way, like Mike and Bob, and others developed a greater sensitivity to these issues after they simplified their lives for different reasons. Which comes first? The visionary philosopher, Edmond Bordeaux Szekely, suggested that our innate selves are naturally connected to the earth—that we are genetically programmed to view ourselves as deeply bound with nature and the earth as a whole. With the increasing technological development of the second half of the twentieth century, we have added more and more layers between the earth and us. Our fast-paced lives keep us out of touch with our inner selves, including that part of ourselves that feels a deep connection with the earth. When we slow down and simplify our lives, we reconnect with our

nature-loving natural self, and environmental concerns become a priority.

Back to the City—Jill Osborne

Many people associate simple living with moving from the city to
the country. For Jill Osborne, it has been just the reverse. During the
1970's, Jill and her then husband were inspired to adopt a back-to-
the-land lifestyle. They purchased some land in rural Louisiana,
started building a home, and had two children. It was a struggle.
Their home never quite made it to the finish line. For example, the
kitchen and bathroom had no cabinets and the floors never progressed beyond the plywood stage.

There were other letdowns. Jill felt little connection with other
back-to-the-land people in the area, many of whom had the benefit
of trust funds or other sources of financial security. In contrast, the
Osbornes' money worries were constant. Their only source of income was their home business of making children's clothes out of
cotton and other natural fibers. Jill had mixed feelings about this
enterprise:

*Working at home was great. I believed in my work and loved it. But it
was financially erratic, involved long hours, and had no benefits—no
health care, sick pay, vacation, or retirement benefits.*

Jill found rural living to be anything but simple. In addition to
living in an unfinished home, she hated driving long distances to get
just about anywhere, and homeschooling her older son was a challenge. While Jill enjoyed the peace and beauty of rural living, the
stresses clearly outweighed the benefits.

There is no *right* way to live simply. Jill has not failed at simple
living because she didn't take to a rural lifestyle. You can live
simply in the woods *and* in New York City. Don't try to force

> yourself to live a certain way, but instead pay attention to how you feel living in the city or the country, or somewhere in between. Just as we have unique callings for our purpose in life, we each have an ideal physical environment that will support our efforts to live full lives of balance and purpose.

Seven years ago, the Osborne family moved to a small college town in the Pacific Northwest. They bought a 1,000-square-foot home with a monthly mortgage payment of $500. Jill and her husband continued their children's clothing business for a few more years when they decided to end their marriage. The boys, now fifteen and nine, live with Jill and spend time with their father, who lives nearby, several days a week. Jill works 30 hours a week in data entry at the local college, commuting the two miles to and from work on her bicycle. For Jill, her current more traditional lifestyle beats life in the country, hands down:

I have found life easier and less stressful living in a small college town with a regular job and mortgage for a finished house. I don't drive as much, I have good health insurance (including dental and eye care), and my children are more independent here. The simple life has involved plugging into the system more for me.

Another benefit of Jill's new life is a warm and supportive neighborhood community, including frequent vegetarian, pot luck dinners:

It's so nice that many families in our neighborhood share our values. There is an old fashioned feeling to the neighborhood, with a lot of trust, commitment, and sharing. Often my kids and I borrow one of the neighbor's dogs for a walk and a romp in the leash-free park.

What a refreshing change from the isolation Jill felt in the country! Jill and her sons rely on the library, hiking, gardening, and free events for their leisure. Jill is also very pleased that her children can be much more independent than they were in the country. For example, the boys can walk to school and to their friends' homes.

Jill's job is not ideal—it provides little intellectual or career satis-faction—but it does offer a stable paycheck and benefits. Unlike her home-based business, which tended to consume much of her mental energy, Jill can leave her work at the office at the end of the day. Overall, it is a better choice for Jill, for now. However, she is also eager to make a change to improve the quality of her work life. Recently, Jill renewed her teaching certificate and is exploring jobs in alternative education.

Jill's choices illustrate the use of *deferred gratification* as a tool to getting what you want, ultimately. For the last four years, Jill has set aside her desire for a rewarding career position in exchange for a stable economic environment and an opportunity to live simply and in community with compatible neighbors. Now, she is focusing on improving her work life and hopes to find the ideal teaching position soon. Many of us can have it all—interesting work, enriching relationships, the opportunity to pursue our passions—but sometimes we can't have it all RIGHT NOW. Being comfortable with deferring gratification in some aspects of your life will allow you to enjoy the present fully while building for the future.

Jill's work commitment of 30 hours a week (down from her previous 40-hour work week) has a substantial impact on her family life. Dinnertime is special in Jill's household; she and the boys take time to connect with each other and enjoy their meal. Jill also makes a point to spend time with each of her sons individually at least once a week.

What would you do with an extra ten hours a week of free time? If you believe you cannot possibly quit your job because you want to maintain your current standard of living, what about working out a compromise with yourself? Could you reduce your material wants by 25 percent of your after-tax income and buy yourself that extra ten hours?

The Osborne boys are very aware that having Mom available more means there is less money for material things. Their peers have more money to spend; however, for the most part, the boys do not feel deprived. Rather, they feel grateful when their friends invite them on snowboarding trips and other events that they could not afford themselves.

One of the simplicity study participants shared her view that our hunger for material things is a substitute for emotional cravings that go unsatisfied. This theory is borne out by Jill's sons. Instead of feeling deprived because many of their friends have more material goodies than they do, they feel grateful that their friends often share their blessings. I suspect that this is in part because they are getting their emotional needs met not only from a caring mother, but also from a dedicated father who spends time with the boys every week.

Jill learned the values of living simply and frugally from her mother, a single mom and English teacher. Jill's mother would frequently comment on the waste in other people's lives and point out to her children that their trips to Europe every five years were possible only because they lived frugally. Jill did not feel deprived then nor does she feel deprived now: "I feel I live like a queen on very little money."

Jill is a single mom living on an annual income of $23,000 (including child support). She wants for nothing; in fact, she would be happy living on less. Much of what is working in Jill's life has to do with her physical environment. She chose a town with a moderate climate and reasonable real estate values. She chose a job two miles from her home, allowing her to commute by bicycle. She chose a modest home in a neighborhood with built-in support and companionship. It works for her.

Lessons and Reflections

One thing is clear from hearing the stories of Brent and Ellen Farrow, Mike Warren and Bob Smith, Jill Osborne, and the Duran family—the pros and cons of living in the city or the country are very much a subjective matter of individual preference. The most important lesson here is to try to live without fixed notions of which is better. Try to be open to what works for you and your family. Remove the word "should" from your vocabulary when it comes to these issues.

If you have tried something that did not work out, or are in the middle of such an effort, be encouraged to know that you have company. False starts are common for those who live simply and authentically. The only way to avoid them is to accept whatever lifestyle you start out with in your early adult years, and then never change—not a very appealing option.

Large cities (populations over 500,000) and medium sized urban areas (populations of 100,000 to 500,000) are the home for 46 percent of the simplicity study participants while another 22 percent live in the suburbs of those urban areas. That leaves only 15 percent who live in small towns and 17 percent who live in rural areas. Only a handful of participants expressed any dissatisfaction with their location. To the contrary, most indicated that their current location is a positive factor in their quest for simplicity.

People who enjoy urban life mention city conveniences (often within walking distance), such as the library, cafes, local markets with fresh produce, and public transportation, as factors that support their efforts to live simply. They enjoy the stimulation of other people, places, and events on a regular basis. It is usually their comfort level with the volume of stimulation that determines whether a small town or large city (or something in between) will best suit them.

Those who live in rural areas talk about how much they cherish the natural beauty and quiet that surrounds them. Watching wildlife eating, walking, or playing in their yards is an oft-repeated rave. The focus for some of these ruralists (17 percent) is working their land—growing food, raising animals, restoring the land to its natural state. They appear to settle into a rhythm that corresponds with the seasons, working harder during the spring and summer months, retreating to a more quiet time during the fall and winter. However, most (83 percent) direct their paid work or volunteer efforts to other areas, sometimes in a business out of their home but more often they commute to a traditional job.

All this reminds us that simple living is not a prescribed, defined lifestyle; it is a way of thinking and being in this world. Choosing an environment to settle into is not particularly simple. You need to know a lot about yourself. See if you can answer these questions:

♦ Do you thrive on solitude (lots of it) or do you tend to get lonely if you don't see people (other than your immediate family) on a regular basis?

♦ Are you an outdoor person who likes physical work, or do you prefer to curl up with a book in front of a fire?

♦ Do you crave the stimulation of different surroundings and events or are you content to stay in one place?

♦ Do you get a thrill from taking care of many of your basic needs personally, such as growing and preserving food, cooking, making household repairs, sewing clothes?

♦ What do you like and not like about your current living environment?

The answers to these questions do not necessarily point you in one direction or the other. You can be lonely in a city as easily as you can in the country. But the process of asking and answering these types of questions will lead you to knowing what will work best for you. And finally, don't forget—the only way to truly know anything in this life is to experience it. So, if you can set up a trial experiment before making any radical changes—for example, rent a home in the country for a few months before selling your condo in the city— so much the better.

Chapter Six

Work We Can Live With:
A Balancing Act

Recently my husband and I visited with his son from a prior marriage, a twenty-nine-year-old, earnest young man who also happens to be drop-dead gorgeous, funny, smart, and considerate. We were talking about simple living and my stepson commented, "That's of no interest to me. I have no desire to reduce my expenses so that I don't need to work much. It's important to have goals and ambitions in your life." Jim Jr.'s impressions of living simply bring to mind early media articles on this subject, often depicting people sitting in coffee houses during normal work hours, sipping their lattes, contemplating life, and maybe dashing off a poem or two.

While this sounds like a lovely way to spend an afternoon, it is not a lifestyle favored by the participants in the simplicity study. Purposeful work is important to the vast majority of people who live simply. The problem in discussing the subject of work is that we do not share a common definition of what it is. Webster's dictionary defines work as "physical or mental effort exerted to do or make something." Of course, this definition would include almost all activity during our waking hours. In the context of simple living, work can be best defined as purposeful activity that (1) uses a person's skills and abilities (2) to contribute to the welfare of the person, other people or other life forms (3) in a manner that is in tune with the person's values and (4) is in balance with the rest of his or her life. Whether an activity generates compensation or societal recognition is not material to the true essence of work. In the end, each individual—and only that person—must determine whether a given activity constitutes a form of work.

Success a la Brophy—Victoria and Tom Brophy

Some people would describe Victoria and Tom Brophy as a "DINK" couple—double income, no kids. At forty-five and forty-one, Victoria and Tom are successful, respected professionals. Victoria is a physician, specializing in pediatrics. Tom obtained a master's degree in counseling and now works as a counselor. However, the Brophys' lifestyle bears little resemblance to the typical DINK professional couple.

Soon after they married 12 years ago, Victoria entered a residency program at Temple University in Philadelphia. After she completed her residency, the Brophys moved to a medium-sized urban area in the Northeast where Victoria joined a small practice with two other women physicians. At that point, it was Tom's turn to pursue his academic interests. He entered a master's program in counseling.

Tom and Victoria became involved in the various communities that formed their lives—medical, university, and church. Their social calendar blossomed. The Brophys soon discovered that there was a prescribed lifestyle for physicians—dining in expensive restaurants, drinking exquisite wines, and attending posh theater events. The dress code for some of these affairs was quite elegant. For example, Victoria bought a new, long dress each year for an extravagant, society affair.

Speaking of clothes, one of Victoria's partners disapproved of her wardrobe, constantly harping on Victoria to dress more in the style of a successful physician. Victoria succumbed to societal pressure to the point that one year she spent over $7,000 on clothes.

Your style of dress is a form of artistic expression and should be tailored (pun intended) to reflect your artistic self. Some of us spend great amounts of time and money dressing to please others and not so much to please ourselves. Our purpose in grooming (other than warmth and some minimal level of appropriate dress) should be the smile on our faces when we look in the mirror, a smile that results from the aesthetic pleasure of what we see, not from the anticipation of approval by others. And this is why a certain style of grooming will be pure pleasure for one person and a burden for another. For example, consider the practice of a woman polishing her nails, either by doing it herself or paying someone else to do it. It may cost a little or a lot, but either way it takes time and energy. Does it enhance her life any? Does she experience an artistic or aesthetic pleasure from it? Does she enjoy the actual activity of polishing her nails? Or does she feel that it's just one more thing that she needs to fit into her already busy life so that she can satisfy her image of what a properly groomed woman in our society should look like? Does she feel guilty if she skips it? Living simply involves taking a hard look at how we spend our time and money and making sure our activities reflect our authentic values and deepest satisfactions.

For a while, Tom and Victoria willingly participated in the quintessential American Dream—buying more than they needed or wanted—because, after all, Victoria was a physician and that's what physicians did. For example, the Brophys bought a 2,900-square-foot home in a prestigious neighborhood without considering whether they really needed or wanted that much space. And true to the lifestyle of the successful physician, the Brophys purchased a boat and slip on a nearby lake.

Eventually, Tom and Victoria's inner voices led them to the realization that their lives were high on consumption and low on fulfillment. This realization came gradually, in small increments. Victoria missed having the time to meditate, garden, and simply spend a lazy day curled up with a book. Their Catholic faith had always been an important priority for them and although they attended Mass regularly, they didn't feel much connection with their faith.

They sensed that their lives were not quite right, but it was not until after a later move that they were able to fully understand what was missing. Tom explained,

Our lifestyle forced us to compartmentalize what we believed in and how we lived. I complained about quite a few things in the church, but knew that the biggest problem was with me, not the church. However, it was not until we later moved to Pennsylvania that I was able to slow down, take account of things, reassess, and make changes. Some things (like a house) can be changed easily. The change of making my faith and church a more central part of my life took a geographical move—a new start.

The Brophys were also concerned about their expanding appetite for spending, in part due to their childhood experiences. Victoria experienced a series of family financial crises growing up, leaving her with a feeling of tremendous economic insecurity. Tom grew up in a family that could barely afford the basic necessities. Financial security is a high priority for both of them.

The Brophys eventually grew weary of feeling stressed about all the possessions they owned; they worried about them being stolen or lost in a fire. They felt the burden of high mortgage payments and the long work hours needed to support their lifestyle. They were also dissatisfied with how little they were saving. Victoria was feeling burned out with her work as a physician. She wanted to take a break from her practice, but they needed her income to pay for their physician's lifestyle. It was time to make some changes.

In 1992, Tom and Victoria sold their large, custom home and downsized to a 1,300-square-foot tract home. The reactions of the Brophys' friends and colleagues were intense. Many of them were horrified at their decision to buy a home in a neighborhood that was populated by teachers and policemen rather than lawyers and doctors. Some expressed surprise and dismay that they did not buy "a doctor's home." Others speculated that maybe Tom and Victoria were having marital trouble and needed to downsize as a prelude to a separation. It became clear that many of these friendships were built around a certain lifestyle, rather than on genuine concern and caring. It is no surprise that some of these relationships did not survive the Brophys' transition. Living simply can sometimes be a lonely and isolating journey.

Unfortunately, the reactions of the Brophys' friends and acquaintances are not that unusual. To the extent that people seek validation of their values from their peers, it is not surprising that when one member of a community or social group makes radical changes, the others may feel a sense of unease. Sometimes they might feel threatened; this is often expressed in hostility towards the person who is changing the rules. It takes a good deal of fortitude to strike out on your own path. The level of support varies. For further discussion of the support experienced by the simplicity study participants, see Chapter Fourteen, *The Pierce Simplicity Study: Reflections and Inspiration*.

It was not just the Brophys' friends who failed to understand. Tom and Victoria's choices contradicted the essence of the American dream. For example, their mortgage lender insisted that the Brophys write a letter explaining why they were borrowing so much less than they could afford; their behavior was clearly suspect.

However, all this resistance and judgment did not keep the Brophys from making substantial changes in their lives. After Tom obtained his master's degree in 1994, the Brophys moved to central Pennsylvania where Tom accepted a position in an established counseling practice. Victoria planned to take a year off from practicing medicine. This time, they bought a home they could pay for in cash.

Victoria thoroughly enjoyed the break from practicing medicine. She spent her days setting up their new home and just *being*—landscaping, cooking, gardening, relaxing, reading, thinking, and listening to music. On some days Victoria took off to explore the area, with no planned itinerary.

After about six months, Victoria started thinking about practicing medicine again. She came to realize it wasn't medicine she disliked; it was working full-time in a stressful, high-pressure practice that did not sit well with her soul. She found that she missed caring for patients. Even as a child, Victoria always knew that she wanted to be a doctor and that was still true. She decided to search for an opportunity to practice medicine on a part-time basis, a rare commodity in the field of medicine. She received one lucrative offer but turned it down because it came with an hour and a half commute. Then one day, Victoria was chatting with her neighbor who suggested that Victoria contact her children's pediatrician, a woman physician in a small practice in a town only 30 minutes away. Victoria called this doctor and explained what she was looking for—a part-time job share arrangement. There was a long pause after Victoria finished talking and then the doctor responded, "I can't believe it. I have a two-year-old and have been looking for exactly this arrangement for two years. Please come down here as soon as you can." Victoria was thrilled.

Victoria is now well settled in her 20-hour per week job share practice. It's working out very well. Tom is enjoying his counseling practice. The Brophys' living expenses are considerably less than they were in their former lifestyle. They plan to keep their eight-year and 11-year-old cars until they die a natural death. They have no debt. They are saving as much as possible and anticipate reaching financial freedom—being able to live off the income from their savings—in seven or eight years.

In the meantime, Tom and Victoria enjoy life tremendously. In addition to a slower paced life at home, they have the time and resources to travel—their favorite passion. They adore Europe. In the last five years, they have traveled to Portugal, Spain, France, and Italy. Backpacking, roaming around on rail passes, and staying at hostels enlivens their travel experiences. Gone are the four-star hotels and expensive cuisine. Their frequent flier mileage helps to keep the cost of airfare reasonable. They charge most of their living expenses to their credit card to earn miles. Of course, they pay the balance off each month.

They enjoy Europe so much that they may move there at some point, perhaps living in Spain or Italy. Their dream is to have a home base in Europe and then take off to work on various volunteer projects throughout the world. One great benefit of the medical profession is that Victoria's skills are portable. She could volunteer with organizations such as Doctors without Borders or the Red Cross. The Brophys are choosing to live on considerably less than they earn to make this dream come true.

The benefits of living more simply have touched all areas of the Brophys' lives. They enjoy locally grown produce, eat less processed food, and have time to exercise three times a week. Living simply has also led to a deepening spirituality for them. Victoria feels it is connected with having more time. While the Brophys have always been active in their Catholic church, Victoria now has time during the week for inner growth—meditation, spiritual reading, centering prayer, and mindfulness. She suspects that people who are spiritually inclined might also be attracted to simplicity and vice versa. That theory is certainly confirmed by the experiences of the simplicity study participants.

The changes in the Brophys' lives have been deeply gratifying. However, the resistance and judgment from some friends, colleagues, and family continues. For a while, Tom and Victoria gave family and friends gifts of *experiences* like movie tickets, gifts of their labor, and magazine subscriptions instead of *things*. They use a software program to make their own birthday and special occasion cards. A holiday newsletter, sent by e-mail if possible, has replaced Christmas cards. Victoria comments that, "I just can't stand the waste anymore." Unfortunately, some of the Brophys' family and friends have interpreted these gifts of *experiences* instead of *things* as an indication of less care or love from the Brophys. The Brophys have made some changes to accommodate the feelings of their loved ones:

We are going to exchange gifts with family and some close friends, but with the theme that it be a single, meaningful gift. The ordeal of trying to explain simplicity came across as stinginess, and it just wasn't worth it.

People still want the holidays to be special, and gift giving is an essential part of it.

Recently, Tom told his mother that he would like a certain book for his birthday present, trying to ward off another gift of stuff that was neither needed nor wanted. Tom's mother complained in exasperation, "Everything I buy for you is something you absolutely want!" A long pause followed. Then she started laughing, realizing what she had said.

The Brophys are aware that others often perceive them as unusual or weird and don't know quite how to react to them. The nurses are shocked that Victoria brings her own lunch to work; Victoria just doesn't fit the profile of the successful physician. Once Tom was in Victoria's office and her male colleagues asked Tom if he played golf. When Tom responded in the negative, they really didn't know what to say next. The social culture of the medical community centers on skiing, golf, money, and second homes.

Most of the Brophys' friends and family have no interest in what they are doing or don't want to discuss it. Some of them think it's "cute" because "after all, they have the money and ability to make this choice." Other than meeting with a group of people to share their experiences of living simply, they don't get a tremendous amount of support. As a result, they no longer share their enthusiasm for voluntary simplicity unless they sense that others share their values. The Brophys have no interest in preaching to others; they prefer to model their lifestyle, and let others choose what works best for them.

Living simply can sometimes be a lonely and isolating experience. Many participants in the simplicity study report that their friends, family, and associates cannot relate to their life of simplicity. If you are surrounded by people who at best think you are nuts, or, at worst, feel hostile towards you for the choices that you make, consider joining a simplicity circle. A simplicity circle is a small group of people (maybe six to eight) who share similar values about living simply and who meet regu-

larly to share and learn from each other. If there isn't an existing simplicity circle in your area, start one. For information
on simplicity circles, see the Resource Guide at the end of this
book.

Tom and Victoria view this way of life as a process, not a destination. As Victoria explains,

*It has been a step-by-step growth process down the path of simplicity.
I somehow thought that it might just happen—that it would be a place—
but I am constantly reminded that is it not a place; it is a process. The
daily living of it is a choice and it involves growth, thought, further reading, and sharing of experiences. What other people think or do is not a
reflection on me. I am not bound to follow their path. Our goal is to work
at whatever we do because we want to, not because our choices in spend-
ing/lifestyle have made us.*

And that is exactly what Tom and Victoria Brophy are doing.

Most Likely to Succeed—John Andersen

As John Andersen stepped up to the podium at his high school graduation, everyone knew that this young man was destined to fulfill the
American Dream. His achievements were numerous and impressive,
including his role of Salutatorian of a senior class of over 600 students. Even his classmates recognized his potential, voting him "most
likely to succeed." John's opportunities were unlimited—he had the
intellectual abilities and disciplinary skills to achieve anything he set
out to do. Lawyer, doctor, scientist, corporate mogul—he could take
his pick. No door would be closed to him.

Not surprisingly, John excelled in college, graduating with a degree in German literature. But true to John's independent nature,
he did not follow the normal pattern of attending college for four or
five consecutive years. He took a break after his freshman year to
work as a missionary in Germany for 18 months. His exposure to

another culture opened his eyes to other worlds and awakened in him a love for adventure and a passion for learning about people.

John returned to the states, completed his undergraduate work, and contemplated his future. He decided to give the Air Force a try; it would provide financing for further education and give him the opportunity to travel. After completing officer training, John accepted a four-year assignment in England, where he met and married his wife, Mandy.

John's military performance was exemplary. He even found time to earn an MBA through a university extension program on his base. After four years, he was offered a promotion to captain and was told that he would be augmented to the regular Air Force, the equivalent of earning tenure at a university. To everyone's amazement, he declined this promotion.

During this period of high achievement, John was also learning about himself. He was discovering who he really was—not what society or his parents or his friends or anyone else thought he was, or could be, or should be. For example, he gradually realized that he did not feel very comfortable in the military environment. He felt at odds with the values emphasized by the military—team playing, formal hierarchical relationships, and submerging individual expression.

John unearthed a little rebel within, but he needed to silence that rebel in order to perform well in the military environment. Outwardly, he was a model Air Force officer, performing as expected, but feeling trapped inside. He came to understand that what society defined as *career success* not only fell short of his needs for personal fulfillment, but also forced him to adopt a persona in his work life that was not authentic. In short, his strong desire for individual freedom and expression found no home in the military.

Because of this lack of congruence between his true self and the needs of the military, John turned down the promotion that was offered to him. He recalls the shock on the commanding officer's face when John responded to the announcement of his promotion with his own news that he was leaving the military. Clearly, it was not commonplace for someone who performed as well as John to not take the next step. Imagine the dinner conversation between that commanding officer and his wife that evening, "Dear, you are not going to believe this, but this promising young officer...."

The commanding officer's shock on hearing of John's resignation is telling. In our American culture, we assume not only that *more is better* in terms of material possessions, but that *more is better* with regard to career achievements and status. Who told us this? Did our founding fathers teach us that our goal in life should be to achieve as much career status and position as we possibly can? What about life, liberty, and the pursuit of happiness? Who equated those values with career achievements and status?

When John left the military in 1990, he and Mandy returned to the states where John entered a graduate program in German literature at Purdue University in Indiana. For the next few years, John and Mandy lived on his earnings as a graduate teaching assistant, reserve duty pay, and GI Bill benefits.

John obtained his master's degree and was teaching in a summer school program when he started to have second thoughts about his career choice. He became discouraged when he saw that others who had obtained their Ph.D.'s in German literature were struggling to compete for the few good jobs that were available. With Mandy pregnant with their second child, he was concerned about whether he could earn sufficient income to support his family. For John, once again it was time to reevaluate—a familiar step for those who walk the path of simplicity.

The journey to simplicity is often a circuitous one, with many detours along the way. To live simply, mindfully, and authentically requires courage. It takes courage to seek our own paths,

> rather than live the *all-American dream*—a life of work and
> spend—on autopilot. As there are no roadmaps, we inevitably
> will take some wrong turns along the way.

John's next step was a corporate job with potential for a good
income and upward mobility. But again, he felt a clash between his
desires to work in a setting that rewarded individual thinking and
what he perceived was the modus operandi of the corporate world—
submerge the individual to blend into the corporate culture and value
system. He realized he would need to dig deeper to find work that
would both support his family and reflect the person he truly is.

It was John's mother who first suggested that he look at options
for self-employment. He dove into researching these options with
enthusiasm, applying his refined, intellectual and organizational skills
to the task. John eventually decided to buy a franchise, a cleaning
and restoration business.

How could someone in his mid-thirties with an impressive educational and work history end up cleaning other people's homes and
businesses? Did John see himself as a failure? What did his friends
and family think about this change? Wasn't this intelligent, high-
achiever terribly bored with his new choice?

Over the next few years, John had many conversations with himself about the meaning of success. He observed his reactions to his
new work life carefully, gaining insights on what brought him true
satisfaction. He basked in the freedom of being his own boss. He
could set his own hours and often took a few hours off during the
middle of the day. He savored the experience of listening to books
on tape as he drove to his different appointments throughout the
day. What a terrific fringe benefit for someone who reads books like
the rest of us eat our breakfast cereal—one year John read (or listened on tape) to 122 books!

Being his own boss in a business with flexible hours allowed John
to take on other work and explore many personal interests. John
and Mandy share a passion for life-long learning and they have instilled this passion in their children. John also tutors students in
German and math, does some freelance writing, and organized a

German club for homeschooling students. He prefers to work in several capacities on a freelance basis: "I've found that when I'm forced to put most of my time into just one activity, it often becomes boring and loses its appeal."

Another appealing aspect of John's particular business is the opportunity to interact with engaging people who have intriguing stories of their own to share. Over one period of several months, his customers included landlords, doctors, real estate agents, homemakers, school teachers, writers, an interior designer, a drapery manufacturer, stockbrokers, a sculptor, an opera singer, an executive recruiter, and a professional storyteller. Any prejudices a customer might have against people who work in manual labor are erased quickly when John engages them in conversations about their work, travels, or art interests. One typical day included a conversation with an attorney about the beautiful, stained glass and wood flooring in his home, a conversation with an eighty-three-year-old man about his experiences of living through the Depression, and finally, an exchange with an Indian family about their Hindu faith. For John, his work life is an adventure, offering constant opportunities for learning and exploring. He starts out each morning not knowing what interesting people he will meet or what new areas or places he will discover.

While the work of cleaning and restoration is not always intellectually riveting, it does provide John with the time and the environment to *just be* with his thoughts. As he observes, "The mind is a fun place to go."

There appears to be something inherently satisfying with working in ways that use both our heads and our hands. People talk about how fulfilling it is to sew their own clothes, repair their own homes and cars, bake their own bread, and grow food in their gardens. The question is why. One reason may be that working with our hands (sewing, cooking, carpentry, gardening, even housecleaning) supports our inner lives and spirituality more than the typical desk or sales job. For one thing, the mental activity involved in physical work is for the most part slower and less demanding, less constant, than the

mental activity in a desk job. This may allow us to stay more
connected to our real selves and to feel less alienated. It may
also explain why some people who make more than enough
money to pay others to clean their homes and wash their cars
prefer to do these things themselves.

John also enjoys a sense of accomplishment when he completes a
job and can see the tangible results of his work. His customers appreciate the end result, too, and tell him so. A job well done and
appreciated by his customers—simple, straightforward—it suits John
very well. What a contrast to the ill-defined, intangible objectives of
the corporate and military work environments! John no longer
spends his evenings and weekends processing and recovering from
the tensions and conflicts inherent in organizational politics.

John also recognizes that his business requires brainpower. As he
explains, "As an entrepreneur, you get to wear many hats: production, marketing, public relations, accountant, repair person,
purchaser, janitor, etc. With such a range of tasks, it's hard to get
bored, and even possible to get smarter."

John did not come to appreciate the benefits of his new work
choice overnight. It took several years and considerable soul searching to let go of the success model of his teenage and early adult
years. He replaced that model of success with the value of authenticity—a work life that allows him to be the person he is, a staunch
individualist who loves his freedom. Being able to integrate personal
interests into his work is a bonus.

Feeling positive about his choice of work is an ongoing process
for John. He is not unmindful of the fact that, "If I were to go to my
20-year high school reunion, or see some of my old college buddies,
many would probably be shocked to hear what I'm doing for a living."

John's story teaches us many things about the role of work in our
lives. Our western culture promotes certain notions about the relative value of different types of work, such as the belief that
white-collar work is more valuable than manual labor. Undoubtedly, many people would be perplexed by the choices made by John,

a man who could have succeeded in a white-collar environment. This is where living simply departs from the *all-American dream*. It is time to give ourselves and others permission to take on work that reflects our authentic selves. Work that is enjoyable and does not drain you of all emotional and physical energy is an essential aspect of living simply.

An Inside Job—Gloria and Peter Kimball

A casual observer might not notice the dramatic changes in the work lives of Gloria and Peter Kimball. Even their bosses may not fully comprehend the differences. After all, each morning they show up at their same offices and perform many of the same tasks they did before their changes.

Gloria and Peter are financial planners who have worked for the same investment firm for nearly 12 years. During their courtship and early years of marriage, they traveled on the same career path— both very talented, productive, fast-track professionals who worked hard, putting in substantial overtime. Their employer recognized their outstanding performances with regular promotions and salary increases. The Kimballs never questioned their yuppie, fast-track work life; they seemed to be born to follow this path. Ironically, in hindsight, Gloria reflects, "It seems like we were restless and bored and very unhappy with our jobs, which weren't *moving fast enough*." They were even thinking of making a job change to accelerate their ascent up the career ladder.

Gloria and Peter dealt with their underlying ennui and dissatisfaction by playing hard and well, rewarding themselves with frequent restaurant meals, movies, shopping, vacations and ski trips. As Gloria looks back on this stage of their lives, she comments, "We were *renegade spendthrifts* who had gone to college, gotten decent jobs, and were spending money as fast as we made it." They racked up almost $10,000 in credit card debt, had two car loans, and almost no savings. When they bought their home five years ago, they could barely scrape together a five- percent down payment.

Gloria and Peter were addicted to the rush of a speeded-up life. The adrenaline from their fast-track jobs carried over into their personal lives. The thrills in their lives were intense but fleeting. When each new exciting event or thing faded, emptiness settled in until the next thrill showed up. Does this sound familiar? How do you wean yourself off the rush of a speeded-up life? To start, do one thing at a time. You can't possibly focus on your life experiences while they are happening if you are trying to do two or more things at a time. How many times do we eat breakfast while reading the paper, watch TV while eating dinner, and talk on the portable phone while cooking or folding laundry? No need to take this to an extreme. Some experiences are enhanced when combined with others. For example, eating a leisurely dinner by candlelight can be more enjoyable when shared with another. Or there's nothing quite like lying in a hammock on a beautiful day while reading a book, allowing your consciousness to float back and forth between the book and the splendid beauty surrounding you.

Three years ago, the Kimballs' daughter, Nicole, was born. Gloria took four months off work for a maternity leave. She then faced the heart-wrenching need to return to work to support their prior lifestyle of debt and excess. This experience was a serious wake-up call for the Kimballs. They started to read simplicity books and fantasized about living on one income. They no longer wanted to fill their lives with work and spending; they had someone much more important to focus on, and her name was Nicole.

So, what to do? Move to the country, buy an old farmhouse, take on odd jobs to make ends meet? No, the first order of business was to take a hard look at what they had. Fortunately, they bought their California home at a low point in the market, resulting in mortgage payments that were lower than rent would be for a similar home. They were hesitant to walk away from this affordable housing option.

Next, they examined the pros and cons of their existing jobs. They calculated their true hourly wage, adding in the additional hours required to support their jobs and deducting job-related expenses from their salaries. They realized that their jobs could support their objectives of living balanced lives as parents if they made certain adjustments. For example, letting go of their attachment to the managerial fast track could result in profound benefits. The overtime hours would disappear from their normal routines. They could dress casually, spending little time or money on dry-cleaning, ironing, and expensive wardrobes.

The Kimballs considered other appealing aspects of their jobs. Their commute was negligible, as their home was only a short distance from their office. They had earned substantial autonomy and flexibility in their jobs, allowing them to meet the firm's performance expectations without watching the clock. Lunch at home reduced midday restaurant expenses, not to mention the convenience of having time midday to plan for or prepare dinner, or do a little housecleaning. When considering all the hidden costs of jobs, they realized that their current employment could meet their goals. They decided to keep their jobs, but let go of their aspirations for advancement, along with the long hours and stress that went with those yearnings. Their level of contentment in the slow lane at work is quite a contrast to the frustration they felt in the same jobs when they weren't "moving fast enough."

Hmnnn.....To quit, or not to quit—that is often the question we wrestle with when we are in a job that exhausts us and excites us at the same time. Maybe there is another option. Perhaps we can "quit" the portions of the job that deplete us, and still have enough left in the job to provide some rewards, including a paycheck. Even if what remains does not engage your passions, it may still serve as a bridge to a future time when your work and passions are one and the same.

It was not that difficult emotionally for Gloria and Peter to let go of the yuppie, fast-track, mind set. When Nicole came along, their priorities crystallized for them. Their former work-and-spend lifestyle felt so inappropriate; they just naturally lost interest in it. For the most part, the Kimballs did not feel judged or ostracized by friends and colleagues for opting out of the career fast track. They credit this acceptance to the general tolerance for alternative lifestyles in California. On the other hand, Gloria's mother does have some negative judgments about their changes, particularly with regard to what Peter should be doing to provide for his family. This is not surprising; living simply goes against the grain of mainstream values in America. One has to have considerable inner fortitude to forge this path.

Perhaps the only thing Peter and Gloria miss from their prior lives is the traveling they enjoyed before Nicole came along. For now, their goals are to have another child and at that point, live on Peter's income so that Gloria is available to be a full-time mom and family manager. The Kimballs hope to resume their travel adventures once the children are a little older.

In the last three years, the Kimballs have made substantial progress in reaching their financial goals. The credit card debt and car loans are paid off, they have saved and invested another $35,000, and the equity in their home has doubled. Their lives feel in balance now. Nicole is in pre-school three days a week (which her parents feel is very beneficial), and Gloria's sister takes care of Nicole the other two work days. Gloria and Peter work staggered hours which allows Nicole to spend time with her dad part of each workday morning and be with her mom during the late afternoons.

Living simply often generates small discoveries and little presents that surprise us. For Gloria, the financial incentive to handle more of the family's practical needs has been a positive experience. For example, when Gloria feels tired after a day in the garden or doing home repairs, it's a satisfying, "good tired" feeling. What a contrast to the enervating, numbing experience after a long day at the office when watching TV passively was all Gloria was good for. It has also been an experience of self-discovery for Gloria:

I have always had an interest in home repairs, but I used to feel my time was too valuable when I could just pay someone else to do things. Learning that I could hand wash virtually every item I used to dry-clean, and do without the rest, was amazing to me.

Other changes have occurred. Gloria and Peter are much more interested in preserving the earth's resources since they embarked on the path of voluntary simplicity. Having a child seems to affect many people in this way. Gloria explains: "Realizing in a concrete way that the world needed to go on beyond our life times made us want to live more lightly on the earth." It's interesting how this works. Gloria and Peter both lived in California through the 1970's and were educated about the ways in which our society's activities were harming the environment. Yet, as Gloria reflects, "We were not personally engaged in the issues, figuring that somehow other people were taking care of these problems."

In addition to having a child, other factors contributed to the Kimballs' increased interest in environmental issues. Gloria noticed that when she did things to save money (for example, combining her errands to save on gas), she became more aware of the environmental benefits of her new lifestyle. Her increased awareness of environmental issues reinforced her concern for preserving the earth's resources, which in turn enhanced her awareness.

Many people report a similar circular pattern. They may start out doing something to save money, or improve their health, or relieve stress. Gradually, they realize that these actions also help the environment. This awareness produces a feeling of satisfaction, a feeling of doing something that benefits others, and this feeling in turn reinforces their actions. For further discussion of this phenomenon, see Chapter Thirteen, *Environmental Champions: A Passionate Love for the Earth*.

We have much to learn from Gloria and Peter. Sometimes the changes we need to make are all on the inside. In contrast to John Andersen (see story above), the Kimballs didn't need to change jobs to enhance the quality of their lives. Instead, a change in their mental attitudes about their work was their creative work solution. They needed to look at the glass (their jobs) as half full (a sweet deal) instead of half empty (not moving fast enough). As we will see time and again, the types of changes the Kimballs are making take years, not weeks or months. They are getting close to their ultimate goal of living on one income, but the process takes time, patience, and hard work. In the meantime, their lives are infinitely richer and more satisfying than before the birth of their daughter. Their lives illustrate the true concept of simple living—an authentic life of balance, purpose, and joy.

Soulful Work—Sally Armstrong

Five years ago, Sally Armstrong held a position of power and autonomy in a large, prestigious accounting firm. Over a period of seven years, she not only established her professional expertise, but she also functioned as an excellent team leader on complex, long-term projects. Her work experiences instilled in Sally a strong sense of self-esteem, something sorely missing in her life due to a troubling childhood. She had been drawn to the accounting profession as a way to round herself out—to develop analytical skills and general competence in the business world. Being able to function in the world of business, and do it admirably, was terribly important to her: "I needed to prove to myself that I can do anything I want to do."

Sally's mastery of the business world did not require her to forego a personal life. For example, Sally's spirituality had been the driving force in her life for 25 years. Even during her years as a star accountant, she continued her yoga and meditation practices. At the same time, she immersed herself in the consumer lifestyle associated with material success. She now finds it difficult to identify with the person she was back then: "I know that deep down I was very unhappy with the lifestyle, even though I enjoyed it. I was always looking for someone or something to fill the gap."

Gradually, Sally's desire to develop her spiritual practices, especially meditation, became a paramount concern in her life. She was also passionate about sculpting. Once she derived the self-esteem benefits from her business success, her work provided less ongoing value for her. Eventually, she came to realize that it was all the complexity in her life that prevented her from living as she wanted to.

The turning point for Sally was a visit with friends on a Caribbean island. This holiday turned into a retreat of sorts:

I seriously looked at how dissatisfied I was with the life I was leading, even though from the outside it was so successful. I couldn't save any money because I had bought into the lifestyle of everyone around me.

Sally concluded that she would need to make some drastic changes. Before she ventured into the business world, she had worked with children for many years in various capacities, including work in day care centers and as a nanny. It occurred to Sally that working as a live-in nanny would be very compatible with her interests in meditation and sculpting. She accepted a position as a live-in nanny four years ago with a family who had a new baby boy. Now, that boy is four years old and has a two-year-old sister.

Today, nothing in Sally's life resembles her prior life. Well, almost nothing. She still has two days a week off, although that wasn't always true in her accounting job. She lives with her employer's family in an affluent suburb of Cincinnati, surrounded by acres of woods. Her work day may be long (10-12 hours), but there is considerable flexibility built into that work day. For example, she can easily do her laundry and grocery shopping while taking care of the children. That leaves her non-work time completely free to engage in her true vocations of artist and spiritual seeker. As Sally observes, "I have large blocks of time to sculpt; I can structure my day so there's time to meditate morning and evening; I read a lot and spend two nights a week in meditation circles or with friends." Unlike many of us, she does not spend her Saturdays on chores and shopping.

Sally's work as a live-in nanny is an excellent illustration of a job that supports, rather than detracts from, a person's true vocations—in this case, Sally's art and spiritual practices. We need to start thinking "outside the boxes." What would you love to do if you didn't have to work? Is there a job you could do that would free up some time to do those things? If you are passionate about something you can do at home, have you considered a position as a caretaker (see the Resource Guide, Newsletters section, at the end of this book)? If you want to stay home with your children, but also want an income, what about taking care of other children at the same time? Keep on thinking, keep on trying, don't give up, follow your dreams.

Sally appreciates the simplicity in the infrastructure of her new lifestyle. She has no commute. The dress code is wide open and dry cleaning is a distant memory. She prepares her own, simple meals in the family kitchen. Her living quarters consist of one 20-foot x 15-foot room and a bathroom. The time and energy for cleaning is minimal. She spends no time or energy hassling with those never-ending, pesky home maintenance chores like repairing appliances, getting bids for exterior painting, or trudging around to stores looking for draperies. Her employer, who also employs a gardener, a chef, and a housecleaner, handles it all. In many ways, Sally is shielded from all the normal stresses of daily living, which frees her to focus on her work with the children and her personal interests in art and meditation.

We often think about the hours we put in at our jobs, and sometimes we are even conscious of the time to support that work—time for commuting, dressing, and decompressing. But do you really know how much you spend on the infrastructure of your life? How much time do you spend each week cooking, housecleaning, doing laundry, shopping for groceries and other household items, making home repairs and improvements, doing yard work, washing your car, not to mention all the paper-heavy, time consuming tasks like reviewing insurance options, paying bills, and arranging for all the services, like cable TV, that have become a standard part of our American lives? Whew! Now, some of these tasks can be very satisfying. If you enjoy cooking and gardening, for example (I actually have a friend who claims to love housecleaning), these tasks should be placed in the credit column of life rather than on the debit side. On the other hand, if you don't get a kick out of spending all afternoon searching for the right tools to repair your broken garage door, this task should be placed on the debit side of your life energy chart. The bestselling book *Your Money or Your Life* popularized the concept of viewing your paid work as life energy you exchange for money. Likewise, you would do well to consider all the other tasks in your life to determine which tasks are forms of life energy that you are trading for something else (like cleaning a large home), and which tasks are satisfying and enjoyable in and of themselves. Then you are in a position to evaluate whether you are getting sufficient value for the life energy you expend on those tasks. For example, is spending six or more hours a week cleaning a large home (or hiring and supervising a person to do it) worth having that size of home?

Sally has rediscovered the pleasures and satisfaction of working with children. She sees her work with the children as "soul work," connecting with and nurturing the spiritual sides of her charges. She feels her role is to help the child hold onto the spirituality we all are born with and too often lose as a seemingly inevitable part of growing up in our western culture. She describes her role as "very invisible work, but also deeply satisfying."

Conscious of the substantial influence a nanny has in a child's early years, Sally focuses on modeling a lifestyle of integrity and love. She teaches environmental awareness to the children through songs, watching nature shows, and creating a ritual of waiting together for the recycling truck to come. She delights in spending many hours

outdoors with the children, taking them on the trails in the woods
and to the neighborhood park. She proudly reports that, "The-two-
year-old can manage two miles without a fuss."

Sally's work with the children in her care gives her a deep, purposeful meaning to her life. She knows that she is making a
contribution, a difference. She feels a great deal of satisfaction from
making an impact that is real and long lasting. Her inner sense of
purpose is strong: "I have had several light-filled dreams where I
know that the work I do with children is far more important to the
planet than anything I did in the corporate world."

Sally's work as a nanny provides the structure for Sally to deepen
her commitment to her spirituality. Even though she is a self-described hermit by nature, her spirituality is *other-directed*; her energy
is directed towards others. As she explains,

*I am going through a shift of consciousness right now regarding my
responsibility towards what I bring to the planet. This means that who I
am at all times becomes important in terms of thoughts and attitudes. I
believe that through my work with a few children and weekly meditation
circles with others holding the planet in light I can have an impact far
greater than I can imagine.*

When asked about the source of her spirituality, Sally responds
that she has always had a sense of it being an integral part of who
she is. She says that she is highly sensitive to her environment and
to other people's emotions. As a child, she learned to go inside of
herself to survive a difficult childhood. She sees herself as introverted,
investing substantial time and energy in reflection, although she
would not describe herself as shy. In fact, her relationships with
friends are an essential part of her life. As an adult, Sally has worked
with a number of spiritual teachers and has trained in various traditions. Her voracious reading in the spiritual area has deepened her
spiritual experiences further.

Letting go of the material trappings of her former lifestyle has not
been particularly difficult for Sally. Her spiritual path is her life. She
worked on the nature of desire, primarily by studying her thoughts
and emotions. As a natural result of this inner work, her attachment

to personal ambition and acquisition lessened. When she left the business world and moved out of her apartment, Sally held a massive garage sale and sold or gave away three-quarters of all her possessions. She looks back on it with little regret: "At a certain point everything became very meaningless to me—it was all only *things*, after all." Now, she enjoys visiting her friends and seeing her former furniture, sculpture, and pottery: "It feels like we are still connected, even though I now live in another state." And even though she personally owns very few possessions, she is living in a beautiful home surrounded by nature's bounty. She has not assumed the lifestyle of a medieval monk.

Sally also views her artistic endeavors as "soul work." Her objective is to produce sculpture that instills a sense of inner harmony and peace in the viewer, rather than art that is primarily an expression of her own persona. Again, her ego and personal ambition in her art is a mere shadow, if that. Her monetary objective in selling her sculpture is to make enough money to pay for the materials. It's not that she would reject additional money for her sculpture, but making money through her art is not her intention or focus.

Because her basic material needs are provided largely by her employer, Sally is able to save money for her retirement years. Ironically, when she was making four times her current salary as an accountant, she couldn't seem to save anything. Her job security derives from her skills and competence in her work. Now in her mid-forties, Sally's experience and maturity can command choice positions. She also works on keeping her body agile and fit, an essential requirement for keeping up with an active two-year-old. These factors all reinforce her feeling of job security.

Sally, a single woman in her mid-forties, is living a lifestyle that is not for everyone. And it may not be Sally's choice forever, either. What is clear, however, is that her current lifestyle is ideal for Sally at this time in her life. Her spiritual path is paramount in her life, and I suspect that it always will be. Whether that path will lead her to different lifestyles in the future is an open question. For example, Sally has been involved in romantic relationships in the past, including one marriage, and is open to the possibility that a primary relationship may again be a part of her life.

In the meantime, being single is not the kiss of death for Sally—far from it. She recalls that as a teenager, she felt despair and alienation because she could not relate to friends whose entire focus in life was getting married and having children. One day Sally and her mother went to visit a neighbor, an older, single woman. Sally was very impressed with this woman who appeared to be happy, at peace with herself, and content with her life. Sally learned that day that living as a single person is a perfectly acceptable way of being.

One personality characteristic that is common to most of the simplicity study participants is a high level of self-esteem. It is not that these people feel at all superior to anyone else. Quite the contrary. They are more likely to believe that the more they learn, the more they realize how little they know. But perhaps because they have worked hard to seek out their unique paths, surviving the highs and lows of such a journey, they develop an inner sense of confidence, a sense that they will not only survive but flourish. They are surprised to discover new strengths in themselves. Self-esteem is a natural outcome of this process.

For Sally, working as a live-in nanny, with most of her material needs provided for, creates an infrastructure for her spiritual life. It is that simple. She is blessed to have discovered what is truly meaningful to her and to have created a lifestyle that allows her to be who she is.

Lessons and Reflections

As we can see from the stories of Tom and Victoria Brophy, John Andersen, Gloria and Peter Kimball, and Sally Armstrong, working simply comes in many shapes and sizes. Full-time work, part-time work, family manager, and parenting are all viable work options. There is no limit to the creative work practices devised by people who live simply. Examples from other simplicity study participants include:

◆ Faye Atkinson, a married woman, CPA, and mother of two teenagers, does accounting work for four months each year during the tax season and spends the balance of the year pursuing other interests, including building up a small homestead on the family's rural property in North Dakota.

◆ Selena Bertino of Everett, Washington, a self-employed nurse and single mother of two children, takes care of a disabled man in her home so she can limit her work hours outside the home to one day a week.

◆ Haley Peter, a married woman with two children, lives frugally with her family in their dream home, a Victorian style farmhouse designed by Haley and her husband. She provides daycare services so she can stay at home with her own children and enjoy her home.

◆ Patricia Rollins, a married woman whose husband is disabled, homeschools her daughter and tutors other children 25 hours a week so she can be at home with her daughter and husband.

Many myths surround the subject of work and simple living. For example, some people assume that a person seeking financial independence—an objective for some but not all simplicity lovers—is motivated by laziness. As a general rule, this is simply not true, not even close. Financial independence brings freedom—freedom to engage in work that is interesting, fulfilling, and congruent with our deepest values. It brings freedom to integrate our work into the rest of our lives; we can more easily select the hours, location, and style of our work. We can choose to work for monetary compensation or as a volunteer.

Most of us still seek the rewards of meaningful work even if we don't need the income. We seem to be naturally predisposed to want to test ourselves, to stretch and grow, to develop whatever talents and skills we have, to make a contribution.

Coming up with a definition of *work* is no small challenge. Work can be defined broadly as activity that makes a contribution by utilizing a person's talents and skills. This could also include sustained efforts to develop skills and talents through attending educational or vocational programs. What about a hobby? If I study nature photography with no intention of selling my work or even sharing my photographs with others, is that work? I think you would have to say that work, like beauty, is in the eyes of the beholder.

The chart in Figure 6-1 illustrates the types of activities (and percentages for each) chosen by the simplicity study participants as their primary form of work.

Figure 6-1: Types of Work Activities

71%	Traditional forms of work for compensation, including entrepreneurial activities
10%	Full-time parenting/family manager
5%	Volunteer work on a committed, regular basis
3%	College and postgraduate studies
1%	Homesteading (as in living off the land, not staking a claim)

This accounts for 90 percent of the study participants. The remaining ten percent are not engaged in what we might call *work* as broadly defined above. Some, but not all, of this latter group are financially independent. Others have spouses whose incomes are sufficient to meet the family's economic needs. A few are disabled and are supported by disability payments.

This group of non-workers spends time pursuing personal interests, such as reading, life-long learning activities, gardening (and other nesting activities), visiting with family and friends, and traveling.

They may engage in hobbies or volunteer work, but not on an ongoing basis. Some of these people have adopted this way of life for the long haul. Others see it as a temporary phase until something comes along that really interests them.

The diversity of occupations engaged in by the participants is impressive. Here is just a sampling: accountant, administrative assistant, architect, artist, attorney, banker, bookkeeper, carpenter, chaplain, chemist, choir director, college professor, community volunteer, computer programmer, construction manager, consultant, counselor, database administrator, day care provider, dentist, desktop publisher, dietician, draftsman/person, editor, educational researcher, electronics technician, engineer, forester, government administrator, graphics and web designer, homesteader, hydrologist, investment banking analyst, janitorial services company owner, librarian, massage therapist, motel clerk, nanny, non-profit worker, nurse, owner of retail store, parent/family manager, Ph.D. student, pharmacist, photographer, physical therapist, physician, professional organizer, radio personality, rancher, real estate agent, sales person, school bus driver, secretary, shipper, social worker, statistician, stock market investor, systems analyst, systems engineer, technical software support operator, theatrical event planner, and writer.

So, if you think that working and simple living don't mix, think again. Simplicity impacts our work lives in several ways. For example, we are less likely to work to exhaustion, preferring to balance our work energy with time spent on relationships and other personal interests. One half of the simplicity study participants who work for compensation work less than a full-time job. The chart in Figure 6-2 lists the weekly hours the participants work.

Figure 6-2: Number of Hours Participants Work Each Week

25%	20 hours or less
25%	More than 20 hours, fewer than 40
40%	40 to 45 hours
10%	More than 45 hours

It is tough to work 40 or more hours a week and still have sufficient time and energy for a balanced life—a life of quality relationships
with friends and family, nutritious meals, daily exercise, the pursuit
of passions, interests, and hobbies, a spiritual life, and some regular
doses of pure relaxation. I am not saying it is impossible, but I think
you would need an unusually high level of energy to pull this off.
When you choose to work full-time or more, it is important to realize what parts of your life you are sacrificing for that privilege, and
then consciously make that choice.

But wait, you might say, what about those people who truly love
their work—people who are energized by 70-hour work weeks,
people who feel exhilarated rather than enervated by their jobs?
What's wrong with working crazy hours if you love it?

Are these people in denial or are they blessed with unusually
high physical and mental energy? Perhaps some of each, but I suspect there may be more of the former than the latter. Anne Morrow
Lindbergh, in her classic book, *Gift From the Sea*, reflects on the negative aspects of a life cluttered with activity. In contemplating the
beauty in life, Lindbergh observes, "For it is only framed in space
that beauty blooms." Lindbergh refers to the beauty of a tree framed
against the empty sky. She reflects that a note in music gains significance from the silences on either side, and that a candle flowers in
the space of the night. Lindbergh concludes that her life lacks these
qualities—and therefore beauty—because there is so little empty
space. So few empty hours on her calendar, or empty rooms in her
life in which to stand alone. Too many activities, too many people,
too many things. Clearly, our activities as well as material possessions can clutter our lives. If all our energy is devoted to our work, if
there are no "spaces" around that work, where is the beauty in our
lives?

According to Juliet Schor, Harvard economist and author of *The
Overworked American*, the United States doubled its economic output
from 1948 to the early 1990's. In theory, we should be able to work
half the hours we do today and enjoy the same standard of living we
had at mid-century. Instead, our society has opted to work more
hours and spend more money. To live a full life, to live a life of sim-

plicity and authenticity, consider limiting your weekly work hours to a maximum of 30 (20 if you are also a parent with children at home). If you search hard enough, you can find flexible, part-time work arrangements. Thousands of people have managed this; you can, too.

People who live simply tend to think outside the box when it comes to traditional notions of what a successful work life should look like. Their work is important, not only for the income it produces (in most cases), but also for the sense of purpose and meaning it brings to their lives. Generally, they do not define themselves by what they do for a living, nor are they attached to any status or prestige associated with their work.

The key is figuring out who you are inside. Then you are in a position to build a work life that reflects the real you and meets your needs. Start by listening to what you say to yourself and others about your current work. Gradually, you will figure out what type of work will bring you the most satisfaction. If you feel overwhelmed by this process, read the book *Follow Your Bliss*, by Hal Zina Bennett, Ph.D. and Susan J. Sparrow. This book can be an excellent tool to help you unearth your unique passions and life purpose.

As a society, we have a long way to go. How many years will it take before the following conversation is commonplace in our corporate offices?

BOSS: I'd like to talk to you about the possibility of assuming a new position with greater responsibility and a salary increase. We think you would be great for the job and we hope you will accept it. It will involve more time, more stress, more travel, but it will also provide more compensation, more challenge and (perhaps) more satisfaction.

EMPLOYEE: Thanks for the offer! I appreciate your vote of confidence in my abilities, and I will give it careful consideration. As you know, money is only one factor that motivates me to work, so I will need to carefully weigh the potential enhanced satisfaction and fulfillment of the new position against the investment of additional time and energy that will be required.

Fortunately, as an individual, you don't need to wait for society to catch up with you. You can make your life work for you right now. You are in control.

Chapter Seven

On the Road to Simplicity: Travelers in Transition

L iving simply is a ongoing journey, not a fixed goal or destination. In that sense, every person profiled in this book is in transition. Ideally, each day we engage in the process of becoming a more authentic embodiment of our true selves. Simplicity provides the personal freedom to further that life process. We are changing, for better or worse, constantly. Sometimes the changes are subtle, occurring gradually over the years. At other times, we make sweeping changes to our lives, often in the areas of work, home, and family, within a relatively short period of time. It is during those times of dramatic change that we are most aware that we are in transition.

A Dad for All Seasons—Armando Quintero

Growing up as the eldest child in a large, Mexican-American family, Armando Quintero was drawn to the natural world—a self-described "nature nerd." He loved to be outside as a child. When not outside, he spent many hours traveling vicariously by reading *National Geographic* and memorizing whole sections on animals and birds from an old set of *Encyclopedia Britannica*.

While attending college, Armando started working for the National Park Service. Fulfilling his life-long dream, he excelled in his work as a naturalist and park ranger. Over the next 20 years, his supervisors recognized Armando's talents and hard work with successive promotions. When I first interviewed Armando, his position was one of managerial and administrative responsibilities, an ego-gratifying position that provided both exciting challenges and stress.

It's interesting how frequently you see people whose first love (in Armando's case, nature) and talents are rewarded with increasing responsibility, often in the form of management positions, effectively removing the person from the work he was drawn to in the first place. While some people thrive on positions of leadership and management, not all of us do. When offered promotions of this kind, most of us tend to accept them automatically. But sometimes these choices backfire on us: While we may gain prestige and a higher salary, we lose the very thing we love—the work we enjoy. We need to educate ourselves and our employers that moving up the hierarchical ladder may or may not be desirable.

When Armando was in his mid-twenties, he reunited with his high school sweetheart, Brigid, after not seeing her for several years. They married and settled into a comfortable lifestyle of a professional working couple. With a business and accounting degree in hand, Brigid launched a career that now earns her a six-figure income in a prestigious high-level position for a bank. She and Armando bought a small home in the suburbs of the Northern California Bay Area and endured the long commute to their jobs in San Francisco. With their long hours and tiring commute, they ate more meals in restaurants than at home. Brigid loves high quality clothes and shoes; for many years, her favorite pastime was shopping. Together they made plenty of money, but always seemed to spend just a little more than they earned. Credit card companies were delighted to have them as perennial customers.

By their mid-thirties, Armando and Brigid were eager to start a family. They struggled to conceive for a few years, then suffered through an emotionally painful late-stage miscarriage. But at last they gave birth to a beautiful healthy girl, Lily. They adored their daughter and cherished every moment they could spend with her. Even so, adding a child to their already full lives of two full-time jobs with long commutes was a challenge. They were exhausted but proud and happy parents.

A few years later another daughter, Bella, was born. Now with two children in daycare, their physical stamina was really being put to a test. They rose at 4:30 or 5:00 in the morning to get the children and themselves ready for the day, dropped the kids off at day care, and then drove the hour-long, congested commute to their jobs. In the evenings, they picked up the kids from daycare, stopped for groceries, takeout or a restaurant meal and arrived home at 7:00 or 8:00 P.M. They barely had the energy to feed and bathe the children and put them to bed before they collapsed themselves. Then it was up at 4:30 the next morning to repeat the routine.

Weekends were a little better, but not much. They hated living in a home that was in constant turmoil and messiness but they rarely had the energy to deal with it. The communication and intimacy Armando and Brigid had enjoyed for years had all but disappeared. They were living in survival mode.

Over the next few years, Armando and Brigid became increasingly dissatisfied with their marathon lifestyle. They became keenly aware of what was missing from their lives—time and energy to enjoy each other and their children. As Armando saw it, "We had the feeling that time was slipping away faster than we could enjoy it." By then they had purchased a larger, more expensive home for their growing family. How could they possibly reduce their work hours and income when they barely had enough money to pay their bills!

When you are living on overload, it may seem impossible to carve out the breathing space to examine your life and consider other alternatives. Sometimes illness or losing a job will force the issue. Try to preempt that likelihood by taking a little time here and there—maybe a weekend—to get away, preferably in nature where you and your spouse can walk, and talk,

or simply gaze at the sunset. The answers are all inside of you.
Remain still, listen patiently, and they will come.

Armando and Brigid kept at it; they kept thinking and looking for
ways to change their lives. They acknowledged that their spending
habits were out of control. Since they had no time or energy to tend
to the home fires, they tried to meet their needs with money, be it an
expensive restaurant meal for the family's dinner, or a costly birthday party for one of their kids. Slowly it occurred to them that if one
of them worked fewer hours, that spouse could also do a lot to reduce expenses. Since Brigid's job brought in considerably more
income than Armando's, they started imagining a life where Armando
would quit work and stay home to take care of the children, eliminating costs such as day care, meals out, and the special "treats" we
buy hoping they will compensate for our stress.

Initially Armando took a four-month leave of absence from his
job to see what life would look like as a stay-at-home dad. He took
the children out of daycare, resulting in immediate savings of $1,200
a month. During this trial period, Armando and Brigid discovered
that their intuitive sense of what they needed to live on was way
off—they were astonished at how much less money they spent.
Armando prepared inexpensive and delicious meals at home, using
fresh ingredients. He kissed Brigid goodbye many mornings, sending her off with a container of leftovers for her lunch. Armando had
the time and the skills to undertake several remodel projects for their
home, saving the family thousands of dollars. He also helped various
extended family members with remodeling and repair projects. His
trial experiment was a resounding success:

*In my entire career I had never felt so satisfied as I did when I was
able to focus 100 percent of my time and energy on my family. My wife
and I read several signals clearly during this time:*

We were happier.
We did OK on one income.
Our kids were happier.

We felt that we could be of value to the people we cherish most in our lives. The things I can accomplish with my time at this point in our lives (two young children, new home, two mature careers, aging parents and a large, extended family) makes us realize that I am more valuable to our families (financially and emotionally) if I dedicate myself full time to family needs.

After the four-month trial period, they jumped off the high dive—Armando quit his job. It was scary and thrilling at the same time. They were still not 100 percent sure they could make it on a lower income over the long run. Armando was at the peak of his career; people were shocked that he had just walked away from it. One colleague told Armando that what he was doing was "unacceptable and irresponsible." Another former coworker described Armando's actions as subversive!

> Frequently, people who simplify their lives face negative reactions from friends and acquaintances but "subversive" is a new one for me. In a way, I see Armando's coworker's point. Armando's actions contradict some of America's most cherished values of the twentieth century—a traditional breadwinner role for men, the fruits of which are to be enjoyed by the entire family in the form of never-ending consumer spending. Is it possible that people who react so intensely to those who simplify are threatened by the notion that the all-American dream they work so hard to achieve may be an illusion?

The Quintero family now has a life they thoroughly enjoy. No more pre-dawn risings in this household. Brigid is more relaxed than she has been in years. She has started walking for exercise, something she never had time or energy for before. One weekend, soon after starting their new life together, she enjoyed making Christmas decorations by hand—something that had seemed impossible in years past.

Armando is having a ball with his daughters. The kids, now five and three, are also learning life skills from their dad. Armando shares his pleasure in teaching them:

With two young children at home I am taking every opportunity to involve them in the discussion, planning and work on home projects. I recently constructed a chicken coop and pen. The kids decided that they wanted the chicken house to look like a barn in one of their storybooks. We sat outside, drew the barn design on paper, picked the site in the yard for the coop and small pen. My kids then helped me select the materials (all used and recycled) that we used to build the barn and pen. That is an experience I could not buy.

Armando is also teaching Lily and Bella that the joys in life are not tied to how much money you spend:

The kids always want toys (and pets!), of course. We do a couple of things to deal with this. We purchase toys at garage sales. I regularly take the kids to the local Humane Society so they can see all the pets that people are trying to give away. We play with the puppies, kittens, rabbits, and guinea pigs. We look at the snakes, iguanas, parrots, full grown and old dogs, horses, ducks, geese, peacocks and other creatures. It offers a great opportunity to educate the kids about the numbers and kinds of animals that people think they want for pets but then give up. It is great, they get their animal fix, they see a variety of animals and we don't spend any money.

Nature is an everyday extension of our lives. I have encouraged the kids to be curious about the natural world and I am trying to teach them that "everything" is a part of that world. My children know most of the common birds by name and have learned a number of flower names and insect names. When they see something new they want to know its name. They are not satisfied to hear, "Oh, that is a birdie or a bug." Recently, our three year-old got mad at my wife and me. She called us "crabs." Then she paused and asked me, "Dad, what kind of crabs are those that put little pieces of stuff on their shells?" I answered, "Decorator Crabs."

She then moved back into her mad voice and said, "You guys are Decorator Crabs!"

As a child, can you imagine a better deal than having a stay-at-home dad who is a naturalist? I can't. Maybe a circus performer would rate as a close second. It's clear that Armando enjoys the time he spends with his daughters enormously. Not all of us are wired that way. There are no roadmaps that dictate how to live our lives. We need to find our own paths. But observing others can spark our imaginations and give us new perspectives on the many ways to experience joy and fulfillment in our lives.

It is clear that the family rewards are substantial but what about Armando's career? Can he just walk away from it without feeling a loss? What if something happens to Brigid (or her job) and Armando needs to reenter the work force in five years? Will he still have marketable skills? Doesn't he miss the intellectual stimulation and challenge of his job?

These questions are all still being answered. Armando is in transition right now. At the time he responded to the simplicity survey, he was only six weeks into his new role, admittedly "still in the honeymoon stage." So far, his sense of self is secure and comfortable without his career. But he does want to stay connected to the world of work, and opportunities have already presented themselves. One of his favorites is leading nature walks in his area, working through a friend who has a business offering guided nature tours. Intellectual and creative stimulation are still present in Armando's life. Recently, he accepted a position as a citizen's commissioner for the county parks system. He plans to set up an art studio in the garage to indulge his lifelong artistic passions. Maybe he will try his hand at writing children's books. He has experimented with creative writing for over a year now, meeting with a writer's group weekly. Armando also enjoys a lively and supportive men's group that has been meeting for over 12 years.

It's interesting that Armando's self-esteem is not tied to his career—a characteristic he shares with most of the simplicity study participants. Of course, having 20 years of career success behind him doesn't hurt. He voluntarily chose to leave his career at a time when he had already achieved a sense of personal satisfaction with that part of his life. Thanks to the experience he already has in his field, he could easily get another job in his field if he wanted to. The real test will be the test of time. Will Armando continue to feel fulfilled in his role as househusband and father? Will he be able to find occasional, meaningful work to maintain his connection to the career he developed? Only time will tell.

Who knows where Armando's talents will lead him? At this point, he is staying open, exploring opportunities that are compatible with his primary goals of enjoying a rich, family life:

Simplifying has not meant that we are living "less." In fact we feel richer. I feel like I can put my arms around the experiences and time that are of great importance to us. In the last month, Brigid and I have had several "million dollar days"— at least that is how we refer to time that is so precious that it feels invaluable. We regularly talk about the value of a day. The experiences and the stuff we are alive for. We have gone to sleep several times in the last month in agreement that we had just had a "million dollar day." I have said on a few of those days that what I received in that day was worth (easily) a year's salary.

Enough Already!—Rebecca Bowles

When Rebecca responded to the simplicity survey, she had just quit her long-term (13 years) job as a postal worker—first as a letter sorter, then a letter carrier—four days before. At forty-one, she decided she'd had enough—she could no longer take what she experienced as "the repetitive, boring, mundane, no-brainer atmosphere." She was ready to step out into the void and reinvent her life.

Rebecca had struggled over the years with the dissatisfaction she felt in her job. Growing up in a poor household, she had been attracted to the post office job for its good salary and benefits. Then, as she became progressively more bored and frustrated with her job, her friends encouraged her to take advantage of the money she earned and treat herself to nice things as a way to balance out the drudgery of her work. She bought a beautiful, 3,000-square-foot home in the country and decorated it in a way that would make Martha Stewart proud. But, after an initial burst of excitement, the beautiful home didn't do the trick—happiness still eluded Rebecca. On top of that, she found that she felt uncomfortable taking up so much space as a single person. Her fantasies of entertaining friends in her spacious home never seemed to materialize. As much as Rebecca loved her home and the beauty of the countryside, she was lonely.

As we saw in Chapter Five, *Urban or Rural Simplicity: Choosing a Nurturing Milieu*, figuring out whether you want to live in an urban or rural setting—or somewhere in between—is not always a simple task. Most of us love being surrounded by nature, but some of us also like the stimulation of an urban environment—close proximity to libraries, theater, and friends, or the spontaneity and ease of something as simple as buying fresh produce daily from a neighborhood grocer. And in many cases, as in Rebecca's case, what we think we will like turns out to be less than ideal. It reminds me of watching my women friends with their first child. It seems almost impossible to predict who among them will thoroughly enjoy the parenting experience and want to focus all her energies on her child, and who will long to get back to a work environment with adult stimulation. Their own pre-parenting feelings seem to have little to do with the final outcome. So, if you are living in the city or in the country and find you dislike it, take heart—many have

walked that path before you. And, unlike having a child, making a change in this area is much easier!

Eventually, Rebecca realized that fulfilling, meaningful work was
more valuable to her than the dollar, although she acknowledges
that, "Both at the same time would be ideal!" She planned her escape carefully. First, she sold her large home and bought a much
smaller one (1,000 square feet) at a nearby lake resort area, about
an hour's drive from Columbus, Ohio. With the profit from the sale
of her larger home, combined with her savings, she was able to buy
her new home mortgage free. At that point, she also had enough
savings for a year's living expenses. Three months later she made
her break—she quit her job, and for the first time in her life, experienced total freedom.

Initially, Rebecca planned to take up to a year off from working.
Her choice to live at the lake was ideal—it was a beautiful spot to
enjoy her "extended vacation," closer to the city where she hoped
eventually to find another, more meaningful job. She figured that
once she had reestablished herself in the working world, she would
make another move to be closer to her job and to the city. For now,
the lake was a perfect environment for this critical transitional phase
of her life.

To conserve her resources, Rebecca reduced her living expenses
substantially to $500 to $700 a month. Spending less did not make
her feel deprived at all; to the contrary, her freedom gave her a feeling of wealth. This was also a time of peacefulness and reflection for
her. She spent time reading, running, and enjoying the beauty of
her lakeside environment. For Rebecca, her long runs around the
lake became a form of meditation. This period gave her an opportunity to become centered—to connect with her inner self—before
venturing out in the world of work again.

Taking an extended period of time (at least three months) off
from work and other obligations can be an excellent tool for
personal growth. It is not even necessary to concentrate on

your life's issues during this period. In fact, "working hard" on the big issues in your life can be counterproductive, much in the same way as concentrating on hitting a golf or tennis ball perfectly can produce some pathetic shots. Just spending time relaxing will allow your inner self to bring clarity and courage to your conscious self. You should follow your heart during this period, spending time on activities that nourish you physically, emotionally, and spiritually. As it did with Rebecca, it will help you center yourself, and almost as if by magic you will come away with new insights and direction for your life.

After three or four months, Rebecca noticed that the fear of financial insecurity started to creep up within her. She wondered how long it would take to find the right job and didn't want to reduce her financial resources, her cushion, too much. She decided to explore opportunities for meaningful work. For Rebecca, this meant working for an organization that contributed to a better world. She was prepared to take an entry-level position in a new field as long as her efforts contributed to a good purpose. She accepted a clerical position in a non-profit organization that paid far less than her postal job.

When I checked back with Rebecca after she had been in this job for six months, she reported mixed feelings. She felt that monetary issues played a greater role in her employer's operations than she would prefer. In terms of working for a purpose, she questioned whether the rewards justified giving up her higher salary. As she sees it, "I just learned a lesson—you may not just step into the right job. It may take a few jobs to get the right one." She continues to explore other options, but going back to the post office job with its higher salary is not one of them.

Structuring a life of simplicity is a unique challenge for each of us. Think of it as experimenting with a recipe. You may start out with the basics of a recipe from a cookbook, or perhaps you enjoyed an excellent dish at a friend's home. It tastes good, but you start wondering what it would taste like with some of your own favorite foods in it. So, you substitute one thing for another, and maybe borrow a part of another recipe that you think will work, and then start the fiddling process. Eventually, you come up with something that tastes better than all the other variations. And this is what simple living is like— you try one thing, and then another, discarding what doesn't work, borrowing from something else, until you end up with something delicious.

With the vote still out on her new job, Rebecca also started to tire of her hour-long commute to and from her job. When she bought her home at the lake, she thought she could tolerate the long commute to the city for a winter or two, but she found herself very frustrated with it after only two months. She also found she was ready for a more stimulating and nurturing environment. She longed to connect with people of like minds—people who are interested in spiritual and simplicity issues. Her situation wasn't helped by the fact that many residents at the lake resort take off for warmer parts of the country during the winter. She decided to accelerate her plans to move closer to the city.

After a year at the lake, Rebecca sold her home and bought another one of similar size and price closer to the city. Her commute is now only 25 minutes each way. She lives in a suburb of Columbus, enjoying the urban amenities that are available to her. She has joined several running clubs and spiritually related study groups. There are nearby parks and a high school track for running, and the library is within walking distance.

Rebecca's experience is a classic example of *transitioning* into a simpler, more satisfying lifestyle. Within 15 months, she quit one job, discovered her new job is not likely to be a long-term affair, and bought and sold two homes. It is not that she is a flaky person; you don't stay in a job for 13 years if you are flaky. No, Rebecca's story is one of creating a new life of greater satisfaction, experimenting with the variables of work, home, and commute until she finds the right combination. At the heart of living simply is a personal commitment to structure a life of deep satisfaction in all major areas of our lives. This is a tall order and is likely to require some experimentation and changes along the way.

Many of Rebecca's friends and co-workers do not understand why she bought a less expensive home than she could afford. Her father, having struggled all his life to provide for the basics in life, cannot comprehend why Rebecca would give up her higher paying postal job. For many people, going against the grain of the American ideal can be an isolating experience. Rebecca reports that sometimes people react with hostility: "It seems that some people feel almost insulted by my choices—they are slaves to their jobs and are envious that I am not."

Sometimes, Rebecca feels tempted to start accumulating more things again. Her working peer group has changed from blue-collar to professional; she is surrounded by people who spend money on material things. She has to remind herself, "Oh yeah, it's not worth it to me to live that lifestyle."

In *The Overspent American*, Juliet Schor suggests that our materialistic desires and urges are motivated by our need to compete with, and be accepted by, our peer group. We want to be viewed favorably in the eyes of our peers. Rebecca could feel this desire herself when she started to work with people who spent more money on material things. People who embark on the path to simplicity inevitably have (or are fast developing) a high level of self-esteem. Simplicity requires you to look to your own values to define yourself, rather than relying on external measures of success—money, possessions, power, and prestige. If you define yourself primarily by how you measure up on these factors, simplicity will not work for you.

Rebecca is well on her way. She jumped off the high dive when she quit her long-term, secure job, and has resurfaced with vitality and enthusiasm.

Returning Home—Joe Judge

At the time Joe Judge responded to the simplicity survey, he was living in a small, rural desert community in Southern California. He refers to this period in his life as "detoxification." He lived alone, renting a home on five acres from a friend. His days were filled with reading and walking—lots of walking, often two to four hours a day— through the beautiful desert landscape. He eschewed television and newspapers, following the suggestion of Andrew Weil in his book, *8 Weeks to Optimum Health*, to go on a "news fast."

In many ways, Joe was living the life he dreamed of as a child. When people asked him what he wanted to be when he grew up, he responded, "A cloistered monk." Joe explains: "I loved the simple way of life depicted in Thomas Merton's *The Waters of Siloe*." Although this was not to be his calling, living a contemplative life was ideal for Joe for this time in his life—a time of transition, of detoxification from a lifestyle that was too disparate, too disharmonious, with who Joe really is. He cherishes solitude and freedom:

Voluntary simplicity allows me time alone. When I was forced to in- teract with people at work (beyond my tolerance for interaction), I sometimes became bitchy or competitive, then subsequently guilty. Now I control my amount of interaction. I interact with people when I know I'm able to be fully present and responsive. And usually the interaction is in a situation we want to be in—rather than a stressful job, bureaucratic details, etc.

Joe describes himself as an introvert. While personality characteristics were not specifically queried on the simplicity survey, many participants revealed their introspective nature in responding to the survey. There are a number of interesting speculations why this may be so. Does simplicity, which necessarily requires one to live consciously and mindfully, attract people who are by nature more inner-directed, more inclined towards reflection? Perhaps, but not necessarily. It certainly is possible to be an extrovert, finding pleasure and satisfaction in frequent interactions with people, and live mindfully. But to the extent that simplicity is a way of looking at the world, of living a life that, in the words of author Duane Elgin, is *outwardly simple, inwardly rich*, it makes sense that it would appeal to the introvert personality type.

Joe grew up in a Catholic family of professional helpers—teachers, doctors, nurses, nuns, and social workers. While he eventually rejected Catholicism, Joe retained his family's affinity for the service professions. He obtained a master's degree to teach English as a second language and spent a number of years teaching in the Mideast. His most rewarding work experience was a job in Egypt under a Fulbright program, instructing teachers in rural areas how to teach English. When he was downsized out of that job due to funding losses, he accepted a teaching position for an oil company in Saudi Arabia. While this job offered him a high tax-free salary, it clashed with his values. He felt he was working for the privileged class of a society whose values were at odds with his own. The only real reward was his high salary, and money was not enough to satisfy Joe.

While he was still in the Mideast, Joe became aware of the voluntary simplicity philosophy. First, he read the book *Voluntary Simplicity* by Duane Elgin, which inspired him. Then he read *Your Money or Your Life*, by Joe Dominguez and Vicki Robin, which lit a fire under him. He was ready to make his move. He wanted to experience what it

was like to live only with what he truly needed. When a friend offered to rent Joe his home in the southern California desert, he
jumped at it. At the same time, he purged his life of possessions that
were a burden to him:

*After dragging a ton of books, etc. from continent to continent, and
probably paying thousands of dollars to ship them, I just "let go"— aban-
doned it. Some of the stuff was hard to let go of—journals, photos—but it
was both a burden and an expense. I told friends, "I'm going to fit my life
into two suitcases and a carry-on!" And I have.*

> When I first read in Joe's survey that he abandoned his jour-
> nals and photos, I let out an involuntary gasp. Even though I
> rarely read my journals or look at the photographs taken over
> the years (much less take the time to put them in albums), I
> feel attached to these records of my life. I imagine myself in
> my eighties or nineties sitting in my rocking chair, reliving my
> life as I gaze at my photographs and read through my jour-
> nals. I admit that it is equally plausible that I will be too focused
> on living in the present during these final decades to bother,
> much as I am today. Perhaps Joe's action of letting these sym-
> bols of his past go facilitated his transition to a life of greater
> fulfillment. A year after our first correspondence, I asked Joe
> if he ever regretted that decision. He replied that there were
> times he wished he had this or that, but overall he felt fine
> with giving it all up. Once again, there is no right or wrong
> here, no action that is more ideal, more in tune with simplic-
> ity, than another. The key is to figure out what material
> possessions are important in your life, cherish and preserve
> them, and let go of the rest.

Joe was determined to see how far he could reduce his living
expenses, writing down every penny he spent. When he first moved
to the desert, he bought a used truck, but then sold it after only a
few months. He explains why:

I bought a truck but decided it wasn't worth the expense. What's the main purpose of a personal vehicle? I think, mainly, to transport Americans to centers of consumption. Most people could use public transportation to commute. If they don't, their real hourly wage is drastically reduced.

The rural environment in which Joe lived supported his efforts of "detoxification" from the consumer culture. If he got bored, he could not easily go out and spend money on something to lift his spirits— places to spend money were few in number. The small strip mall a few miles from his home held little appeal. Most of the people living in this area had little money to spend so there was no peer pressure to keep up with the Joneses. One day, Joe was hitching a ride into town from a neighbor and proudly announced to her that he bought this fabulous pair of shoes at the thrift store for $1. His chauffeur gave him that "you fool!" look, explaining that no one around here spent money at the thrift stores when you can get everything you need at the dump.

Simple living does *not* require you to frequent thrift stores or the dump. This is entirely a matter of personal preference. Some people enjoy the thrill of stumbling on a find—something of quality for considerably less money that what you might pay at a retail store. They also enjoy the shopping experience of seeking out those deals. Others could care less. For example, I detest shopping of any sort. I have to force myself to buy clothes, usually at the behest of my husband or friends who are tired of looking at the same old thing. Many of my clothes are hand-me-downs from friends. I have also found a local consignment store that usually has what I need.

The key to spending simply is to spend wisely and consciously, focusing on high-quality, durable items that are truly valued. The people in the simplicity study who are well off financially do not spend money impulsively or carelessly. They would rather give away their wealth than fritter it away.

The editor of this book, Hal Zina Bennett, being a talkative sort of guy with a keen sense of humor, often entertained me with little stories and jokes in between his ubiquitous red markings that covered my manuscript. While some of his jokes are too wicked to print (gotcha, Hal!), his technique for buying cars is worth repeating:

When I buy a car, it's never a new one. I go to wealthy areas—like Atherton or Los Gatos [in California]—and look through their local classified tabloids. Their cars are usually cheap, well maintained, and of good quality to begin with. The last car I bought like this was my Volvo, which had 65,000 miles on it. It cost me $3,500. It now has 165,000 miles and is still going strong!

Weaning himself off the consumer treadmill affected Joe in ways that were common to many of the simplicity study participants. One could view the process he and others went through as environmental education through the back door. Joe describes how it worked for him:

Originally I was attracted to voluntary simplicity for selfish reasons. My life—my time—is invaluable; no amount of salary can compensate for wasting the little time I have on earth on boring, stressful or meaningless tasks. However, as I've seen how little I actually need, I am appalled—yes, appalled!—at the waste I see around me. Especially since I've spent the past few years in the Third World where people live with very little. I can't fault Americans; I was once as blithely unaware as they are, but I can see the need for educating people to be environmentally concerned.

Joe's living expenses for his rural lifestyle were approximately $800 a month. Almost $500 of that was spent on rent with another $100 going for health insurance. He had sufficient savings from his prior teaching positions to provide interest income to cover basic living expenses. This lifestyle was a dramatic change for Joe. Given

that any change, positive or negative, can be stressful, it is no surprise to hear that the changes Joe underwent engendered doubts
and fears:

*I have misgivings about voluntary simplicity. Will I have regrets that
I didn't work harder, save more? Am I simply lazy? Also, voluntary simplicity is a Western effete trend. Letting go of "stuff" and job pressures has
been liberating for me, but it's very different to be simple by choice as
opposed to the forced simplicity of poverty. I also hope I don't become
judgmental and dogmatic of people hypnotized by the consumer culture.
It's very seductive and difficult to combat.*

*Voluntary simplicity is not for everyone. I've had many advantages
that others don't have, including supportive friends, a middle class upbringing, health, not having to fight racial prejudice, and a lot of luck,
like the raging bull market of the past few years.*

Joe's time living in the desert community served him well as a
transitional period, but he also needed and wanted the support of
others during this time of change. Longing to connect with people
who share his interests and values, he started attending meetings of
a voluntary simplicity circle group in nearby San Diego. The support
of this group is essential for him: "I do worry about going into a
panic and racing off to the Mideast again for a high tax-free salary.
I'm looking to the Simplicity Circle I'm involved with to help me
with that concern."

After six months in the desert, Joe moved to San Diego and is
now sharing a home with a friend who also believes in living simply.
Joe continues to monitor every expenditure and delights in finding
deals and living well on little. When he heard about *Buy Nothing Day*,
a national program that encourages people to spend nothing on one
day of the year, the day after Thanksgiving, he incorporated that
concept into his daily life. He loves to count his consecutive *Buy
Nothing Days*—it brings a smile to his face when four or five days pass
during which he makes no purchases.

Joe's move to the city also opened up a door for his return to the
teaching profession he loves. He now teaches English as a second

language to adults in a private school sixteen hours a week. The school's students come from all over, not only from nearby Mexico but also Japan, Saudi Arabia, Russia, China, Brazil, and Korea. The combination of highly motivated students, a high level of autonomy for the teachers, and cooperative co-workers provides the perfect work environment for Joe: "The small staff works as a team rather than a hierarchy. We are all mutually supportive, not competitive. I have a sense of community there."

Even though Joe's savings are sufficient to cover his current living expenses, he is pleased to be working again. He was starting to feel a bit stale, which prompted him to seek out meaningful work. The volunteer positions he explored did not pan out, and he was delighted to receive the offer from the language school.

Financially, Joe would also like to build up his nest egg a bit more, not knowing exactly what the future will bring. Now in his late forties, he likely has many years ahead of him. He also enjoys earning income so he can give away more to friends, family, and worthwhile causes. Last year, he gave away $2,000 of his annual budget of $10,000 to others. He would like to be able to give away more.

When I asked Joe what were the primary events or influences that motivated him to simplify his life, he responded,

One word answer here: Death! I've had friends in their forties and fifties die of cancer and heart attacks after spending years in jobs they hated, waiting to live in some future that never happened.

The scarcer a resource is, the more valuable it is. The time each of us has on earth compared to the vastness of eternity is very scarce indeed. Is it worth spending that time at a job where you earn only minimum wage? For that matter, would it even be a fair trade for Bill Gates' salary?

I lived two years in Egypt. The middle class there is quite poor compared to the U.S. They look to meaningful human relationships for contentment rather than stuff. Clothes shopping is limited to one new outfit a year for the feast after Ramadan [an Islamic tradition of fasting for one month]. They make do, repair, etc., rather than replacing with the newest and the latest.

It's interesting to look at what influences those who choose simplicity as a way of life. Often, as in Joe's case, a complex set of factors is at work. Remember that in his childhood Joe was surrounded by people who placed a high value on helping others and being of service to the community. Those influences were apparently much stronger for him than the pursuit of money, power, and status. Also, living in third world countries had an enormous impact on Joe's thinking. I don't think it is possible to live in a third world country for any length of time and not seriously question the patterns of consumption in the United States. Finally, reading books at certain times in our lives can trigger changes that are ripening within us. In Joe's case, reading *Your Money or Your Life* was just such a triggering factor.

Lessons and Reflections

The people profiled in this chapter, Armando Quintero, Rebecca Bowles, and Joe Judge, are all in transition. They are consciously trying out new ventures to simplify their lives. When we are in transition, we often embark on something that holds tremendous promise, but also has a highly unpredictable outcome. We approach these types of adventures with excitement and some trepidation. It is quite the opposite of feeling like you are in a rut. These experiences are the trademark of those who accept simplicity into their lives.

In some cases, you may try something new for a limited period of time, as a stepping stone to a life of simplicity. For example, some people will work additional hours for a certain period of time to provide more leisure time in the future. Kevin Jenkins, a thirty-four-year-old software developer, often works more than 65 hours a week with the goal of paying off all debt, including his mortgage, within a short time. His wife works part-time as a schoolteacher and cares for their three-month old baby. Together their income exceeds

$100,000 a year. This plan should allow Kevin to drop down to part-time work (25 to 35 hours a week) for the rest of his life, starting in the year 2000.

Other examples of participants in the simplicity study who are clearly in *transition* include:

♦ Michelle Holliday, a twenty-six-year-old single woman who recently left a prestigious, high-paying marketing position with a U.S. company in Moscow, Russia, is now back in the states to start a new life and career, focusing on providing seminars on life and career planning. This was no small feat for someone in her twenties who, according to our cultural norms, should be working hard to climb the corporate ladder. As she explains, "Walking away from a good job with a good salary was seen as irresponsible and foolish. It took me almost a year to realize that I could and should listen to my own convictions. I feel liberated, triumphant, and as if I've made a great discovery; I've discovered myself under the clutter."

♦ Bonne Dix is a sixty-year-old woman and former grade school teacher whose chronic multiple sclerosis has progressed to the point she can no longer work. She is taking a course on writing for children—a positive step in her life: "I feel very good about this; my illness has caused me to slow down and notice what is going on in the world for the first time in my life."

♦ Dennis Oliver is a thirty-seven-year-old single man who recently quit his 50+ hour a week (including commuting time) job as a dentist in a busy clinic to take over a part-time (three days a week) practice in a poor community. He is the only dentist in the area and treats many children who would have no dental care if he were not there. He plans to sell his current home and buy a less expensive home closer to his work.

Many people who choose an entrepreneurial route to a simpler life feel considerable financial anxiety at first. Here is how one participant explained it:

I still experience some anxiety about financial subsistence. In my first year of self-employment [1996], I made only enough to cover the costs of my business. So far, 1997 is looking a bit better, but I'm more or less in a dead heat trying to generate enough income to stanch the hemorrhage from my savings. I'm doing this at the same time I'm continually on the lookout for ways to simplify our lives and reduce financial demands without imposing hardships on the family.

As your childhood piano teacher taught you, "practice, practice, practice." That's what we are all doing here. We are practicing the art of living, the art of living well, living in tune with our values, bringing peace and fulfillment to our own lives, and service and love to others. Change is not always pleasant, but if it will help you finely tune the artistic notes of your unique life, embrace it.

Chapter Eight

Long Timers:
People Who Have Always Lived Simply

Although interest in simple living has been building through the 1990's, the simplicity movement is not merely a recent trend. As David Shi points out in his book, *The Simple Life: Plain Living and High Thinking in American Culture*, the fervor and passion for simplicity has risen and fallen in cycles during the last three hundred years. In the twentieth century, interest in simpler ways of living reached a peak during the 1960's, the so-called *hippie* era. Some people were inspired to move back to the land by homesteading visionaries such as Scott and Helen Nearing, authors of *Living the Good Life: How to Live Simply and Sanely in a Troubled World*. However, people who live homesteading lifestyles are in the minority. The vast majority of people who live simply choose more conventional lifestyles; they hold traditional jobs and reside in cities, suburbs, and small towns.

In this chapter, we will meet people who have always lived simply, certainly during their adult lives, and in some cases, even as children. For them, simplicity was an ideal before it became a popular trend.

Overwhelming Joy, Peace, and Contentment—Holli-Anne Passmore

In only five minutes of talking with Holli-Anne Passmore, you become aware that this woman can hardly contain her excitement and joy in simply being alive. A casual observer might be perplexed about the source of her happiness, since Holli-Anne was born with a rare neuromuscular disorder, bestowing on her lifelong emotional and physical challenges. As a child she wore braces on her legs, and we all have seen how a child who is different struggles to become accepted by her peers. Now in her mid-thirties, Holli-Anne still wears leg braces, but that doesn't slow her down one bit.

In some ways, Holli-Anne's physical limitations contributed to an enriching childhood. For one thing, because of her physical disability, Holli-Anne's mother showered her with abundant loving care. And it was this relationship that gave Holli-Anne the foundation for the person she is today—a woman in the prime of her life, blessed with a healthy dose of self-esteem and the simple joy of living.

Holli-Anne's mother modeled the essence of simple living. Holli-Anne remembers her mom fondly: "She was incredible. She could find joy in cleaning up the dog doo in the yard! Really, everything was so special and such an adventure—she really taught me to approach life that way."

Holli-Anne remembers her childhood in a middle class family as wonderful. She learned early on that happiness does not come from money or material possessions:

We weren't scraping for pennies or struggling by any means, but we weren't inundated with material goods either. The camping trips were just as much fun as the big trip to Disneyland. I think it was a good balance.

In Chapter Four, *A Parent's Choice: Savoring Life with Our Children*, I discuss the impact of parents modeling a love of simplicity on their children. Holli-Anne's upbringing is a classic example of how this can work.

Holli-Anne believes that the joy in living simply is not related to income level at all. She sees it more as a frame of mind, a way of looking at the world: "Hiking in the mountains, watching the sunrise, walking the dog, reading a book, writing, creating—all these are simple pleasures that income doesn't affect."

It is not that Holli-Anne leads a fairy-tale life; she has had her fair share of the traumas and frustrations experienced by most people. For example, Holli-Anne reports that her much-loved mother now suffers from Alzheimer's disease and no longer recognizes Holli-Anne. Holli-Anne also survived a painful divorce and has felt betrayed by people who have taken advantage of her strong faith and trusting nature.

Like many of us, her career has had its ups and downs. For many years, she worked in a somewhat unfulfilling administrative job while studying at night to be an accountant. Eventually, she came to realize that even though she excelled at accounting, "It just wasn't me." Now she works full-time as an on-line editorial specialist, a job she enjoys. In addition to her full-time job, Holli-Anne takes on a variety of freelance marketing and other creative projects, including writing advertising copy, designing brochures, writing articles, conducting workshops, and designing web pages. She looks forward to the time her freelance work grows to a level that will support her. But realistically, that may take years. In the meantime, she describes her work as "very exciting, challenging, creative, varied, responsible and fun!" She is not suffering while she waits for her dreams to come true; she is living life fully in the present, enjoying almost every minute of it.

All this is to say that Holli-Anne has no business living every day as if she had just won the lottery or received an academy award— that is, if you measure her life against our conditioned standards of what should make us happy. While she has never been deprived of her essential needs for food, clothing, and shelter, she has faced the same (or greater) trials and tribulations as the rest of us. Yet, it is her ability to appreciate the simple pleasures in life that brings her to such high plateaus in her daily experiences.

Holli-Anne's income and her expenses are both moderate. She lives in Edmonton, Alberta, Canada in the 900-square-foot home she owns, a home she acknowledges as less than perfect: "It has cracks in the walls and a basement that leaks if it rains too hard, and windows that leak if we don't shovel the roof." But Holli-Anne can hardly finish that sentence without rushing to exclaim, "It's so cute, just the right size. It's unique, has nice hardwood floors that are wonderful to wax and polish, very soothing, and very beautiful wooden doors. And I've got photos and mementos from trips all over the walls." Holli-Anne is a living example of the principles espoused by Timothy Miller in his inspirational book, *How to Want What You Have: Discovering the Magic and Grandeur of Ordinary Existence.*

> It is clear that aesthetics play an important role in Holli-Anne's life. Some people associate simple living with austerity, plainness, and the absence of man-made beauty. Nothing could be further from the truth. Simplicity attracts beauty—both the natural and man-made varieties. In the bestselling book, *Simple Abundance*, Sarah Ban Breathnach talks about the Aesthetic Movement in the 1870's and 1880's on both sides of the Atlantic. This cultural trend was based on the idea that one can nurture the soul through beautiful surroundings. To favor simplicity over materialism does not in any way negate the beauty in life. If we limit the number of our material belongings, they can still be beautiful and inspire our souls. How important is aesthetics in your home and immediate surroundings? This will vary from person to person. If you believe that beauty can be found only with a high price tag, you will miss out on the beauty in your life right now.

To save on expenses, Holli-Anne shares her home with a roommate and rents out the basement apartment. She spends little on food, entertainment, or material possessions, preferring to allocate her monetary resources for adventures rather than things—travel, an occasional movie at the dollar theater, hiking and canoe trips, and the cheap seats at the symphony. She seldom eats out, preferring her simple, inexpensive, primarily vegetarian diet. Her lifestyle has been pretty consistent throughout her life; she has always lived simply.

Holli-Anne's energy level is awesome. In addition to her full-time job and her part-time freelance work, she loves to hike—albeit slowly due to her physical limitations—swim, camp, and travel, staying in hostels not only to save money but also to "meet such interesting people." She responds to her physical disability matter of factly: "I've never known anything different, and my case is mild compared to others." She doesn't focus on the fact that her right hand is weakening, resulting in considerable difficulty with buttons and writing with a pen. Instead, she concentrates on all the delightful experiences and people in her life.

As I got to know more of this remarkable person, I kept wondering how she did this. How does Holli-Anne pull this off? It turns out that she has worked hard for the state of mind she enjoys. True, she was blessed with a loving mother who instilled in Holli-Anne a strong sense of self-esteem. But she has developed her inner self on her own. Ever since she was about twelve years old, Holli-Anne has studied psychology and philosophy. She has always been fascinated with how our minds and emotions work. She not only reads on these topics, she works with her own emotions and thought patterns. For example, when she is hurting emotionally, she pays attention to what she is feeling and thinking. She brings a sense of discipline to her inner life, asking herself why she is thinking a certain way, or feeling a certain way. As she becomes more aware of her patterns of thinking, she has the opportunity to catch herself and change her thoughts, which in turn affect her emotional state in a positive way. For Holli-Anne, it's all about focus, paying attention, and learning about herself.

Another source of Holli-Anne's personal strength and energy is her focus and attention on her physical well-being. In addition to her regular, vigorous exercise from swimming and hiking, she is very conscious of how she eats. She said good-bye to caffeine and alcohol years ago and ingests only a limited amount of sugar.

Holli-Anne is not the only participant in the simplicity study who indicated that her use of caffeine and alcohol decreased as she took steps to live simply. When asked why this happened, many said that it happened naturally, without force or discipline. In fact, it seems to flow naturally from a process that Holli-Anne does so well—mindful living, paying attention, focusing on what is happening in the present. For example, if you feel terrible the morning after drinking alcohol, and you have the presence of mind to acknowledge that to yourself, it may be only a matter of time before you reduce or eliminate alcohol from your diet. After all, the consensus among psychologists is that our natural response is to seek pleasure and avoid pain.

Like a grazing animal, Holli-Anne nibbles on small amounts of food throughout the day rather than consume three large meals. She believes that the food we ingest has a much stronger affect on us than we realize. She also feels that it is a simple matter to figure out what our bodies need. In Holli-Anne's experience, all it takes is paying attention to how you feel after you eat or drink something, or after you exercise. She has naturally gravitated to those health practices that make her feel terrific and has experienced no sense of deprivation in the process.

Living in harmony with our natural rhythms is a marvelous fringe benefit of living simply. Once a reporter asked me, "What has made the biggest impact in your life as a result of simplifying?" Without giving much thought to the question, I immediately responded, "Sleep." I now get enough sleep, in sharp contrast to my years of working as a lawyer, dragging myself out of bed each morning after having been awake half the night fretting over some work issue. Now I go to sleep when I'm tired and I wake up when my mind and body are ready to embrace the day. I do not use an alarm clock unless I have an early morning appointment, which is rare. To me, waking up after a good night's sleep is one of the finest pleasures in life.

Holli-Anne has always lived simply, even as a child. As an adult, she has gone beyond *simple living* and has embraced *mindful living* with an intensity and enthusiasm that is rare in our western culture. She is an inspiration to all who know her.

The Art of Deferred Gratification—Edward Saunders

Edward Saunders retired a few years ago at the ripe, young age of forty-seven. He and his wife, Diane, have two grown children who are away at college. Edward and Diane enjoy a stress-free life, spending their time on activities that nourish their bodies and souls, including daily walks on the beach where, in Edward's words, "All sounds are natural: surf, wind, birds, and the stones on the beach crunching as one walks on them." Edward will tell you that he has never been more content and at peace than he is right now. His retirement at age forty-seven is about 20 years earlier than most people expect to gain their freedom. How did he pull this off? To answer that question, we need to go back 30 years.

After Edward graduated from high school, he enlisted in the army. He was assigned to Fort Richardson, outside of Anchorage, Alaska—an event that would alter the course of his life. Having grown up as a city boy, breathing in polluted air and feeling stressed from living in a high-density environment, Edward's encounter with Alaska was love at first sight. The wildness of Alaska—its virgin lands and pristine resources—all made his heart sing.

Not surprisingly, after completing his military tour and graduating from college, Edward immediately moved to Alaska, settling down in a small fishing community. He accepted a teaching position in the local high school and continued in the same job for 23 years. Within the first few years of living in Alaska, he met and married Diane. They built their own home over 20 years ago and raised two happy children.

Edward's story is interesting in that unlike many of us, he not only seemed to know what he wanted as a young adult, but he was able to create his dream with few detours. No *false starts* for Edward. So, what is the secret to his success? Why has Edward's life unfolded so simply and cleanly, while so many of us struggle to balance it all—how to find meaning and purpose in our lives, how to survive economically, physically, mentally, and spiritually?

The factors that influenced Edward's journey are worth reviewing. Edward was blessed with clarity of vision at an early age. Perhaps this gift is similar to other personal attributes such as a high I.Q., superior athletic ability, or a creative talent. While a person may be born with these gifts, it is still up to that person to learn to use them well.

Edward was raised in a fairly typical, American middle class family by parents who placed a high value on material things. However, Edward evolved into a young man who questioned those values, perhaps due to the fact that he came of age during the 1960's, a period in which the youth of this country questioned traditional values. Many of Edward's contemporaries adopted a liberal, contrary stance toward mainstream American values.

Mark Twain once said, "Civilization is a limitless multiplication of unnecessary necessities." This quote made a lasting impression on Edward as a young man. He never did jump on the *more-is-better* bandwagon, but instead, from early on, focused on defining and creating a certain quality of life for himself and his family.

Edward feels his current lifestyle of freedom was made possible by his ability and affinity for long-term planning—his ability to set a goal and then take steps to make it happen. It was his understanding of *deferred gratification* that allowed him to retire early at age forty-seven. He credits his army experience with helping him to develop these attributes. He describes himself as a "concrete sequential personality-type," a person who takes a practical, step-by-step, long-term planning approach to making his dreams come true.

Not all of us are wired to live our lives according to a plan. Oh, we might set up a plan all right, but following that plan is another story. I, for one, have numerous financial plans saved in the spreadsheet directory of my computer—spreadsheets outlining financial plans for various schemes, buying various homes, buying a home with rental unit, buying apartment houses, traveling around the country in a recreational vehicle, business plans for various short-lived careers. Each time I come up with a new plan, I enthusiastically present it to my husband, who smiles and says, "That's nice, dear," knowing full well that the likelihood of the plan coming to fruition is slim. I need to plan as I go along, and not get too far ahead of myself. Others are more successful at what Edward has done—making his dreams come true through conscious, systematic steps over a relatively long period of time.

When Edward first moved to Alaska in 1972, he focused on securing a piece of land to homestead. He had a vision. His plan was first to save enough cash to buy the land and the materials for his home, and then to build the home with his own labor, at his own pace. A mortgage was not part of the plan.

In 1974, Edward bought a ten-acre plot for $4,000. He married Diane the next year and they started their married life out in a cozy yet comfortable 8-foot by 30-foot trailer on the land they owned. Their willingness to live in such a relatively small space for a year or so in order to achieve their goals is a good illustration of *deferred gratification*. Yet, when they look back on that time in their lives, it doesn't look all that bad. Diane observes with amusement and approval, "We have been camping out in the wilderness since we were married."

The Saunders' desire to have children motivated them to start building their home. Raising children in a small trailer would have felt more like *deprivation* than *deferred gratification* for Edward and Diane. They bought the required materials (primarily from catalogs) for $10,000 in cash and then built a 600-square-foot home themselves. Over the years they expanded their home to include a total of 1,000 square feet. They raised their two children in this home and continue to live there today. Two adults, two children, 1,000 square feet, and no one in this family reports any feelings of deprivation, even though their friends have tried to persuade them they need a larger place.

It makes you wonder. If we all, or even a substantial number of us, felt content with 1,000 square feet of living space for a family of four, what possibilities might that open up? If our appetite to accumulate other material possessions were similarly downsized, we certainly could live comfortably on a lot less income than we need today. As a society, we would have the economic option to give our children the gift of full-time parenting, either by allowing one parent to be at home full-time, or by enabling both parents to work part-time and share the parenting during normal work hours. Or, we could choose to work fewer hours and develop those interests, hobbies and passions we fantasize about during the slow or stressful periods in our jobs. We would not feel so stressed with the demands of modern life, trying to juggle not only our jobs and family responsibilities, but also our desires to contribute to our communities, to nourish adult friendships, and to explore our spiritual selves. What type of society would we live in if so many of us were not feeling so burned out? What would our world be like if we all got enough sleep? Would we have the time and energy to start caring for each other more? It makes you wonder.

Edward could envision the benefits of *deferred gratification* at the start of his journey. He was willing to trade off some material benefits during the last 23 years in exchange for the freedom he now enjoys. It is not that he deprived himself of material or other things that were important to him; it's just that he and his family understood what they really needed and wanted. As Edward sees it, "I believe material possessions own the owners. What you have should benefit your life, not be a burden to you or anyone else."

In addition to having their basic material needs met, the overall quality of the Saunders' lives was very satisfying throughout this period of *deferred gratification*. They thoroughly enjoyed living in a world of wondrous natural beauty and wildlife, with bear and moose as frequent visitors. They could afford to live on one income, which allowed Diane to be a full-time mother and family manager. Her contribution provided a sense of balance and tranquillity to this family's life. Edward is proud to report, "Our family doesn't quite fit the normal family mold of today. Our children are the winners for it."

Teaching high school was a mixed experience for Edward. He loved working with the students and enjoyed having his own children in his classes. However, as the years passed, he experienced changes in the teaching profession that resulted in his feeling less free to create and improvise, with fewer resources generally. Even though Edward didn't realize it at the time, he was feeling stressed from the pressures of his job. The stress showed up as back problems and asthma-type symptoms. Still, in retrospect, Edward feels the benefits outweighed the costs. His teaching career laid the foundation for his early retirement at age forty-seven, complete with his life-long pension and health care benefits.

Now free of stress, Edward works his land, restoring it to its natural vegetative state after a spruce bark beetle infestation. The manual labor feels good to him. He volunteers at the library one day a week and is active in the community. And he has the time to satisfy his voracious appetite for reading. He enjoys reading so much more now—if he gets immersed in a great book, he can actually spend the whole day reading it if he wants to. His daily five to ten mile walks have done wonders for his health, including losing the excess weight he gained from his physically inactive teaching years. Not surprisingly, his back problems and breathing difficulties have disappeared. He has not been sick a single day since he retired.

Edward's choice to work his land and in the community exemplifies the principle that we have a need for purposeful, meaningful work, quite apart from earning income to support ourselves. His life dispels the myth that people who value simple living are interested only in a life of leisure. What distinguishes people who live simply from the rest of America on the issue of work is that (1) the former group often has the option to work in areas that are more fulfilling to them, and (2) they also tend to work less than the typical work week of 40 hours plus five to ten additional hours for commuting, preparing for, and unwinding from work.

Edward and Diane are reaping the rewards of living frugally for over 20 years, of not moving up to a larger and more luxurious home when they could afford it, and of saving their money instead of squandering it on all sorts of material enhancements. Each of their children has saved enough money for four years of college at the University of Alaska. This family's life of simplicity may not have always been easy, but it has certainly been deeply satisfying and rewarding.

It's true, you may be thinking, that many of us would not want to move to a rural area and buy a relatively inexpensive plot of land, or build a home with our own hands. But maybe there are other tradeoffs we could make, other forms of *deferred gratification*, that would make sense in our lives. Maybe there are creature comforts we could give up in exchange for a more satisfying, fulfilling lifestyle than the American prototype of working in jobs that lack fulfillment until we retire or die.

The concepts of *deferred gratification* and *deprivation* are distinct ideas. With the former, the emphasis is on gratification, albeit at a later date. *Deprivation*, on the other hand, is not associated with any benefits at all. One challenge of modern life is finding the right balance between immediate satisfaction and gratification for today—after all, we may only have today—

and deferring some of the gratification for a more fulfilling tomorrow.

Free and Fiercely Independent—Dixie Lynn Darr

Dixie Lynn Darr is a single, fifty-year-old woman. She has always lived simply. As she observes, "Not everybody who has chosen a simple lifestyle is some former fast-track yuppie who saw the light and downscaled. The truth is many of us have always lived this way. I learned a long ago that time and freedom were much more important to me than money and material goods."

For the last 20 years (except for a two-year stint in a full-time job), Dixie has worked about "20 to 25 hours a week, frequently less and occasionally more." Dixie is a *portfolio* worker—she uses her portfolio of skills and expertise to create a variety of work opportunities. Currently, she publishes *The Accidental Entrepreneur*™, a newsletter for "self-employed corporate refugees," teaches part-time at a local university (one course a semester), and writes and conducts business research for corporations. She thrives on the diversity and intellectual stimulation of her work and is especially keen about the fact that she can work primarily from her home. Her annual income varies from $15,000 to $40,000.

It is interesting that Dixie has arrived at this stage of middle life with professional skills and expertise equivalent to those who paid their dues in full-time, often stressful careers. Dixie never bought into the presumed necessity for such a career; still, she has scored stimulating, professional work. Too many times, we think in black and white, neglecting life's great array of shades and colors. We think our choices are either to commit to a full-blown career of long hours and hard work, or settle for something less than what would satisfy us. Dixie's experience shows us there are other possibilities.

When Dixie is not working, she enjoys reading, gardening, meeting friends for a bite to eat at local cafes, and walking in the surrounding neighborhoods, gazing at all the beautiful homes and gardens. Living in one of Denver's inner city neighborhoods, she is close to the library, museums, and other cultural amenities. She prefers living as a single person; it provides the quiet and solitude she cherishes.

Dixie's lifestyle is a quality blending of work, leisure, and relationships. Even though it has taken her years to develop the professional expertise to procure stimulating and rewarding work, her vision has been consistent throughout her journey. In addition to time and freedom, living and working independently has always been at the top of her wish list. The rigid structure of college courses did not sit well with Dixie and she detested the clerical jobs she held in her twenties. Her first job of a professional nature left her feeling miserable; the office politics and hostility drove her nuts. To say that Dixie is fiercely independent would be an understatement. It took not only vision but also perseverance and frugality for Dixie to create the independent, balanced life she enjoys today.

Living frugally has not been a huge sacrifice for Dixie; she has never been attracted to shopping as a way to fill a void in her life. She rarely goes to shopping malls, and then only if she needs something that can only be found there. Even so, she is a bit of a pack rat, and getting rid of excess stuff is an on-going process:

One recent idea is that when I get the urge to go to a flea market, garage sale, or thrift shop (some of my favorite places to shop), instead I shop through my own stuff. I don't throw much away because I like to recycle, so I always have unused things in the garage or storeroom that I might be able to use in a different way so it's new to me. This is much more creative and satisfying than going to the mall and buying something that anybody could buy.

Dixie's aversion to shopping stems in part from her concern for the earth: "One of the reasons I live simply is because of my concern for the environment. I've always been disgusted by our society's overwhelming materialism and selfishness."

Time and again, we will see that people who live simply are motivated in part (and in some cases primarily) by their concerns about the earth. It is not that these people are altruistic do-gooders who are busily trying to save the world. No, their concerns stem from a connection they feel to the earth. They sense that we humans are all part of a life force that includes people, animals, and plant life. They understand in their hearts, not just intellectually, that living in ways that destroy the earth is self-destructive behavior. Their values on this subject reflect the common spiritual belief that *we are all one*.

Dixie has also managed the infrastructure expenses of her life very well. Eleven years ago, she bought an inexpensive, small (900 square feet) home in an inner-city neighborhood that has since gained considerable popularity, resulting in higher property values. Her mortgage is less than the current rent for a one-bedroom apartment in her area. Dixie's eight-year-old compact car suits her just fine. And since she works primarily out of her home and walks to restaurants and local businesses, her car maintenance expenses are minimal. Her lifestyle allows her to wear sweats in the winter and shorts and T-shirts in the summer, so her clothing expenses are minuscule.

Dixie is fortunate to have known what she wanted early in her adulthood. Unlike many of us, she did not spend much money on material things, incur substantial debt, or buy more of a home than she could afford on a part-time income. The sooner you start living simply, the sooner you will enjoy the time and freedom to create your ideal life. Check out Chapter Nine, *Starting Out Simply: Generation X Takes a U-Turn*, for the inspiring stories of young people who are starting out simply.

Dixie's lifestyle, like those of others profiled in this book, is not for everyone. For example, her income does not allow much for retirement savings, which might be a serious concern for others. However, she enjoys her work so much she doesn't see herself retiring. Considering the type of work Dixie does—teaching, writing, and consulting—she may very well be able to continue working for the rest of her life.

Surprisingly, saving for retirement or reaching total financial independence is not a high priority for some of the simplicity study participants. One reason for this is that they have reduced their monetary needs and desires to a level that doesn't require an enormous nest egg. There is another, less tangible reason. People who incorporate the principles of simplicity into their lives appear to be blessed with an unusually high level of self-confidence and sense of personal security. Typically, they enjoy their work and intend to continue working well into their senior years. They have mastered the art of creative living—they know how to obtain their basic necessities with little money. In essence, they have removed themselves, at least partially, from our monetary culture. Whether saving for retirement is an important priority depends in part on your risk tolerance level. Like the question of whether to carry health insurance, this decision must be made by each individual and family based on their unique circumstances and comfort levels with risk.

Like many people who choose simplicity, Dixie reports that her friends and family see her as an oddball of sorts:

My family and friends all work at regular jobs and don't really understand what I do. I think it makes them uncomfortable. A few close friends understand me, but at the same time, they think I'm nuts. I have been an oddball all my life, but I sort of like it that way.

Clearly, Dixie values her freedom and independence highly. And she walks her talk.

Lessons and Reflections

What can we learn from these long-timers? Just knowing that there are those who have walked this path before us is reassuring. Simplicity is not just a fad, a trend that will disappear in a year or two. Living simply can be very satisfying over the long haul. In fact, it appears that the longer one applies the principles of simplicity to his or her life, the greater the satisfaction.

Perhaps the most distinguishing feature of those who have lived simply all their adult lives is their early clarity of vision. It is unusual in our society to know much about who you are or what is important in your life as a young adult. Most of us experience significant transformational changes during our twenties and early thirties, often accompanied by a divorce or major career changes. Until we have a clearer idea of what makes each of us the unique human being we are, we are not likely to create a cohesive, satisfying way of life for ourselves. As the old saying goes, "If you don't know where you are going, any road will get you there." Holli-Anne Passmore, Edward Saunders, and Dixie Lynn Darr are blessed to have found their paths early in their lives.

Chapter Nine

Starting Out Simply:
Generation X Takes a U-Turn

Twenty-three percent of the survey participants fall into the age group known as Generation X—people in their twenties or early thirties at the time of the simplicity study. The stories of these younger people are refreshing in part because so many of their peers are in-tent on trying to prove their self-worth by amassing possessions, status symbols, and career prestige without considering the tradeoffs. While it is common for people in middle life to reevaluate the meaning and purpose of their lives, these young people stand out for doing so early in their life's journey.

The Promise of Youth—Jessica Coleman

Jessica Coleman is starting out simply. At twenty-two, she and her husband, Ian, have no desire to chase the American Dream. Living in a one-bedroom apartment in downtown Portland, Oregon, they see no reason to burden themselves with an automobile. As Jessica says, "Car payments, insurance, repairs, parking, traffic citations, accidents…who needs it?" Having been an avid bus rider since she was fourteen, Jessica enjoys her hassle free commute on the bus. She and Ian often ride the same bus to work. They walk or ride their bicycles just about anywhere else they want to go.

When Jessica and Ian first started dating, things were different. They went out to dinner almost every night and never missed the newest film releases in the theaters. Now they spend about $3 a

month on movies and $40 a month dining out. They entertain them-
selves with reading, walking, talking, spending time with family and
friends, and playing with their two pet parrots. Jessica has never
owned a TV, and Ian doesn't miss the TV he gave up when he married Jessica. As Jessica observes, "Life itself, just the breathing and
seeing out of your own two eyes all the incredible things there are,
the fascination of steering a human body around through the world—
that can be pretty entertaining all by itself."

I am impressed that a twenty-two-year-old person made the
above statement. It displays a wisdom, an inner knowledge,
that is beyond her years. How and why Jessica became the
person she is today is not easily answered. Who we grow up
to be is the result of many factors and complex relationships.
As we will see later in this story, Jessica's childhood experiences can be viewed both as grooming her for a life of
consumerism and traditional American values (work 'n' spend
'till you drop), or as leading her to create an original, satisfying lifestyle based on her unique interests, skills, and passions.
Jessica chose the latter route.

Jessica's wardrobe has also undergone a major transformation
since her high school days:

*When I moved out on my own five years ago, my clothes would have
taken up most of a truck bed. I won a bet in high school that I wouldn't
be able to go two entire months without wearing any duplicate articles of
clothing other than underwear. Now all my clothes fit into a small dresser
and my half of a small closet, and every accessory I own fits into the same
hatbox (including hats). Over the last two or three years, I have gradually replaced my impulsively-purchased "orphans" with clothes I can
mix and match with almost anything else I own. I stick with a small
palette of colors I know are attractive on me, and I never buy anything
that requires dry-cleaning. I have one winter dress for special occasions*

like family dinners, one summer dress for the same, and one all-purpose
black velvet evening dress for parties.

Jessica recognizes that she and Ian have made, as she puts it,
"pretty major changes for two kids who grew up staring at the TV all
day:"

I mean, really, all we did was stare at the TV all day, eat processed
food, and fight with our siblings. Now we have traded boredom, ennui,
dissatisfaction, and depression for a sense of wholeness and purpose. Some-
times we talk to our coworkers and it just seems like they have become
zombies, tearing themselves from their televisions only long enough to
order pizzas delivered or wander around some shopping mall getting them-
selves further into credit card debt. To think that used to be us! It's very
humbling.

Well, watching TV *all the time* isn't totally accurate. Her family
also went on camping trips during the summer. It is no surprise that
a key motivation for Jessica to live simply is her deep concern for the
earth, stemming in part from the appreciation of nature she developed on those family camping trips. She recalls one vivid memory
when she and her brothers were walking in the woods and came
across a tiny shrew:

The shrew was holding very still on the ground, trying to blend in,
and we could easily have stepped on it. What was so touching for us was
realizing how vulnerable the little guy was. There was a sense of awe at
how easily it could have been killed. It was directly in our path, and less
observant hikers probably would not have seen it. It amazed me that
something so small could be alive, have eyes and tiny feet. I realized that
God cared enough about this shrew to give it a heart and lungs—there-
fore, we people might not be as important as we thought.

As a child, Jessica was open to being touched deeply by the wonder of nature. These types of experiences formed essential aspects of
her character as an adult. Her passion for the earth is strong:

How could anyone not be interested in environmental issues? One thing I have learned from living with birds is that you don't pollute your own nest, or your food or water supplies either. I think part of the problem is that we humans feel that we are separate from the rest of life. We are killing species of animals before we even meet them. I am devoted to our planet, and I serve her as a steward as best I can.

In some ways, Jessica feels that her generation was "handed a dirty plate" by her parents' generation—a dirty plate that needs to be cleaned before it can be used. Jessica focuses on what she can do, one small step at a time. Some of the actions she takes to preserve the earth's resources include eating a vegan diet, buying in bulk to save on packaging, buying used instead of new clothing and other goods, using natural cleansers, and reusing lunch bags, grocery bags and cloth napkins. And, especially, not driving or owning a car. She talks with others about these issues when it feels appropriate, but does not try to impose her beliefs on others.

Jessica's concern for the earth strongly influenced her choice to live simply. Others develop ecological interests as a result of living simply. For 13 percent of the simplicity study participants, concern for the environment was the dominant motivating factor leading them to simplicity. However, 82 percent of the participants have a moderate to strong interest in environmental issues. Clearly, while not all participants were drawn to simplicity out of concern for the earth, most of them are sensitive to ecological matters. For further discussion of the relationship between simplicity and environmental concerns, see Chapter Thirteen, *Environmental Champions: A Passionate Love for the Earth.*

Living simply and frugally also serves Jessica and Ian's personal goals in life. Ultimately, they would both like to work fewer hours, leaving more time for volunteer work and pursuing other interests.

For now though, in addition to a full-time job, Jessica is taking a full college load and would like to teach English as a second language. They are working full-time to save money for a home with a nice yard so that they can have a garden and grow some of their own food.

Jessica's lifestyle does not speak of simplicity in terms of her activity level. She is working full-time while maintaining a full college course program. With this schedule, there is not a lot of room for long, unbroken stretches of leisure, for stopping to smell the roses. So, what does this mean? Does Jessica fail the simplicity test? No, because there is no simplicity test! There are no "10 rules to follow to become a full-fledged member of the simplicity movement." The answer lies in how a person feels about her life. Jessica enjoys her life enormously. She cherishes the time she spends playing with her pet parrots and walking and talking with Ian. And, Jessica does not plan to keep up this schedule forever. She and Ian believe they will be able to buy their home in about 18 months, at which point they can reduce their work hours.

In the meantime, they appreciate the benefits of apartment living in a downtown setting:

Apartment living can certainly be simpler than home ownership; we never have to worry about wiring, plumbing, roofing, lawn-mowing, painting, broken appliances, exterminators, storm windows, or property taxes. We are also protected from annoying door-to-door solicitors. The front desk is there for us if we forget our keys, and we don't have to worry about packages left on our doorstep getting lost.

Jessica and Ian are looking forward to their first home for what it offers in terms of potential equity appreciation, a feeling of stability, and an opportunity to grow vegetables. They are not striving to buy a home as a way to prove to themselves or others that they are successful in life. In fact, as noted above, they are mindful of the pros and cons of apartment renting versus home ownership, and are basing their choices on the real benefits of each option.

Many of Jessica and Ian's friends and family view them as rather eccentric, or at least as oddballs. In addition to what Jessica describes as "our obvious apathy regarding the national pursuit of wealth," Jessica and Ian's vegan diet and lack of desire for automobiles sometimes trigger negative reactions from the people in their lives. But Jessica has been trained well in the art of being different. Growing up as the poorest kid in the neighborhood, she learned early in life that being different is not a curse:

My parents, who are not simplicity mavens, taught me as a child never to be afraid to be different from other people, and to do whatever I wanted to do as long as I was prepared to accept the consequences of my actions. This background left me open for inspiration. I read Walden *as a teenager and loved it, but it didn't seem like a life I could start for myself. Then at age nineteen, I read Elaine St. James'* Simplify Your Life. *The life she described seemed not only attractive, but also easily attainable, and thus my journey began. I do not miss any part of my old complex life—that cluttered life filled with social obligations that filled me with anxiety, attitudes that restricted me, and possessions that smothered me.*

Jessica displays the conscious living characteristics more common in the middle to later stages of life, in stark contrast to the typical mindset of those in their early twenties. Undoubtedly, her values are a combination of many things: her parents' influence, the affect of her bond with nature, and her inner wisdom. Perhaps we are all born with this wisdom, which most of us slowly lose as we grow up. Jessica may have just held on to it better than most.

At the end of our interview, I asked Jessica if there was anything else she would like to share about her experience of living simply. She responded by asking me to relay this message to you, the reader of this book:

It's really not as hard as you think it is. Living simply gives you the time to think—the time to look at what your life is all about. If you think it is too much work to chop vegetables—well, it won't be, once you slow down a bit. It will be worth it. Just do it.

A Focused Start in Life—Melissa Reid

Melissa Reid lives a life of freedom—freedom to work or not to work, to spend each day exactly as she wants to. Now in her early thirties, she lives in the home she purchased ten years ago, paying off her mortgage in just a few years. She has built up a nest egg that generates sufficient income to pay her living expenses.

At first glance, I would guess that Melissa might be the daughter of a privileged family. I might well imagine that her family has money, probably old money, with various family trusts to help the kids get a good start in life. I can imagine a paid-for college education at a prestigious university, a generous gift of a down payment on Melissa's first home, perhaps some strategic family investments to provide financial security early in her life.

Well, nothing could be further from the truth. Melissa's story has nothing to do with privilege or family trusts. It has everything to do with focus and clarity at an early age. Her story is striking not only because her accomplishments are so remarkable for a young adult in our culture but also because what she has accomplished is so simple—so very attainable and sensible.

Melissa decided early on what was most important to her and then proceeded to make it happen. After high school, she earned a bachelor's degree at a local university. She was awarded a full scholarship that paid her basic college expenses. Her parents gave her free room and board at home. She also worked part-time during college and was able to save up a sizable down payment for the home she now owns. Immediately upon graduation, Melissa bought a small, brick house for $30,000 in Madison, Wisconsin.

I can imagine some readers muttering under their breaths that *they* did not have the benefit of a full college scholarship. No, they would say, they barely had enough money to put food on the table, much less save for a down payment on a house. Maybe so. But how many of us choose to live away from home during college, incurring extra expenses for room and board, because we simply must get away? This may be a worthwhile choice, but remember it is a choice and in most cases, not a necessity. How many students attend high-priced universities when a less expensive local college would serve them well? How many families explore colleges in less expensive states where a relative or a part-time, live-in caretaker position could provide room and board? We may not want to do any of these things, but they are options. And, of course, there is always the option of not attending college at all, which may be the best choice for some people. The point here is that we tend to think narrowly about our choices in life; we need to learn to think outside the boxes, to broaden our horizons and consider uncommon alternatives.

After graduating from college, Melissa tried several jobs, eventually settling on a position with a marketing research firm. This work suited her very well; she loved being surrounded by intellectually stimulating people and enjoyed the pace and activity level of her job. During this period, she paid off her mortgage and was able to save up a good-sized nest egg. When she realized she had sufficient savings to support herself from the interest income, she started to sense the call of freedom, first as a distant murmur and then as an increasingly louder and appealing option.

In 1998, Melissa quit her full-time job as a research assistant. She now earns a small amount of money taking care of a friend's daughter a few evenings a week. However, Melissa doesn't need the money to live on; her savings are sufficient to cover her basic expenses, which run from $200 to $500 a month. But how can you possibly support yourself on that level in this country? What kind of living conditions can this meager amount buy? Let's take a look at Melissa's life.

Melissa's home purchase is a key aspect of her success at living simply:

Simplification definitely played a part in choosing what my new home would be. My overall goal was to buy a cheap, small, low-maintenance house that I could pay off very quickly so I would no longer have house payments and could move on to building up enough savings to become financially independent.

Melissa's home is 700 square feet and consists of a bedroom, a bathroom, a large kitchen, and a small living room/office. The house has many windows, very few furnishings (most of which are give-aways or garage sale finds), and is decorated sparingly. Melissa derives enormous comfort and aesthetic pleasure from her home:

I'm very affected by architecture, light, color, arrangement of furniture, decor, etc. My house has just the right mix of these elements, and I enjoy spending time there. It's a quiet sanctuary when I'm alone and a welcoming space for family and friends as well.

Reminder: voluntary simplicity is not about deprivation. Melissa does not feel deprived living in a 700-square-foot home. Between 1950 and 1997 the average size of the new single-family home built in America has almost doubled—from 1,100 square feet to 2,150 square feet. How much of our desire for larger homes comes from what truly brings us comfort and pleasure? Or is our desire for *bigger and better* the product of conditioning generated by expert marketing professionals retained by corporations whose growth is dependent on our continually increasing hunger for consumption?

It takes more than a paid-off mortgage to live on $200 to $500 a month. Transportation, for example, could run that amount alone. But not for Melissa. For one thing, she has never owned a car. Her primary source of transportation is a second hand bicycle. She also walks regularly, gets rides from family and friends, or uses public transportation during inclement weather. For Melissa, her transportation choices are all about freedom:

For many people I know, having a car seems closely intertwined with their sense of freedom—freedom to go where they want, at any time they want. In my life it's the opposite. I feel free without a car—free from car payments, maintenance, and traffic tickets. And I have the freedom to park my bicycle practically anywhere!

I think that a bicycle is the essence of simple, effective technology. There's very little to learn about riding or maintaining one, and much of that is readily apparent. I also get a physical workout in the process of running errands, visiting friends, etc., without having to make time to fit one in.

When my husband and I travel abroad, we never rent a car, choosing instead to rely on public transportation and our own four feet. In those settings, I don't feel deprived at all, whereas I cannot imagine my life at home without a car. When I think about it, I realize that the key difference is that when I'm travelling, I'm not working, and if it takes me an hour and a half to get from point A to point B, who cares? It's all part of the experience. I love walking, and using public transportation can be a great opportunity for people watching, to take time to just think, to just be. In fact, as odd as it sounds, it can be a great time to be alone. No phone calls, no one you need to talk to, no problems to solve—just sit and watch the scenery or amuse yourself with your thoughts.

All this reminds me how much the perceived necessity for a car in our society is tied to our work. Even if you don't use your car to commute to work, you need your car for errands, recreation, and trips, all of which must be squeezed into tight time frames because your job leaves you only a very limited amount of free time! So, if you quit your job, you could probably quit your car at the same time. You may have no interest in doing either of these things, but it is important to realize that your car is a work-related expense, whether you use your car to commute to work or not.

Melissa has lived comfortably on very little for ten years. During her working years, she routinely saved over half her salary. She doesn't recall feeling deprived at all:

Saving up money was (and still is) exciting and not depressing for me, because it was tangible evidence of movement towards a dream. I'm sure I spend much less nowadays than I did even at that time. I have had years of studying my needs and gradually paring down on things that don't give me the added enjoyment or comfort to match their price tags. I also think I'm lucky in that there are certain common American commodities that I really just never had a desire to own, like a car, a dishwasher, a surround-sound stereo system, etc.

It's much harder to give up things you've gotten used to having around or that you have become attached to. I went through major withdrawal symptoms the first few weeks I was experimenting with giving up television. Nowadays I don't even think about television but at the time I was practically bouncing off the walls trying to fill in the gap left by my "TV time." All things considered, I'm very glad I made the decision to give it up, because for me it had become a negative addiction.

The impact of television in our lives is a popular subject among those who live simply. The TV-watching experiences of the simplicity study participants are discussed in Chapter Fourteen, *The Pierce Simplicity Study: Reflections and Inspiration.*

Living frugally has come fairly easily for Melissa. In contrast, the transition from full-time work to an unstructured life of considerable freedom has been much more challenging. Before taking the leap and leaving her job, Melissa took a few weeks' vacation to think it over and try living as if she didn't have a job. The time away was very enjoyable for her and helped firm up her resolve. She gave notice upon returning to work and left her job shortly thereafter. However, it took her some time after that to get her bearings:

At first I spent a lot of time sleeping. My body took some time adjusting to a more organic schedule and not having the wind-up/wind-down from work cycles. I also realized I used the job as a crutch and an excuse for all the things I would do if I didn't have to work.

Self-esteem wasn't an issue. Me, myself and I get along pretty well together. However, the identity thing was a little tricky because I felt like I needed to redefine my place in the universe. I don't think it was so much that my work as a research assistant was any more important than other things I did in my life, but that there was something about it that gave me a sense of my own importance, however accurate or inaccurate that may have been. It also gave me a sense of movement because of constantly doing tasks to achieve certain goals. Even though some of my work activity actually led me around in circles or even backwards at times, the physical and mental movement involved in my work gave me an illusion of constant forward motion.

If I had to pick the one hardest thing about not having a job, it's coming face to face with myself, with no buffers in between, no handy excuses or rationalizing. I've started seeing myself as I really am with no limits, and it can be pretty surprising and disturbing. I am learning to just live more in the flow of the day. There are things on my list that I haven't gotten to and probably won't, but then other things have taken their place. I think for me the lesson is to relax into my life and learn to live it more, instead of spending so much time planning to live it.

I experienced similar inner turmoil when I first left the world of real jobs to focus on writing. At last I had the freedom I had always dreamed of; I could literally do anything I wanted to. With a supportive husband and no children, I had few obligations—keeping house and caring for two dogs. And yet I found it difficult to embrace my hard-earned freedom. I discovered I was uncomfortable without the structure of external expectations. Instead of throwing myself into all those activities that filled my fantasies of freedom, I found myself frittering away a lot of time, doing things like playing solitaire on the computer. Freedom, total freedom, is daunting. There is tremendous responsibility involved in creating your entire life. You don't have 40 hours (or more) a week of structured expectations with built-in feedback. If I am in a job where my performance will be noticed, it is easy to respond with work and more work. In essence, I turn over some of my own freedom to the expectations of others. When that structure is removed, I am left with myself. Time is the ultimate form of riches, but it takes courage and responsibility to realize that wealth. It took me about nine months to learn how to provide structure for myself and settle into a balanced life of productivity and leisure.

In addition to the internal adjustments she was making, Melissa also began to relate differently to others in her new role:

Family and a handful of good friends have been very interested and supportive about what I'm doing once they got used to the idea (although I think many of them consider me odd in a nice, familiar sort of way). However, as far as strangers go, I still have a tough time deciding what to say when someone asks me what I do. It's handy to be able to say I do daycare (for the time I spend taking care of my friend's daughter) because it's an acceptable one-word answer that doesn't require a lot of explaining. I think the "What do you do?" question is mainly a shorthand categorizing system that we use to place people anyway, and not usually something we ask because we really want to know the answer. At least I know that for me, it's kind of a knee-jerk question I ask on first meeting someone.

So, what does Melissa do with her time? Her typical day starts with rising early and spending some quiet time reading or meditating. She then progresses to her puttering phase—listening to the radio while she waters the plants, doing some light housekeeping or sewing, filing papers, or taking care of minor household repairs. After a light breakfast, Melissa might tend the garden or start baking a few loaves of bread, followed by some time on her computer, either writing letters, organizing recipes, or helping out a local charitable organization by entering data on spreadsheets for them.

By late morning, Melissa takes off on her bicycle to visit family or friends, go to the library (where she spends time on personal research projects), or run errands. Lunch and dinner are usually simple one-dish affairs, made from scratch. She spends her afternoons and evenings either taking care of her friend's daughter or "working on whatever I happen to be interested in, whether it be learning a new computer program, poring over candle-making catalogs, cleaning out the bathroom closet, or knitting a scarf. I go to bed fairly early and usually read again until I get tired. It's a low-key life, but very satisfying for me."

I asked Melissa what appealed to her most about voluntary simplicity:

One word—freedom. I wanted freedom above all else, and was willing to do whatever it would take to get it. By freedom, I mean the sense of being able, in my mind, to feel confident that I don't need to compromise myself or my values in any way in order to be able to survive financially. I also wanted freedom from the kind of societal games we are taught to play—first in school, then at work— in order to get the prize, either the grades or the paycheck. Of course, intellectually, I know I've had that freedom all along— it's something that comes from within—but voluntary simplicity makes it feel more concrete to me.

I also wanted to develop my own sense of competency in the art of living, if that makes sense. I think so many of us have forgotten what the true necessities of life are and have accumulated many artificial needs that we really believe we would be unable to live without. I found (and continue to find!) plenty of these in my life. We panic when the power goes out. Well, a hundred years ago, the power was out all the time! I'm not paring back because I'm a technophobe (I love working with computers) but rather because I don't want to mistake the technology in my life for being essential to my survival. I want to become more conscious of voluntarily choosing to use it, not because I need to, but because I want to.

Which leads me to another major reason: consciousness, becoming more aware of what I'm doing, and why I'm doing it, instead of just going through my days on autopilot. Doing things like baking bread instead of buying it, needing to allow extra time to use a bicycle to run errands, and using a wind-up radio…these are the kind of things that are really helpful for me. In each of those cases, I have to make a conscious decision to act in order to get the desired result. There's a built-in pause between wanting something and actually getting it, and the pause involves some effort on my part.

Melissa lives the way she does because it pleases her; her actions are not inspired by altruism, sacrifice, or willpower: "Some of the things I enjoy doing also happen to benefit others, the environment, and my community. I'm glad of that, of course, but overall I do what's best for my spirit first and the rest follows."

Some people are fortunate to know what they want in life at an early age. Melissa's reading of *Walden* by Henry David Thoreau in high school impacted her greatly: "I was blown away by Thoreau's radical approach to life, and found an answer in his writings to how to live my own." She has systematically followed a plan of simple living ever since.

Simplicity with Ease—Beth Heins

For Beth Heins, twenty-six, living simply is natural, easy, and normal. Unlike many of the simplicity study participants, she does not experience the tension between the norms of American culture and her chosen way of life. Rather, she seems to attract people into her life who share her view of the world.

For example, take Beth's living arrangements. She shares a four-bedroom, one-bath home with three single roommates, two women and one man, all in their twenties or early thirties, and all committed to living simply. They live in a residential city neighborhood of Portland, Oregon, within easy access to downtown. The group agreed up front not to have a TV in their home. They prefer to spend their leisure time talking, reading, cooking, visiting with friends, going out for an occasional beer, hiking, and camping.

> Sharing housing serves many purposes. Obviously, it is often less expensive, allowing you to save significant money for other priorities, such as travel, education, or your freedom. It also makes a real contribution to conserving the earth's resources. One refrigerator, one washer and dryer, and one stereo are all better than four of these things. Sharing housing also opens up possibilities for sharing cars more easily, again resulting in a reduced impact on the earth.
>
> Sharing a home also provides the opportunity to spend less time and money on the infrastructure of your life, leaving you more quality time for more enjoyable activities unless, of course, you really enjoy housecleaning, repairs, and yard work—in which case I have room for you in my home!

Living with others also provides a built-in community. Beth has her own simplicity support group under the same roof. It seems true but unfortunate in our society that as we age, we seem to become set in our ways, less flexible, and less able to enjoy a cohousing situation. If you are young enough or free enough, consider the option of sharing housing with others. There are cohousing communities available but you can also do something small and simple, like rent or buy a home with just a few other people. For information on cohousing and other intentional communities, see the Resource Guide (Web Sites section) at the end of this book.

Condominium and apartment living are modified forms of cohousing. There are savings in construction materials (with shared walls, garages) and appliances. My husband and I live in a 16-unit condominium complex with a laundry room that has four washing machines and four dryers. It is only a small contribution, but I like the fact that we have 12 fewer washers and dryers than if we all lived in single family homes. Not that we do any fewer loads of laundry, but at least the construction materials for those saved appliances will not be coming from nonrenewable resources.

Beth drives an older Toyota and commutes to work with one of her roommates. While she does not view her current job for a software company as her *right livelihood* or ultimate career goal, she does enjoy the people she works with and the casual dress code. Dressing casually is a real bonus for Beth during the warmer months when she rides her bicycle to work (22 miles roundtrip) once or twice a week.

When I asked Beth how she came to feel so comfortable with living simply, she replied that initially it was a matter of economic necessity. She was short of funds when she graduated from college and needed to live frugally. Then she discovered it felt great to live that way—to live lightly and not be burdened with mountains of stuff. As her economic situation improved, she did not expand her spending habits, but instead embraced simplicity as a way of life, rather than as an economic necessity. She is now saving about 40 percent of her salary and intends to use that money for retirement, and possibly travel, but has no desire to spend money on bigger or better material possessions.

Many people in their twenties don't even think of saving for retirement. Beth is smart. This is the most important decade of her life for saving. The "magic" of compounding will turn her savings into a nice nest egg much more effectively than saving equivalent amounts later in her life.

The word "retirement" is burdened with negative connotations for many people. Few among us want to "retire" from life. We may want to retire from a less than satisfying job, but most of us crave some form of meaningful work. Retirement or financial independence gives us the freedom to work for non-monetary rewards at a pace that works for us.

For Beth, simplicity is more than opting out of a debt-laden, consumer lifestyle. Equally important is quality of life. For example, up until a year and a half ago, Beth lived on the East Coast, most recently in Boston. Even though she was living simply in terms of her spending habits, she felt stuck in her life. She was not making new friends and had the feeling that, "There was something better than just working and marking time as life passed me by:"

I wanted a better life, with more activities, more friends, more time outdoors in a city I could love. I moved from Boston to Portland for these reasons and have been happier than I had dreamed possible. I was choosing to better my life, not simplify it, but have found that the two are actually one.

Beth loves the natural beauty in and around Portland. Every day, she appreciates the natural gifts of her environment—the green hills and trees throughout the Portland area. She often gazes with delight at the mountains during her commute to work. Hiking and camping in the Pacific Northwest have made living in this area very special for her.

I have often said that simple living is not always easy. And many of the experiences of the simplicity study participants attest to this fact. However, there are exceptions to every rule. For Beth, at this point in her life, living simply is easy, normal, natural, and rewarding.

Lessons and Reflections

Many refreshing facts are revealed by the simplicity survey responses. One of them is that the simplicity lifestyle trend is not dominated by middle-aged, burned out, yuppie professionals who have built up a nest egg and now want to cut back and start smelling the roses. In fact, only ten percent of the simplicity study participants fit this profile.

Fourteen percent of the study participants are young people in their twenties. They are designing their lives based on inner callings rather than following what our commercial culture has suggested for them. They are not "dropping out" of society; rather, they are tuning into themselves. Here are some other examples:

♦ Abby Rivera is a twenty-two-year-old married woman who is a Ph.D. student and assistant teacher at a major, prestigious university. Recently, she decided not to pursue a professorship at this university (with its corresponding high paycheck, prestige, stress, and long hours). Instead she will seek a position at a small college, acknowledging that, "My advisors and mentors are going to be very disappointed in me." As she explains, "My health and my marriage are more important to me than having a huge house with cherry furniture and being revered as a nationally-known professor."

♦ After spending three years on a banking career path, John Stott, twenty-seven, was inspired by his readings in voluntary simplicity to abandon a career he did not like. He entered a full-time graduate program in urban planning, a field he thinks he will enjoy for the long term. This move required a drastic change in his spending habits, which he describes as reckless. (I would have to agree that his collection of 25 pairs of shoes, many exceeding $100 a pair, sounds a bit excessive!)

♦ Kelly Powell, twenty-one, dropped out of college in her junior year and now works at numerous freelance and temporary jobs. Not being tied down to an office job, she has embarked on an odyssey: "I have begun to travel more and explore ways of supporting myself in unconventional ways." She lives very frugally so she can enjoy a measure of freedom in her life, primarily to pursue her passion for dance.

What is notable about the twenty-something people I have interviewed is that they follow their hearts in their quest to find their special niche in life. They are less likely to be influenced by parental expectations for a specific career or by what society deems to be worthwhile or prestigious. They have already figured out that amassing great sums of money, power, and prestige is not the path to happiness.

Chapter Ten

Having Enough:
Living Simply with Financial Freedom

Many people associate the desire for financial independence with simple living, in part due to the popularity of the runaway bestseller, *Your Money or Your Life: Transforming Your Relationship with Money and Achieving Financial Independence*, by Joe Dominguez and Vicki Robin. Financial independence frees us to pursue our passions, volunteer our services, or spend more time with friends and family. However, it does not negate the option of working for compensation. It is not an either/or proposition. Too often, people view the desire for financial independence, or financial freedom, as I like to call it, as an escape from work. Doug Brown, a participant in the simplicity study, reflects this view:

> *I notice a trend of Voluntary Simplicity being seen as a way to early retirement and good investment planning. I think this is sad. I see nothing wrong with working until a person is ninety-five, IF they are doing what they want. It's like Yuppies who are tired of working and want to hang out, living off their investments. This approach does not appeal to me personally.*

Of course, the key phrase in Doug's statement is "if they are doing what they want." We love to work when it is fun, fulfilling, and meaningful. We detest work that is stressful. Work can fall into either of these categories whether it is a paid or a volunteer activity. Financial freedom gives us the opportunity to choose meaningful work and avoid stressful work.

In undertaking the simplicity study, I sought the answers to these questions: What has happened in the lives of those who have reached financial independence? Are they in fact just hanging out, living off their investments? These questions beg another—what do we consider valuable, and thus acceptable, activities for an adult in our society? And exactly how do we define work? The stories of the people profiled in this chapter provide fertile material to explore these questions.

A Rich Life in a Coastal Village—Marjan Wazeka

Marjan Wazeka is in her late fifties. Three years ago, she reached her goal of financial independence and moved from the city to a small, coastal town on the Oregon seacoast. Marjan and her brother and sister-in-law combined resources and purchased a pleasant, light-filled, low maintenance home, paying cash for it. Marjan's brother and his wife spend most of their time traveling in their RV (recreational vehicle), leaving Marjan with the home to herself more often than not.

Marjan's life in this coastal village brings to mind the subtitle of Duane Elgin's classic text, *Voluntary Simplicity*—that is, "a way of life that is outwardly simple, inwardly rich." For starters, Marjan, formerly a librarian, no longer works for money. Instead she applies her work energy and aptitudes to volunteer service and writing. Her volunteer work has included lending a hand at the local food bank, assisting in the hospice program, and contributing her time to various school programs and the library. She especially enjoys participating in a "lunch buddy" program at the primary school. With her only child off to college, Marjan finds the special relationship and weekly visits with a first-grader most enjoyable.

Marjan also spends up to 15 hours a week writing. She focuses on memoir writing—not for publication but rather as she describes it, "as a mechanism for life review and wisdom-seeking." For Marjan, writing is a practice that furthers her ongoing and deepening spiritual quest. While she has engaged in spiritual reading, journal writing, and yoga for many years, now she has the time and energy to pursue these interests on a more regular basis. Since she quit her job and moved to her new home, Marjan has expanded her meditation practice, including participating in a weekly meditation group. As Marjan reflects, "I'm not sure which came first, the simplification or the spiritual seeking. Certainly they proceed together." Marjan appreciates the balance she feels in her life, commenting, "The combination of outward service and inward contemplation feels just right."

> The relationship between spirituality and simplicity is a dominant theme in the experiences of the simplicity study participants. We see this frequently in the life stories of the people profiled in this book. Often people view it as a chicken and egg situation—it's a toss up of which comes first, but most agree that simplicity reinforces a sense of spirituality, and spiritual beliefs reinforce the values of simple living. There is considerable overlap between the tenets of simplicity and the beliefs common to many religions. Caring for and being kind to others, for example, is an important value both to people who are religious and to people who value simplicity. Greed and excessive competition also show up on the list of undesirables for both groups.

Perhaps the most precious gift of Marjan's new lifestyle is time. She has the freedom to choose how she spends her time, not only in what she does, but when and how she does it. This luxury is her greatest delight:

I simply revel in having time to read as much as I like, pursue serious spiritual seeking, do all of my walking, running, yoga and tai chi on my own schedule, hike when I want to, write regularly, easily have many house guests, travel in a leisurely fashion, keep up a large correspondence (both via e-mail and regular post), and do the volunteer work that connects me to the community.

Having grown up on an organic farm, Marjan delights in being outside in nature. Her enthusiasm is unmistakable: "Living in this magnificent natural setting, the possible hikes and excursions into wild areas are endless." In addition to her love for walking, hiking, and running, she is an interested birder and an amateur botanist. She reveals that, "It is simply delicious to have the time to pursue some of these things and to be able to savor them."

Life is sweet and very rich for Marjan.

Marjan's life shines with inner peace and fulfillment. She has followed her heart and created an idyllic life for herself. Is her lifestyle any less valuable because she is not engaged in any form of traditional work? I don't think so. Nor does she. Her contributions in volunteer service are obvious. What may be less obvious is the contribution she makes as a person who has found inner peace, a person who has developed her spiritual self and thus experiences a great deal of joy and love. Imagine a world populated by people like Marjan—people who have followed their hearts, found inner peace, and are delighted to share their joy and love with others. Perhaps the most significant contribution we can make during our stay on this planet is the joy and love we bring to others. To the extent we enable ourselves to do that, we are making the most valuable contribution we can make.

Seeing Marjan today, one would never suspect the rocky path she negotiated to reach her relative utopia. Eleven years ago, Marjan and her then husband returned from a seven-year stint of living and working in Italy. After returning to the states, she faced the devastating knowledge that her 21-year marriage was crumbling. Marjan's eighteen-year-old daughter was about to take off for college. Marjan's husband and her daughter moved out of the house the same week. The emptiness of the house mirrored the loss she felt inside. It was this double dose of loss that brought to the surface the undercurrents of change that had been percolating in Marjan's psyche during the previous few years.

What is it that gives a person that final push to start on the path to simplicity? Sometimes it is a person we meet, sometimes a book, sometimes it is a dream that comes in the night. In Marjan's case it was an audio program by the late Joe Dominguez, coauthor of *Your Money or Your Life*. The insights she gleaned from this program led to dramatic changes in Marjan's life. The program described the benefits of living simply and offered a nine-step plan to reach financial independence. Marjan was very impressed with this material; she felt that, "It just made such good sense." As she worked through the program step by step, her discontent with the lifestyle she shared with her husband—spending, consuming, and always doing, always being on the go—grew. The divorce followed soon after.

With her divorce behind her, Marjan worked in earnest on her plan for financial independence. She concentrated on reducing her living expenses to the amount she intended to live on when she became financially independent. She continued her long-term career as a librarian. Rather than buy a home after her divorce, Marjan rented a small apartment in the city, close enough to walk to the library where she worked. The apartment was not aesthetically pleasing, but she reminded herself that it was temporary and living there would further her goal of financial independence. She disciplined herself to save a good chunk of each year's salary, investing it conservatively. It took her seven years to reach financial independence.

Deciding whether to rent or buy a home is a critical issue for those on the path of simplicity. In contrast to the typical American who automatically assumes that home ownership is an inherent right or the ultimate dream, people who live simply make a conscious decision about housing based on their unique needs. Marjan was smart to rent—knowing that she would be moving in the not-too-distant future, she did not take on the risk that the housing market would be in a downturn at the time she would want to sell her home. If you are fairly confident that (1) you will stay put for the long term (at least ten years), *and* (2) you enjoy home and yard maintenance, *and* (3) you want the benefits of home ownership (for example, the freedom to garden just as you please, or the ability to have pets without question), *and* (4) the costs of home ownership in your area do not greatly exceed the cost of renting (including factors such as probable appreciation and income tax savings), consider buying a home. Otherwise, rent and enjoy your freedom from home maintenance, property taxes, and property insurance.

Marjan does not think back on this period in her life as one of suffering and deprivation—far from it. In many ways, living frugally was a natural extension of her spiritual and inner beliefs:

I think one's expenses drop dramatically when one seriously examines the impact of consumption on one's spirit, the earth, other people, and one's time. In that sense, reducing expenses is easy, since once we see the true costs of our actions, the decision to respect life is obvious and painless.

Notice that Marjan did not feel sorry for herself during this period of working and saving. Her reduced standard of living was truly voluntary—it evolved naturally from her inner self, her beliefs and values. It does not work to force yourself to go without certain material pleasures because you think you "should." Or, put another way, if your "should" feeling is coming only from your head, and not also from your heart, it will backfire on you. Witness the universal law of diets: if you force yourself to diet and feel deprived in the process, your chances of gaining weight are excellent.

As if a divorce and having her only child leave the nest did not supply more than adequate opportunity for personal growth, Marjan was diagnosed with breast cancer a year later. Facing and surviving breast cancer was the final catalyst that propelled her to follow through on her plan for financial independence. She looks back on this frightening experience as a blessing. It intensified her search for her life's values—the meaning and purpose to her life. She entered a period of intense spiritual growth and exploration. She came to an understanding that the meaning and purpose of life is "to be good to one another and to learn." Loving and learning pretty much sums up her way of life.

A significant number of simplicity study participants (about 11 percent) experienced an illness, death of a loved one, or other life-shattering event that literally changed their lives (see Chapter Three, *Turning Points: What Motivates Us to Start the Journey?*). Marjan's breast cancer was such an event. When we are forced to slow down and examine our lives—when we become painfully aware of how fragile our physical selves are—we seem naturally to change the way we live. What a shame that sometimes we need these life-threatening events to wake us up to the true meaning of our lives. Try to imagine how you would feel if you or a loved one experienced a serious illness or a close brush with death. What would be most important in your life? How would you want to live differently? Why wait for a crisis to ask these questions? Do it now.

Marjan's experiences of foreign cultures also kindled her interest in simplicity. She recalls with fondness the sense of community she experienced in Pakistan during her Peace Corps tour. Even though the people in Pakistan lacked some of the basic necessities of life, they did not have what Marjan sees as "the awful hunger our culture has." They were not sick with hurry, as we seem to be, but instead seemed to focus on the present moment, enjoying what little they did have. Likewise, when she lived in Italy, she observed that no one was in a hurry. She was favorably impressed with the high quality of life enjoyed by the Italians, a lifestyle lacking the conspicuous consumption and waste commonly found in the United States. For example, most Italians she knew did not live in huge homes; apartment living was more common. But the smaller residences did not reduce their quality of life. It was just the reverse. As Marjan reflects, "They ate well, drank well, appreciated art and music, enjoyed close relationships with family and friends, and benefited from a real sense of community." And they did not need to consume vast amounts of resources to do these things. In Italy, people savored life. Marjan is now doing the same thing, savoring her life, living the life of her dreams.

Obviously, Marjan knows herself very well; she knows what brings her the most satisfaction in life. This did not happen overnight. She spent years tapping into her inner self through journal writing, meditation, and quiet reflection. If this all feels foreign to you, or if you don't know how to start, try writing in a journal:

Write in a journal, daily or almost daily. Write anything and everything. This is for your eyes only. Write about how you feel. You had a business meeting. How did you feel about it? *It went well; it went poorly; Joe had some good ideas; I didn't agree with Mary.* If you feel happy, write about what makes you feel happy. If you are angry with someone, write about what makes you angry. If you feel guilty for feeling angry, write about it. If you feel frustrated, write about it. If you don't know what you feel, except that you feel that journal writing is a dumb exercise, write about how dumb you think it is. Promise yourself that if you still feel the same way in 60 days you'll give it up. If you don't know how to write about your feelings, just start out describing your activities the prior day. *I got up and took a shower. Then I had breakfast—oatmeal with skim milk, orange juice and toast. I drove to work. The traffic was bad. I listened to my Eric Clapton tape; I like his music, especially in the morning,* or, *I'm getting tired of this same old tape, I need to recycle some more tapes from the house. On my drive to work, I started thinking about how impossible it is to meet my next deadline.* Gradually, you will become more aware of the emotional content of your daily life. The point here is that you are having conversations in your head all day long and this exercise simply starts the process of your becoming aware of these conversations. This is a great way to get to know yourself—to really know what's going on inside your head and your heart. This is the work of the soul.

Marjan's effort to live simply is an ongoing process. Even though she was never particularly fond of accumulating clothes, furniture, or gadgets, gradually she has pared down her material possessions even more. Of course she no longer needs her professional wardrobe. Marjan's entertainment center is a small radio with the capability for a single tape and a single CD. She borrows most of her tapes and CD's from the library. She doesn't need her own car, thanks to her brother and his wife leaving their car for her use during their extended RV trips. Living lightly is a pleasure for Marjan.

Clearly, Marjan has come a long way in her quest to live simply, not only by determining her true values and interests, but also by creating a lifestyle that reflects her passions and values in life. So far, we have considered Marjan's life from the point of view of her personal satisfaction and fulfillment. We are left with the question that often comes up when discussing simple living and financial independence. Is simple living primarily about personal satisfaction, or does it require looking outward to others? What, if any, connection is there between Marjan's journey to manifest a personally fulfilling, satisfying life and the world in which she lives? What about the critical issues of the earth's diminishing resources and the lack of social justice and global equity?

Not everyone asks these questions, of course, but for Marjan, these themes are all interconnected. Her concern for the environment undoubtedly developed as she grew up on an organic, subsistence farm, where the adults in her family had a profound respect for the earth. Her mother and grandmother were gentle people, attentive to all living things, plants and animals alike. It was her mom who first introduced Marjan to the Sierra Club. Marjan expanded her interest when she became an environmental activist in the early 1970's. Today, her unabashed pleasure in soaking up the natural beauty of her environment stems from the same inner place as her interest and commitment in preserving the earth's resources. Even though she is no longer politically active in the environmental arena, her interest has not waned. Marjan's commitment to live a life of lower consumption and higher simplicity, along with her ongoing volunteer and community service, are expressions of her deep concern for the well-being of others and for the earth itself.

> Most of the simplicity study participants (82 percent) are concerned about the environment and take steps to live in ways that preserve the earth's resources. This subject is discussed in more detail in Chapter Thirteen, *Environmental Champions: A Passionate Love for the Earth.*

Marjan's actions reinforce her values, which in turn fuel her actions. For example, she first experimented with a vegetarian diet to see if he she could improve her physical fitness, specifically to lower her racing times as a runner. It worked. Later she discovered the ethical and environmental impacts of eating an animal-based diet, which then reinforced her commitment to vegetarianism. It is increasingly more difficult to separate the personal from the other-directed benefits of Marjan's lifestyle. They are intertwined.

> Author Ernest Callenbach talks about the "green triangle." Imagine a triangle with health, money, and the earth as the three points. If you do anything to improve one of the points, the other two points will likely benefit. So, for example, if you do something to save money (like walking instead of driving a car), your health and the earth will benefit. Or, if you reduce

> or eliminate the meat in your diet to preserve the earth's resources, your health and your budget will also benefit.

Marjan's journey of simplicity is representative of many others in the simplicity study. Major life changes tend to take five to ten years to materialize. These changes are often triggered by inner growth and spiritual seeking, sometimes helped along by a life-altering event, such as an illness, death of a loved one, divorce, or loss of employment. The payoffs include a deepening sense of inner peace and a life filled with profound joy and love.

Dentistry on the Go—Scott Jones

At forty-one, Scott Jones, a dentist by trade, lives a life that sparks the envy of many who know him. Starting about three years ago, Scott has worked from one to five months a year, spending the rest of his time roaming around the world, indulging his life-long wanderlust for international travel. Last year, Scott and his girlfriend spent a few months exploring New Zealand, crewed on a sailboat from New Zealand to Fiji, and then traveled in Fiji for a month.

Even though Scott is now financially independent, he still works as a dentist, sometimes volunteering in third world countries. At other times he will take contract assignments, often in locations that do not have adequate medical services. At the time Scott responded to the simplicity survey, he was working as a dentist on a contract assignment at the McMurdo Station in Antarctica.

If you think that Scott made a bundle of money practicing dentistry, and is now living off a fat savings account, think again. He is not your typical dentist, even though his upbringing certainly groomed him for such a life. Taking the road less traveled has been the hallmark of his life.

Scott was raised in an upper middle class family, the son of a prominent orthodontist in the Midwest. A college education was a given. However, Scott realized early on that the traditional modes of career success held little appeal for him. He had no interest in following in his father's footsteps. What excited him most was international travel and living in foreign countries.

As a college student, he figured out that his best shot at fulfilling his dreams was to develop a skill that could afford him the means to travel, or, as he explains, "even better, to help out in a meaningful way in other countries." Dentistry seemed to be a good fit for Scott; he enjoyed the sciences and he could work anywhere in the world.

Immediately after graduating from dental school, Scott explained, "I quickly painted two houses, sold everything I owned, including my car, and came up with $8,000, enough to travel around the world for ten months." He was not disappointed. In fact, he had the time of his life. He volunteered at a kibbutz in Israel for four months—an experience that made a deep and lasting impression on him. With only the shirt on his back, he reports, "I was happier than I had ever been in my life. Not quite like Mahatma Gandhi but as close as I could get. My life was very simple and very rich." Scott discovered that he could be quite happy living on very little money.

After returning to the states, Scott started working for another dentist. His goal was to pay off his educational debts and build his nest egg. He lived simply and frugally. People thought he was nuts. He had an income that would support a much more comfortable lifestyle, but he chose to rent instead of buying a home, often sharing a rental with others. He drove a used car and bought used furniture. People scratched their heads wondering why a person would go through eight years of dental school and then not reap the rewards of the "good life."

But Scott had his own version of the American Dream and it did not include a Mercedes. Here is how Scott sees it:

If I spend all my money on material things, I could not afford what I really want to buy—my freedom. We Americans think of ourselves as "the land of the free," but I think that people are terrified of freedom. They seem to be more comfortable if they have some guidance, and unfortunately, many times that guidance is debt.

People who have the education and skills to earn mega bucks—doctors and lawyers, for example—are sometimes judged harshly by society if they choose not to pursue the "good life." Talk about going against the grain of American culture! Many people aspire to be wealthy; when someone simply walks away from the potential of wealth, the judgments pour in. *I can't believe that Joe is just throwing away his career*, or, *What a shame that Susan couldn't hack it.* To turn your back on what our culture has defined as *the good life* can be threatening to those who seek that life at considerable personal sacrifice. Some observers of the simplicity movement criticize those who have saved money from well-paying jobs, often commenting, *I could live simply, too, if I had that income.* They totally miss the point. You can live simply at any income level. A person who has the resources to live a disconnected life of consumption and speed and chooses not to, is no less (or more) noble than one who does not have that opportunity in the first place.

Scott paid off his educational debts in three years. He then purchased a dental practice and settled into a satisfying lifestyle. He worked four-day weeks and took off the other three days to indulge his passions for backcountry skiing, mountaineering, biking, and other outdoor adventures. His office overlooked a beautiful mountain vista. Life was good. But Scott had not lost his passion for travel; it was simply taking a back seat in his life.

There is something important to learn from Scott's experience here. He did not sacrifice the present for the future while he worked in a traditional dental practice. While it is true that he was not engaged in his most passionate interest, foreign travel, he enjoyed a balanced life of work and play. Since any one of us could die unexpectedly at any time, it is important not to put all our eggs into the basket of the future. On the other hand, if we live only for the present, we may never realize our dream life. Balance is to simplicity what location is to real estate.

After five years of working in his own dental practice, a few events rekindled Scott's wanderlust. A friend, also a dentist, sold his practice and started traveling. This inspired Scott to consider doing the same. About the same time, Scott had an opportunity to visit two other friends—one living in Japan, the other in Bali. He took a month off from his practice and backpacked through Japan and Indonesia with his girlfriend. This trip was a turning point for him. He realized he was not likely to be doing this type of travel in his sixties, and that the time to do it was now. At age thirty-five, he came back to the states and set a goal for himself—to sell his practice and begin his travels within three years. Four years later, he reached his goal and has been living as an international traveler/dentist/gypsy ever since.

Scott's total living expenses run about $10,000 to $12,000 a year. He has sufficient savings to cover his basic living expenses. With his earnings from his contract work, he continues to build his nest egg. When he is in the states, Scott lives frugally:

I used to spend money on an apartment. Now when I am in the states, I live in a 1972 RV [recreational vehicle] and store it on a friend's farm when I'm out of the country. My expenses in the states are only about one-half of what they used to be.

I have streamlined over the last few years. Everything I own is in my camper. I have not lived in a house with a TV since 1984. I wish I could get rid of even more yet I'm down to the basics.

Can you imagine living on $10,000 to $12,000 a year? How about living in a 1972 recreational vehicle for half the year? Of course, living abroad can change the equation one way or the other depending on the other country's cost of living. But it's clear that Scott is not living a life of material luxury, or anything close to it. And yet, his life is rich with adventure and satisfaction. How much of our so-called *standard of living* is of our own choosing and how much is the result of 20 to 50 years of conditioning required to keep our consumer economy healthy?

Scott has found the balance that works for him: "I cannot imagine working full-time again. I enjoy work; I just don't have time for much of it. I live life." He has much more time for friends and family now. And thanks to e-mail, Scott can communicate frequently with friends and family when he is out of the country. Providing dental services to people in less advantaged countries is also rewarding for Scott. As he sees it, "Our capitalistic society has exported Coca-Cola but it has not exported its health care. So I am taking health care to the people."

At first, it seems amazing that Scott has created this exciting life of adventure and freedom. How many of us in our thirties would have ever dreamed that it would be possible to roam the world, working only one to five months a year? But when you examine his life, you realize that the path he took to get there is nothing extreme or out of the ordinary. He did not deprive himself during the years of preparation for the life he leads now. When I asked Scott to describe the strategy he used to achieve his dream, he summed it up this way:

Systematically spending less than I made, paying off debts, building savings, and living simply. It is a mistake for people to deprive themselves now for financial independence in the future. Correspondingly, it is destructive to spend money carelessly now at the expense of future financial security. The key is balance. People can have their cake and eat it too. It just takes a little routine like going to the health club or jogging.

So, what will become of Scott? Will he continue to live the life of an international gypsy for the rest of his life? Does he have any desires to put down roots, to experience a sense of community? What about marriage and children?

Scott has no definite answers to these questions. He realizes that traveling 365 days a year is not his preference. He enjoys settling down in one place for half the year, experiencing a sense of community. For example, reflecting on a recent contract job he held in Antarctica, he commented: "I am able to socialize with pipeline welders from Montana and scientists from Ivy League universities at the same party." He enjoys developing relationships with others when he stays in one place for a while. He can envision a future that might involve a home base in the states with perhaps part-time work and one or two international jaunts each year. But for the next few years, he expects to explore and live in foreign countries. His girlfriend, Becky, is an archeologist and has opportunities to work in southern France and Greece. That would suit Scott just fine. He has mastered the art of living with planned uncertainty, of living in the present moment.

Living in foreign countries, even for a short time, is a wonderful opportunity for inner growth. I lived for two to three month periods in various non-Western cultures, including Senegal (Africa), the Galapagos Islands, and the South Pacific. Each experience was life altering—a real turning point in my life. Out of each experience, a new direction for my life emerged. It is not that I consciously reflected on my life; in fact, it was just the opposite—I rarely thought of my life back home. Rather, living in a culture so totally different than my own fascinated me, and I found myself focusing on the people, places, and events surrounding me. By living this way, I seemed to connect with the inner core of myself more directly. Out of that connection, the path of my life emerged. Because the pace of life is so much slower in non-Western cultures, it is relatively easy to slow down and live in the present. For one thing, you are physically removed from all the "shoulds" in your life— your daily chores, your obligations to friends and families (other than sending postcards), your work, your household obligations, your normal routines. Even though your conscious thoughts may not be focused on your life's issues, such as work or relationships, by removing all the noise and confusion in your normal life, you can more easily connect with, and hear from, your inner self. If living in a foreign culture appeals to you, don't let a lack of money stand in your way. Explore options such as a home exchange, caretaking, volunteer work that includes housing, or paid work.

As for children, so far the paternal instinct has not surfaced for Scott, much to his mother's disappointment. Who knows what the future will hold? As Soren Kierkegaard said, "Life can only be understood backwards, but must be lived forwards."

All the Money in the World and Nothing to Buy—Ralph Miller

Ralph Miller and his wife, Trish, a couple in their early forties, are blessed with an abundance of financial wealth—enough money that they could choose to never work another day in their lives. Ralph never set out to become wealthy; he considers this state of affairs a matter of good fortune for which he is deeply grateful. Yes, he did work hard and the Millers were conscientious about spending and investing their income wisely. In their twenties when their friends were off on expensive ski trips at Lake Tahoe, Ralph and Trish put almost every cent they had into a down payment on a house, leaving them with $15 in their bank account.

But many people work hard and do not become wealthy. So, Ralph figures he is fortunate. As he sees it, "I just made money doing what came naturally, at a time when the marketplace rewarded such skills." And what he does quite naturally is design software for personal computers.

As a child, Ralph enjoyed tinkering, learning how to make things work, and playing around with electronics. His interests eventually led to a master's degree in engineering, which provided the foundation for his career in electronics. During his twenties, he worked diligently in the personal computer field; focus and discipline were his strengths. For the most part, he enjoyed his work. However, he gradually came to detest the bureaucracy inherent in business, the office politics, and the occasional lack of integrity. Some of those years were grueling, requiring long hours and frequent business travel.

Ralph achieved considerable success in his career, in part due to his own talent, diligence, and hard work. His employer rewarded Ralph's contributions with promotions and substantial stock options. In addition to earning a high salary, Ralph enjoyed considerable autonomy and was in a position to help direct his employer's growth. Throughout this period, he didn't give much thought to his true aspirations in life or his financial goals. He simply applied his father's work ethic to the work he enjoyed. At one point, Ralph took a break from the corporate world to start his own high-tech company. Two years later, he sold this business to a large corporation so he could take on a challenging, new project for his former employer.

Do you ever dream of winning the lottery? Ah, yes, total freedom with more than adequate funds to live in a style to which you would like to become accustomed. Never having to look at a price tag or the cost of a restaurant meal again. The time and financial resources to pursue whatever interests strike your fancy. Never having to work another day in your life. Sounds pretty ideal, right? But would that really make your life perfect? After taking a tour around the world or buying a mansion, what would you do with your time? What would bring meaning to your life? This is what Ralph and Trish Miller needed to find out.

By their early thirties, the Millers were financially set. If they chose to, they could easily live off their investments. But that is not their choice. Ralph is still working, in a manner of speaking. He left his long-term employer and now works for another high-tech computer firm. Rather than contribute his talents as a team player in a corporate environment, he works out of the home he and Trish built four years ago, a home Ralph describes as "complete with a rose garden and Italian fountain bubbling outside my office window." Or sometimes he works from his second home in Kauai. His current work assignment allows him to live in Rome, a city he adores.

No question about it, the Millers do enjoy some of the finer things in life money can buy. But when I asked Ralph about the relationship between his wealth and his happiness, he responded that he was disappointed that money did not bring much increased value to his life. Yes, he enjoys some things money can buy, but he doesn't think he would be less happy without them. What about you? If you had more than enough money for all your needs and wants, do you think it would make an appreciable difference in your sense of happiness and contentment? Would it last? After you bought your dream home, what would you do all day long? What would bring you true joy and satisfaction in life?

When I asked Ralph how many hours he works a week, he hesitated. For one thing, it is not that easy to define what constitutes *work* for Ralph. Much of his job involves thought processing, a sort of mental tinkering. It often takes place at unpredictable, unscheduled times of the day or night. He speculates that maybe he puts in "20 hours a week of concentrated thinking."

When you have Ralph's talent, you can call your own shots. Work and play are intertwined—it's hard to know when one stops and the other starts. Ralph takes his responsibilities seriously but the enormous autonomy he enjoys gives him substantial freedom in how he makes his contribution. When he contemplates the freedom he enjoys in his job, he observes that, "There is nothing to quit!" He is essentially paid to work on projects that interest him. Ralph's work meshes his own intrinsic interests with those of his employer. Even though his current job lacks his ideal level of professional challenge, the total package—his compensation, the freedom he enjoys, and the content of his job—weighs in on the positive side of the equation.

Even though most of us claim the reason we work is to support our families and ourselves, I wonder. How many of us would continue to work, whether for pay or as a volunteer, even if we inherited a bundle from that eccentric aunt no one suspected was loaded? My guess is that most of us would still want to work—to apply our talents and gifts in ways that make a contribution. The primary value of financial freedom is that it opens the door to working for non-monetary rewards. While a few people may enjoy a life with no work, and others may enjoy occasional periods of no work, most of us have desires and needs for meaningful work quite apart from earning income to support ourselves. What type of work would you do if you didn't need to work for a living?

Trish also continues her part-time nursing work at a hospital. She enjoys both the substance of her job and the camaraderie she shares with her co-workers.

The Millers' lifestyle today reveals other interesting paradoxes. Even though they could easily afford it, they do not spend much money on furniture, cars or other material possessions. They just don't see the point. Never have. When asked why, Ralph explained:

It is an issue of mindfulness. If I see a trinket or flashy car, I might reflect, "What does this do for me?" Is this the best use of my money or could someone else use it for better purposes?

Financial freedom and relative wealth have not changed the people the Millers were 20 years ago. Money and material possessions were never the driving force in their lives. Take Ralph's wardrobe, for example. As he explains, "I always wear shorts and Hawaiian shirts if it's warm enough. Always have." Trish's car has traveled 110,000 miles and sports a broken door handle. The Millers plan to replace the car sometime soon, but they said that two years ago. As Ralph reflects,

Standing back and thinking about it, any car is 99.9% perfect com-
pared to walking [long distances].... To me, living simply is not an issue
of how much one owns; it's a question of do you own the possessions or
the other way around?

We do get everything we want, so one might say we live extravagantly.
But that often doesn't take much money because our material possessions
are few. We're not beholden to our possessions, but we do enjoy them,
and most importantly, could live without them, too.... Guess I'm lucky; I
never think about money at all. But we have simple tastes, so it's quite
Zen. All the money in the world and nothing to buy.

Many people react negatively to the notion of simplicity for
the well-to-do. After all, anybody can simplify his life with
plenty of money, right? But think back to our definition of
simplicity: it is a life-long process in which we turn loose of
the quest for more wealth, status, and power in favor of an
authentic life of inner peace and fulfillment. And what does
money have to do with all this? After our basic necessities are
met, very little.

While freedom from financial concerns has not fundamentally
changed the person Ralph is, another event in his life has. Seven
years ago, Ralph survived a nearly fatal motorcycle accident. The
impact of this event on him was dramatic:

Lying in a pool of blood on the highway with your femur sticking
through your jeans does give rise to reflection...as does staring at the
heart monitor in the intensive care unit with your pulse rate stuck at
185...winning the lottery is clearly not a big deal in this situation.

Two years on crutches and several major surgeries followed. Un-
questionably, Ralph's brush with mortality was a turning point in
his life. As is common with people who experience a life-threaten-

ing event, his awareness and appreciation of simple pleasures has intensified. As he explains,

I never did make a real conscious decision to simplify my life, but I did get into mindfulness meditation after the accident. The accident gave me the impetus to try to remove all the mental clutter from my life.

Removing the mental clutter from his life has allowed Ralph to integrate his work and play activities more harmoniously. Work absorbs less of his energy now as he makes room for other passions. One of his passions is music. He has played classical guitar for 17 years, and in the last few years he has studied piano. In addition to his weekly piano lessons he practices an hour each morning and each evening. He also makes time for his favorite recreational activities, including swimming a mile each day, sailing, and gardening.

Ralph's accident also led him to a deeper spiritual awakening—of what he describes as "living in the glory of God, realizing one's part of the whole, and acting accordingly." In addition to practicing mindful meditation, his extensive reading of philosophical and spiritually related books has influenced him. His capacities for mental processing and reflection serve him well in his quest to understand the meaning of his life.

Ralph's experience of mindfulness and spirituality is enhanced further by certain daily practices. He consciously works on practicing mindful breathing throughout the day. He does not listen to the radio when driving. Pagers, cell phones, and watches are not a part of his life, an interesting paradox for someone who grew up with a passion for electronics. Even the ringer on his phone is turned off.

In addition to being addicted to consumerism, Americans have become addicted to productivity and efficiency. We are trying to milk the most out of each minute of the day, talking on the phone while doing something else (like driving), reading the newspaper while eating breakfast, and doing two or three tasks at once in our work. We feel uncomfortable, ill at ease, when our minds are not fully occupied. Unfortunately, this practice leads to unconscious living which in turn leaves us feeling disconnected with ourselves and others. To live simply, we must live mindfully—we must pay attention to what we are doing and feeling throughout the day.

Another practice that is particularly relevant for Ralph is maintaining his focus, or as he puts it, "consciously deciding (in spite of my innate curiosity) not to read this-or-that about a topic that's not really useful to me." Focusing his curiosity is a challenge for Ralph:

I have a very curious mind, and if I have one challenge, it's saying NO to info-garbage, be it PBS shows on gerbil mating habits or being aware enough not to gaze at TV's in restaurants.

In his book, *Breathing Space: Living and Working at a Comfortable Pace in a Sped-Up Society*, author Jeff Davidson discusses the benefits of creating breathing space in your life. He points out that we are in the "over-information age." We are being bombarded with massive amounts of information and choices and have not yet learned how to selectively screen out some of this information. Many of us feel we need to keep up on all that is happening and then we wonder why we feel we don't have any breathing space. Davidson recommends that we choose a few areas of interest that have some meaning and impact in our lives and focus on those.

Ralph's passion for playing classical guitar and piano exemplify the values that describe the man he is today: "There is a deep spiritual element in music that seems missing in much of today's popular music. I'd say that—totally subjectively here of course—learning to appreciate and better interpret Bach is great training for becoming a Zen Roshi." Ralph's musical pursuits are a form of relaxation, meditation, and work. He is mindful of the enduring quality of his musical interests: "I like to invest my time in areas that pay dividends—ways that will allow me to develop and grow in my later years."

Ralph Miller is discovering what is truly satisfying in his life— living mindfully at a relaxed pace, engaging in activities that nourish his soul (music and reading) and that give him a sense of purpose (working and contributing to charities). It is a life-long process. Simplicity for the well-to-do is not an oxymoron.

Ralph has no desire to increase his net worth. Clearly, this is one man whose self-image is not attached to his balance sheet. The Millers do have a nice home—a home they built themselves, acting as their own general contractors. However, they value their home for its functional and aesthetic characteristics and not as a badge of success.

Ralph's view of wealth is inspired by Thoreau's statement: "Wealth is measured not by what one has, but by what one can afford to give away." Ralph derives considerable satisfaction from donating a substantial portion of his income to causes he believes in, such as Medecins Sans Frontieres (Doctors without Borders), and ChildReach. Ralph views his work as "a vehicle to empower nice things to happen."

Financial abundance did not lead Ralph and Trish to go on massive spending sprees or to change their lives in fundamental ways. However, until Ralph experienced his own mortality, laying on the pavement in a pool of his own blood, he was pretty much just going through the motions of his life as it unfolded. Once again, here is someone who came to voluntary simplicity through an awareness of the impermanence of our individual lives.

Lessons and Reflections

As we can see from the life stories of Marjan Wazeka, Scott Jones, and Ralph Miller, living with financial freedom can take many forms. And while it is true that financial independence does provide optimal freedom for structuring our lives, it is by no means required to live simply. It may be one of our life goals, or perhaps not. You can certainly live a very enriching and rewarding life without it.

Only 17 (eight percent) of the 211 people who participated in the simplicity study are financially free—meaning they have sufficient financial resources to cover their basic living expenses without having to work for compensation. Of that group of 17, eight are engaged in regular paid or volunteer work activities. Others are pursuing personal interests such as reading, photography, travel, writing, storytelling, community service, and financial investing. Several work their own self-sustaining farms.

The appeal of financial freedom is directly related to the level of fulfillment we enjoy in our work lives. If we enjoy our work, and especially if we are passionate about our work, and the income from our work is sufficient to meet our physical needs, financial freedom is less of an issue. Similarly, it is no surprise that the simplicity study participants who are passionate about their work tend to have fewer concerns about saving for retirement (see, for example, the profile of Dixie Lynn Darr in Chapter Eight, *Long Timers: People Who Have Always Lived Simply*). They see themselves continuing to work for pay during their retirement years. In an ideal world, we would work in ways that are satisfying in the present, while building for a future of financial freedom. Balance is the byword!

Chapter Eleven

Living Well on Very Little:
Amazing Stories of Courageous People

A s we have seen from the stories in this book, living simply is not about how little we can spend, but how well we can live. Simplicity is about balance—keeping our natural drives to always want more material things in check, which in turn gives us a shot at a life of true inner peace and fulfillment. For a small percentage of people who live simply, that balancing act results in an almost austere lifestyle. For these people, the material side of life recedes into the background; they embody the ultimate expression of living lightly on this earth. While few of us may choose to follow in their footsteps, we can gain perspective and inspiration from their stories.

A Life of Service—Matthew Hennessy

Matthew Hennessy's life is the antithesis of the American dream; in fact, his $3,500 annual income is far below the 1998 poverty threshold of $8,480 for a single individual (based on data from the U.S. Census Bureau). However, his story is not a *down-on-your-luck* tale of woe, but a testament to one person's ability to soar above his economic circumstances to create a life of purpose and joy.

Matthew grew up in a family that he describes as deeply troubled and dysfunctional. His parents divorced when he was a teenager, leaving Matthew a legacy of economic insecurity:

Raised to be a working class hero, I started working in my first public job at the age of thirteen as a clerk, stock boy, and custodian at a convenience store a couple of blocks from home. At one point, the stress of attempting to maintain the image of having attained the elusive American Dream—along with the accompanying envy, jealousy, greed, and bondage—became too much to bear. Under this burden, our post-industrial yet pre-modern family collapsed. The court declared me independent and forced me to choose, at the age of fifteen, which parent would be my guardian. I went with my mother, who signed me out of high school two years later so I could continue to work full-time.

In these circumstances, it is not surprising that Matthew turned inward: "I was drawn to a self-imposed isolation to which I have grown accustomed and fond, the solace and inspiration of solitude, the calm of silence, and the peace of just *being.*" Matthew views his troubling childhood and the subsequent events in his life in a positive light:

Drawn to the contemplative life at an early age in search of an escape or refuge from the inhumanities modern culture perpetrates upon its children, and unfortunately adults as well, I have been spared the herd mentality which bases personal identity upon the social norms of the day. Though contrary to most advice and feedback, I am becoming more and more convinced that I am currently treading the path which destiny, or fate—whichever the case may be (it matters little)—would have me travel. At the age of forty-two, I feel as never before that I am approaching that center of my existence that has eluded me for what seems like an eternity.

Solitude, silence, contemplation. These rejuvenating sources of strength and personal power are rare resources in our fast-paced, rush-to-success, American culture. We race from home to work and back again, only to distract ourselves with television. We fill our weekends with chores and shopping. When we do take a vacation, we bask in the slower pace, the luxury of time—time to reflect, to just *be*. And we cherish those sto-len moments, believing that we can only experience them on vacation. Don't believe it. You can create windows of solitude and silence in your life.

Consider the moment you turn off your light at night to drift off to sleep. Do you think of this moment as the end of your day? Think again. It's really the start of your day; it marks the beginning of the next 24-hour period. This event—the act of going to sleep—has more to do with the quality of your life than most any other moment in your day. As in many aspects of life, timing is everything.

Try this. Select a time to go to sleep that will allow you to get enough sleep *and* rise a half hour before you need to start your day's routine. This is your time of solitude. Use that time to write in a journal, take a walk, meditate or pray, or sit with your cup of tea or coffee and listen to the birds sing. Carve this time out for yourself; don't spend it doing chores or with fam-ily. (After all, they haven't had this time with you up until now; they'll never miss it.) Realize that all you have done is exchange this one half hour for 30 minutes the previous night—30 minutes most likely spent watching TV, working, or just vegetating.

Or try this. If you work in a traditional job, you probably have a lunch hour (whether you take it or not). Instead of going out to lunch with the gang, or running errands, consider tak-ing some solo lunches. Bring your lunch to work and walk to a nearby park, sit quietly and watch people. Or bring your walking shoes and go for a stroll, stopping at some point to eat your bag of goodies. Try to spend the time outside, weather permitting. Being alone in nature enhances our experience of solitude; it accelerates our journey to our inner selves. If you feel restless and bored, don't force yourself, just try it once a week, or once every two weeks, to start. Then as it becomes more familiar, add more solo lunches to your routine.

Undoubtedly, there are other windows of time in your day
during which you can snatch a solitude break. Be creative. It
will make the rest of your life so much sweeter.

Matthew's sense of inner peace and purpose evolved in large part
from a serendipitous event in his life. During his twenties, he felt
very unsure of himself: "I drifted from job to job attempting to discover my true identity and purpose." During this time he met Julian
and Dorothy Parker, a childless, older couple who became dear
friends, taking Matthew under their wings. Matthew worked for
Julian in the dispatcher's office of a trucking business and eventually came to rent a spare bedroom in the older couple's home. Later,
the Parkers moved back to the Colorado mountains of their youth,
and Julian returned to his job as a nationwide truck driver.

About eight years ago, Matthew visited the Parkers in Colorado.
During his visit, Dorothy suffered a stroke that immobilized the left
side of her body. Julian faced a crisis. If he quit his job to care for
Dorothy, they would lose the medical insurance they needed to pay
her medical expenses. When no other friends or family members
came forward to help, Matthew volunteered to be Dorothy's caretaker until Julian's retirement four years later. This experience became
a pivotal event in Matthew's life:

*Though fully aware that this arrangement was the first opportunity
in my life to break away from the conventional mainstream lifestyle, little
did I know just how deeply the experience would change me—to the in-
nermost core of my being. To put it plainly, on that fateful day, I came
face to face with my purpose in life—to help those less fortunate than
myself in whatever ways I can. I have not had a normal job since the day
I found Dorothy incapacitated on her bedroom floor.*

*The transformation of my life since I dropped out of the mainstream
has been monumental. My four-year hermitage in the Colorado mountains gave me the opportunity to read, study, research, meditate, and
contemplate the desires of my heart. It was a journey through the mysteries of life to determine who I really am, what I truly believe, how and*

why I came to be where I am, and where my destiny, and that of the
world, is leading. I'm not saying I have all the answers, but I do know
that when one gives up control of his life, one can only end up where one
belongs in this temporal realm. Life is a paradox.

Dorothy Parker's stroke was a classic turning point, not only
for Dorothy and her husband, but also for Matthew. As you
read the stories in this book, you will notice that many people
made big changes in their lives, in part as a response to some
external event—an illness or accident, death of a loved one,
losing a job, or a divorce. What these events all have in common is that they facilitate a time of contemplation and
reflection. During these traumatic experiences, we are often
left alone. We are essentially forced to think, to spend time on
our own reflecting on who we are and what we are doing in
this life.

After Julian retired and could care for Dorothy himself, Matthew
moved to Arizona to attend college. Now in his senior year, Matthew maintains a 4.0 grade point average. In addition to carrying a
full academic load, Matthew works 15 to 20 hours a week as a
freelance tutor, note taker, scribe, and narrator for disadvantaged
students at a local community college. He specializes in teaching college level mathematics to blind and visually impaired students—work
that Matthew views as "a very satisfying and rewarding livelihood."
Matthew's efforts to assist disadvantaged students complements his
ascetic and spiritual nature:

I'm pretty much a hermit—I've just always enjoyed solitude and si-
lence. At the same time, my destiny seems to be inextricably bound up in
the service of those among us who, through no fault of their own, are less
fortunate. That's how I wage my own little personal war against the
prevailing injustices of the world—one life at a time. It has been written
by sages of old that unless one has conquered solitude, one cannot live in

community; and until one has lived in community, one is incapable of living in solitude. I guess you could say that I have conquered solitude, but have yet to find that community to which I could belong naturally, except the community of all the disadvantaged people of the world for whom I lament and feebly try to advocate. They recognize me in the midst of the hordes of self-seekers. They discern my compassion and empathy from a great distance. They know me. They accept me. They appreciate me. I am one of them, one with them, and glad to be so.

Are people who live simply introverts, tending to live quiet lives alone, or do they reach out to others in various social and community endeavors? They are both, and often both on a daily basis. It is a paradox of sorts. Those who live simply tend to love their solitude, spending time alone in some sort of daily inner-directed activity such as prayer, meditation, journal writing, walking, and nature gazing. At the same time, they enjoy rewarding, joyous, and fulfilling relationships with others, although those relationships may be fewer in number than what might be typical in the mainstream culture. See Chapter Twelve, *Community: Are We Our Brothers' Keepers?* for additional discussion of this issue.

This paradox reminds me of the myth about artists, writers, and other creative types. Artists are often viewed as loners— people who work alone and prefer to spend their leisure time with just a few people. In reality, artists and writers can be real party animals, as evidenced by the lives of Ernest Hemingway, F. Scott Fitzgerald and others. Each of us is both a solitary and a social person. We need to nourish both aspects of ourselves.

The income Matthew earns is minuscule by North American standards, so he improvises. Because he had no income for the four years he cared for Dorothy, he is able to qualify for subsidized housing. He resides at a center for the homeless:

I live in a 12-foot by 15-foot cell with a desk (three boards and a drawer), a chair, a three-foot clothes rod in the corner, an 18 by 24 inch one-way window, perpetually closed, a smoke detector, and a crate-like contraption with a cot-sized mat on top for a bed.

I use the crate as shelving for books, papers, clothes, food, and other necessities. I sleep on the mat in another corner of the room on the floor. The desk is set up for recording books on tape, practicing algebra, and practicing and recording my ever-growing collection of songs—some original, lots of folk, bluegrass, blues, and soft-rock—anything that sounds good on a classical or acoustic guitar. This is why I call the place my studio.

And I've never been happier, except the three years prior to the Colorado experience when I lived in a used 15-foot travel trailer and paid only $55 a month for lot rent. I presently pay rent in the amount of 30 percent of my income, which varies from one college term to the next, depending on student needs.

There is no refrigeration in Matthew's room; to say that his diet is atypical would be an understatement:

My meals consist of cereal with dry milk, honey, and fresh bananas for breakfast, canned beanie weenies or tuna with cheese on wheat crackers for lunch, canned vegetables with fresh onions and packaged noodle soup (heated with an electrical appliance called a "stinger") for supper, and lots of peanuts, oatmeal cookies, and snack-sized candy bars in between.

Let's face it—Matthew's lifestyle is not for everyone. In fact, it would appeal to very few of us who live in North America. We have grown quite accustomed to larger living spaces with different aesthetics. Most of us prefer diets with greater amounts of fresh food. What's important here is how Matthew feels about the way he lives. Does he feel deprived? Is he waiting eagerly until he can afford a more comfortable lifestyle? Surprisingly, he is quite content with his lifestyle.

Matthew's diet suits him well. It leaves him the time to spend on activities that are important to him:

I have no desire to invest the time some Americans spend in the preparation, consumption, and subsequent clean-up ceremony after meals. As a matter of fact, if it were not for the mandatory nature of eating and sleeping, I could accomplish amazing things.

Time has become my number one enemy. That's why I abhor having to take the time to eat and sleep. There's just not enough hours in the day to do all the reading, writing, creative thinking, jamming (music), jogging, and socializing I would like to do.

Similarly, Matthew limits his material possessions to the bare minimum. Other than his books, guitars, cassette recorders and radio, all of which nourish his soul, Matthew needs little to care for his basic physical needs:

I own only one washer load of clothes (made possible by the Arizona climate and the informal nature of my work), one microwaveable bowl (with lid), one spoon, one butter knife, one seldom used fork (mainly for spearing dill pickles from a jar), one 20-ounce plastic cup (with lid and straw), and one insulated cup for mixing dry milk with water-fountain water (a conceded luxury) for cereal in the mornings.

Matthew's feet are his main source of transportation:

I commute one mile to the campus on foot with a twenty-pound pack of books on my back. I walk many miles per week, investing in one good pair of shoes each year. With one exception, I have not driven since October of 1993 and haven't owned a car since August 1989. I enjoy being chauffeured by mass transit when the need arises—more time for study or anti-sleep-deprivation naps. (The three S's for a successful college career: social-deprivation, sleep-deprivation, and self-sacrifice.)

Matthew does not feel poor or deprived; rather, his life embodies the essence of Duane Elgin's subtitle to his seminal book, *Voluntary Simplicity: Toward a Way of Life That is Outwardly Simple, Inwardly Rich.* Indeed, Matthew feels grateful for the riches in his life:

In my heart of hearts, I feel that everything we experience in life is a gift—every breath, each morsel of food, each point of refuge, each moment of time, and even death itself. More money could never change what I have come to believe about the purpose of life, but it could broaden the horizons of those whom I desire so desperately to help along the mysterious journey.

Matthew's lifestyle feels extreme to me—too austere for my tastes. But his story inspires me, not because I am motivated to emulate his lifestyle, but because his life is filled with great purpose and joy. If Matthew can be truly satisfied with the little he has, enjoying a high level of fulfillment in his life, what does that teach us? It is a lesson in perspective—my material wants seem less significant when I see how content Matthew is with what he has. When you think about it, all his basic physical needs are taken care of—food, shelter, clothing. And don't forget, for more than three-fifths of the world's population, his lifestyle would be seen as luxurious.

The enduring inspiration in Matthew's life is his spirituality. He once considered majoring in and teaching world religions, but then realized that,

I have found that the only spirituality I can offer the world is that which I have personally attained in my own life—that which is learned experientially and which cannot be transferred or imparted, but rather is

revealed through one's compassion for and service to other human be-ings.

I could spend the rest of my life in a cave, pondering the spiritual nature of man and chasing after those mountaintop periods of ecstatic union with life. But at the end of this parenthesis in eternity which we call time, I think the mark we have made in this life will be determined not by the so-called evil we have thought or done (karmic law), but by that small amount of good we were able to do in spite of the overwhelm-ing odds of negativity, greed, envy, contention, cynicism, and wrath which seems to be bound up in the human heart and the very atmosphere of the planet on which we dwell. I cannot change this world, but I can and have changed my attitude towards it. I strive to function within it—to be part of the seemingly impossible solution, rather than contributing to the seemingly inevitable self-destructiveness of the problem.

I guess you could say that I practice a spirituality of conscience, which consists of simply listening to the deeper callings of my inner thoughts and feelings and doing those things that are accordingly right for me. I am but a spiritual pilgrim, walking through this temporal realm alone in the multitudes—just like everybody else.

Once again, we see how spirituality and simplicity overlap. Matthew's spirituality informs his life, which is further sup-ported by his simple living. Like many people profiled in this book, it is difficult to determine where one begins and the other ends. For Matthew, spirituality and simplicity are inter-twined.

An Ambassador for Voluntary Simplicity-Q

Like Cher, Q prefers to use only one name, and it is Q. It all came about during a poker game 20 years ago, when Dave Q was one of five other Dave's sitting at the table, one of whom also shared Dave's given last name. Dave was pressed by the scorekeeper to come up with a distinguishing name or initial. He selected "Q" and it stuck. He rather liked the simplicity of his new name, although banks and other institutions don't necessarily share his views—their computers rebel against such simplicity.

Q is intent on living as simply as possible. His style of simplicity leaves little room for paid work. Now forty-five, Q has worked in paid positions less than a total of four years since high school. For three of those years he worked in computer programming, often in chunks of a few months at a time, followed by several years of no paid work. In addition, Q has worked the equivalent of perhaps a year playing poker (not as a dealer but as a gambler), often 10 to 20 hours a week, with one seven-month stint of 40 hours a week. He played at legal casinos and his poker earnings netted anywhere from $8.50 to $20 an hour.

Think outside the box. Who would ever dream of making money as a poker player? Other than Q, that is. For many of us, playing poker (legally or with a few friends) would be more a form of entertainment than employment. Some people have religious or other beliefs that would make any form of gambling unacceptable. Obviously, gambling would not be appropriate for a person likely to become addicted to it. These are not issues for Q. In the context of Q's life, his poker playing is just another illustration of how creative we can be in earning income. Do you have a passion or a special talent? For example, let's say you have always been a clown and you enjoy children. What about performing as a clown at children's birthday parties? Your start-up expenses would be few. A costume or two, maybe a drama course at the local community college to sharpen your performance skills, and *voila*—you can earn some real money (especially in high-income neighborhoods) doing something you love to do.

During the periods Q was not working for money, he describes his work as a "full-time social change activist." His involvement extended beyond the US borders, including participating in the Tienanman Square Demonstration in China, sleeping in a tent in the square the night before the June 4, 1989 massacre. Back home, Q focused on trying to get the news media to include more positive news. Over a five-year period, he campaigned for the major TV networks and *The Los Angeles Times* to include positive, solution-oriented stories in their news coverage.

So how does Q manage to live on the little income he has earned from his brief forays into the world of work? Creative living and conservation of resources have been the keys to his success. And passion. As you will see, Q is a man of many passions.

When Q first responded to the simplicity survey, he was living in the Los Angeles area, renting a room from a friend in Playa del Rey. He enjoyed this "paradise within the jungle," as he describes it, very much, especially the views of the ocean and the Ballona Wetlands where he could watch the egrets play. He did not own a car, preferring to bicycle everywhere, often 40 or more miles a day. For example, he bicycled to Orange County (an 80-mile round trip) twice a week to attend Mensa lunches. He tells me he never would have made those trips in a car—too far, too long, in his view. He figures that riding his bicycle serves many purposes:

It just makes sense. The bicycle is the fastest form of transportation. It takes no extra time to get from A to B. This is because each minute of exercise is a minute added to your lifespan, plus the positive side effect of increased quality of life. No transportation time, I travel on the exercise budget.

Now, there's an interesting twist on our cultural obsession with managing our time. If by living a certain way today (exercising or eating organic, fresh vegetables from my garden), I can live longer, or more importantly, live a more healthy life for

> the years I do have, then maybe it doesn't take longer to ride a bicycle than a car. If we view our transportation choices as opportunities for living more fully in the present, perhaps the time it takes to get from A to B is irrelevant, or at least less critical.

Bicycling long distances is impressive in itself, but it's even more remarkable for Q, who has multiple sclerosis (MS). Several years ago, Q needed a wheelchair to get around safely. He got motion sickness so badly from riding in a car to his social activist meetings that he could barely function mentally. His lowest point came in early 1995 when his symptoms left him bedridden. He spent most of that period researching medical abstracts on the Internet from his bed. He experimented with natural means to recover with considerable success: "Within a one-month period, I went from Wheelchair 101 to functioning just fine in everyday life, with the exception of hard exercise."

Q was excited about regaining his health. He came up with a five-point natural recovery program for MS—positive attitude, exercise, diet (low saturated fat, no gluten or dairy), sunlight, and supplements. His enthusiasm led him to help others who have MS, providing information through his web site. Later, Q bicycled throughout the Western US, taking his message on the road, talking to MS support groups and individuals about natural means of maintaining health with MS. He bicycled 7,500 miles from Los Angeles to Jasper (British Columbia, Canada) and back. The trip took six months.

> Q's life illustrates the principle that most of our so-called limitations (the way we complete the sentence "I can't do such and such because...") are self-imposed. His positive attitude—his can-do approach to life—carries him over the humps of MS and the challenges of living on very little money. And I suspect that Q has much more purpose and joy in his life than the vast majority of Americans who live the traditional life of long work hours, increasing debt, and little quality leisure.

Like Holli-Anne Passmore (see Chapter Eight, *Long Timers: People Who Have Always Lived Simply*), he does not let a physical challenge stop him from living a full and purposeful life.

Q's unstructured bicycling trip, camping wherever he stopped for the evening, rekindled his wanderlust. At the time of our interview, he was getting ready to move on to a new phase in his life. He was going through all his belongings—sorting, packing, and giving stuff away—to prepare for a more open-ended life on the road. He is committed to reducing his belongings to whatever he can fit into a backpack and two panniers that will drape over his bicycle—about 50 pounds total in weight. He still experiences some MS symptoms, but that doesn't stop him from bicycling an average of 45 miles a day. In fact, his primary motivation to bike long distances is to maintain his health.

Ok, I know what you are thinking. Reality check time. You are most likely saying to yourself that you would not, could not, nor do you have any desire to reduce your belongings to what you can fit on your bicycle and take to the road, with or without MS. Well, neither do I. (Although there are people who do just that, and others who are contemplating that option.) But the lesson we can learn from Q is that there are creative ways to live without working traditional jobs. We have a choice. We don't have to live in large, well-appointed homes; we don't have to buy and maintain two cars for each family; we don't have to spend a bundle on all the stuff that fills our homes. We can lighten our load and reduce the need for paid work. We can find ways to take some chunks of time off from work. Little sabbaticals. For example, ask for a leave of absence from your job for the summer. Rent out your home or apartment and take on a caretaking position in some beautiful spot. Or volunteer abroad. Yes, you will earn less money for those three months, but you will spend a lot less, too. If your rental income pays for your fixed housing expenses, you may even come out ahead.

Activism *per se* has less of a hold on Q's heart than it did in the past. He feels he can make his greatest contribution modeling a life of voluntary simplicity and talking to people he meets in his travels. In addition to helping people recover from MS, Q regularly attends the Unity Church, and plans to continue that practice on the road. He appreciates the benefits of the church services: "It gives me time to pause, time to slow down, reflect, appreciate and connect with people I don't know." He is passionate about spreading his message of what the world needs to heal:

It all boils down to two things: simplicity and connection. This is our common project for humanity. What we need is for people to learn to simplify their lives and connect with each other. We need to learn to do this from the ground up, not from the leadership of some spiritual teacher.

Working towards this goal is Q's mission, his purpose in life. He recently completed the Toastmaster's speaking program and is looking forward to speaking in churches, service clubs, and community groups. He has already lined up several speaking engagements. He is trying to live on donations but so far they barely cover a fourth of his monthly living expenses, which run about $500.

Some people would look at Q's life and call him irresponsible. He really doesn't know how he will support himself, and his savings will not last forever. I don't see him as irresponsible. I see him as a man of courage. His life is marked by his generosity. He has worked hard for the causes he believes in—social justice, relief for MS sufferers, and now voluntary simplicity—with little monetary support. In my view, he is not a parasite on society's back, but a hopeful ambassador for a better world. For 25 years, he has found ways to provide for his basic needs for food, shelter, and clothing. I have no doubt he will continue to do so.

Q appreciates the changing nature of his life, and does not rule out the possibility that he may settle down somewhere along the way. If he found a cohousing or other community committed to living simply, he just might decide to stay. In the meantime, living simply on the road is his life and his work:

To me, the most important goal in travel is not where I'm going or where I've gone, but the process—the memories created. We can't take material goods with us when we die; yet we live on through the memories we create for others.

Lessons and Reflections

Many stories of living creatively with little money, of thinking outside the box, were revealed in the simplicity study surveys. One family bought a piece of property in the rural Midwest ten years ago for $12,500. They moved into what they describe as their "rundown shack of a house in the worst condition" and worked on it themselves. They added seven rooms to the house (to make room for their growing family, which eventually included seven children), mostly with materials salvaged from demolishing buildings that other people wanted torn down. The family got the materials at no cost in exchange for their labor to demolish the buildings.

The mother of this family has always stayed at home with her children. She has developed a real knack for finding great deals. Here is one of my favorites:

The other day my sister, who works at [a fast food restaurant], called and said that they were getting rid of some chairs that day only. So, we drove 100 miles and got a matched set of ten wooden captain's chairs in perfect condition just for the gas to go get them.... My kids think it is Christmas every time I bring home any of my free finds.

Matthew Hennessy and Q have a lot in common. They share a strong sense of purpose—they live to help others. Material wants are very low on the totem pole of their desires. Perhaps there is a connection here. Maybe there is an inverse relationship between the level of satisfaction we feel from serving others and the satisfaction we gain from material pleasures. If we derive deep satisfaction from helping others, we seem to be less likely to look to material sources for fulfillment.

However, this is not something you can turn on and off like a faucet. You cannot will yourself to change your focus from material wants to serving others. It must come from within, from your heart, not your brain. And, unless you experience a transformational event in your life that propels you onto a different path, learning to derive fulfillment from serving others is likely to be a gradual process. Listen and observe. Observe yourself and others. When you find yourself helping someone with no expectation of a return, notice the feeling you have around that experience. Smile to yourself and just recognize the pleasure you feel. Start small. Help an elderly person put her groceries into the car. Surprise a friend with an unexpected gift. I have started to do something on my daily three-mile walks along the ocean that gives me a real lift. As I see tourists (often couples) taking pictures of each other with the ocean in the background, I'll stop and offer to take a photograph of both of them together. They seem to be so surprised and grateful for this small gesture. These random acts of kindness often bring more pleasure to the giver than the receiver.

Matthew and Q's lives illustrate the distinction between simplicity and poverty. If their lives were not filled with meaning and purpose, their material circumstances would leave them poor. Instead, they enjoy rich lives that are far more satisfying than those of many people who earn six figure incomes and enjoy the so-called good life of the American dream.

Chapter Twelve

Community:
Are We Our Brothers' Keepers?

In Chapter One, *Why Simplicity?* I discussed two overriding drives of human nature: to seek inner peace and to experience a sense of fulfillment in our lives. The people profiled in this chapter have accomplished both. I believe their deep connection with community is in no small part the reason for that achievement. While extensive community involvement is not the path for each one of us, nor is it a *sine qua non* for finding peace and fulfillment, the stories that follow are persuasive testaments to the potential for finding fulfillment through community.

Self-Sufficiency and Solidarity—Blake Wellington

Blake Wellington, forty-five, is a resourceful, self-reliant guy. Until 1994, he tried one entrepreneurial business after another—everything from selling merchandise at swap meets to promoting conventions. His last enterprise failed miserably, leading him to re-examine his stated goal of "going into business for myself and making a bunch of money." It was a time of confusion and uncertainty. He was living in Denver at the time and decided to return to Oklahoma City where he had grown up.

Blake's lack of entrepreneurial success led him to dig deep into his inner self—to try to bring some meaning into his life. In the process, his spiritual self emerged with a new vitality. He found solace and meaning in the Catholic Church and converted to Catholicism a few months after returning to Oklahoma City. About the same time, he started to work part-time as an organist for the church and later accepted a position as Director of Music.

We all remember the bombing of the federal building in Oklahoma City in April, 1995. This event was a real turning point for Blake. He shares his poignant memories of this life-altering event:

I was living about 25 blocks away and when it happened, I heard the explosion. I also played the organ for the funeral of one of the children who died in the day care center. This entire event changed my life. I had a mystical experience of sorts about two weeks after the bombing. It was the middle of the night. About 2:00 A.M., a clap of thunder woke me up. I couldn't go back to sleep, so I decided to get up and visit the bomb site. It was an eerie scene—many people standing around, occasional thunder and lightening, and huge spot lights on the massive building to guide the rescuers with their cranes. I leaned against a tree and prayed the Rosary. It was very moving for me. The experience was a type of heightened awareness, timelessness, and rapid communication that came on me suddenly while praying the Rosary. I'm still not sure of all the content, but it's still moving me forward today, close to three years later, even though I still don't know where it is heading.

After the bombing, Blake became intimately involved in the community's healing process. As a choir group leader in his church, he converted choir practice sessions into opportunities for the group to share their stories and grief with each other. Blake explained that, "It was the randomness of it all that drove people crazy—why some people died and others did not."

He also created a set of collages to be used for the Catholic Good Friday service of the *Stations of the Cross*. The collages included photographs of the bombing from newspaper and magazine articles, along with other symbols representing the loss of life, the pain, and the healing journey. The Good Friday service became an ecumenical event. It was held in the Oklahoma City University chapel and attended by students of all faiths and leaders of the local Methodist, Catholic, and Baptist churches.

I often marvel at the apparent arbitrary nature of life's events. The Oklahoma City bombing was a transformational experience for Blake. It did not alter the course of his life as much as it deepened the path he was already on. But Blake could have missed it—he might have still lived in Denver, or the perpetrators could have selected a different city. For every one of us, there are events that alter the course of our lives. Maybe they are not tragic events, but sometimes a move to a new city or a different job changes everything. Do you ever wonder what your life would look like today if those events did not happen? Of course, the question of whether our life events are happenstance or part of a divine plan has intrigued spiritual thinkers and teachers for centuries. Our beliefs on this point are probably less significant than how we respond to the life-altering events that form our journey.

Blake's religious faith deepened and eventually led him to St. Louis, Missouri, where he explored joining a religious order. That didn't work out. Instead, he accepted a full-time position as Director of Music, Liturgy, and Social Justice Ministry for a Catholic parish. Social justice is at the core of Blake's religious faith. He works for a mostly-white suburban parish and sees his role as "helping the parishioners marshal their resources and use them effectively in regard to social justice issues."

Blake's social justice ministry extends into his personal life. In fact, he negotiated a reduction of his work hours from 40 to 30 hours a week so he could spend more personal time working for social justice. For starters, he rents a large, older home in a multi-racial neighborhood of poor and working class people. It is important to Blake to live among the people he wants to help:

I live where I do because it's cheap and because I want to be in solidarity with the people who live here. I have a free clothes giveaway from my front porch at irregular intervals—kind of like a free garage sale.

*Clothes are collected from more prosperous neighborhoods and given away.
I try to be a good neighbor.*

Blake shares his home with five other people—a couple with one
child, and two other single guys. His housemates are all trying to get
back on their feet, and they contribute to utilities and the $350
monthly rent whenever they are able to. Blake buys the food and
prepares meals for the entire group, cooking primarily from scratch.
His stable income of less than $20,000 a year goes a long way to
providing the basic support for six people. Blake's informal cohousing
arrangement is consistent with the role that relationships play in his
life:

*I have made a conscious and informed decision to not form a primary
romantic/family relationship or to have children, but rather to remain
celibate. My relationship with my roommates is one of friendship. My life
is enriched by numerous friendships, many of 10 to 15 years duration,
and I keep in touch with a large number of people all over the world
through phone calls, letters, and e-mail.*

Blake feels a calling to serve in a religious vocation. His efforts
to join a religious order were not successful, so essentially he
created his own (including his choice to remain celibate). In
fact, he *lives* his vocation beyond what would be typical for a
Catholic priest—he shares his home with his "parishioners"
rather than living in a rectory with other members of the clergy.
His experience is a good illustration of the creative abilities
within all of us. If you are struggling to find the right job, the
right form or structure to fulfill your right livelihood, consider
creating your own form, your own structure.

Blake's social justice efforts extend into the community as well.
Community has always been important to him; it just gets stronger
as he grows older. In addition to organizing the clothing "give-aways"
from his front porch, he occasionally volunteers for local Catholic

relief organizations. He also promotes various national and international Catholic social justice efforts, such as Operation Rice Bowl, sponsored by Catholic Relief Services. While some of these activities are part of his job, he spends additional personal time on these projects.

And that's not all. Blake is working with a community organization that is attempting to create a program featuring "block bucks." With this program, the kids in the neighborhood could earn block bucks for picking up trash or working on other neighborhood projects. They could then spend their block bucks at local businesses.

Community currency is becoming increasingly popular in America and other parts of the world. For information on community currencies, see the Resource Guide (Web Sites section) at the end of this book. Blake's community has come up with a creative variation—combining the community objectives of exchanging resources, improving the physical condition of the neighborhood, and providing the children an opportunity to feel connected to the community and develop self-esteem. These are the types of programs that will restore to our communities the sense of interconnectedness and pride that were once more a part of our culture.

Blake seems to have an inexhaustible supply of new ideas to improve the quality of life in his community. He wrote a cookbook and almanac of useful information for poor people in Oklahoma City and may publish an updated version for his new community if he can raise the funds for the printing costs. He would then give the cookbooks away to people in need through St. Vincent de Paul and other relief organizations.

People who are called to serve others are blessed. Blake's commitment to help others is not a forced act or a sacrifice. It comes from within, emanating from his religious and spiritual beliefs. I believe that the greatest happiness to be found in this temporal realm is in the service of others, whether we do so because of religious beliefs or out of humanitarian concerns. But, again, it's not something we can will of ourselves—it must come from within. If we search diligently for what truly interests and excites us, we will discover what brings personal satisfaction while simultaneously serving others.

Even Blake's hobbies contribute to community. He makes rosaries from African trade beads and precious stones and gives them away. He could probably sell them but has no desire for more money to come into his life. Even though he could use additional funds for his social ministry activities, he doesn't want to obtain those funds by earning more money personally. He actually prefers to live on a low-income. It's simpler and he is one with the people he is serving. When he first left home as a young man, living in an inexpensive neighborhood was an economic necessity. Over the years, it has become an integral part of his ideology. He places a high value on self-sufficiency and an equitable distribution of resources.

Blake has always lived simply, but the Oklahoma City bombing changed him. It was a transformational experience. Before this event, his simple lifestyle was primarily a result of conditioning and economic necessity; now it is much more intentional. "I see my on-going efforts at simple living as being an integral part of my own social concern and solidarity," he says. It has also brought Blake an inner peace that was missing in his life:

Since becoming more intentional about this life, things have seemed more peaceful. I get angry a lot less, stress is low, and life has a higher level of contentment and calmness, a sense of purpose and fruitfulness. I like to laugh and be surprised by simple things. I enjoy the sight of a full moon low in the sky and the squirrels that play in my back yard. I am concerned about politics, justice, and peace, and how those three interact with love.

The Pied Piper of Cyberspace—Barry Kort

Barry Kort is single, fifty-three, and a self-described introvert. He obtained a Ph.D. at Stanford University (interdisciplinary degree, emphasizing systems theory), an excellent background for his 19 years of research and development at Bell Labs that followed. A career in science, engineering, and technology matched Barry's skills, temperament, and intellectual interests perfectly. He was married once briefly and has no children. Barry brings to mind one of those really bright people who feels more at home in a world of ideas than in a community of people. So, you may ask, what is he doing in the chapter on community? You will soon see.

Barry's story is a tale of living outside the box, of allowing the creativity within each of us to shape a unique and often improbable lifestyle. His story is also a powerful statement of the impact the Internet can have on our lives. Back in 1986, Barry's life took a major turn:

I lost my career job at AT&T Bell Labs [after the breakup of the Bell System] and have never been able to get back into the Ivory Tower since then. About eight years ago I gave up trying to earn a living in the commercial and funded sector and took a sabbatical that I'm still on.

After being laid off by Bell Labs, Barry accepted a research job in another corporation. When he was assigned to work on a military-related project, it did not sit well with his soul. As he explains, "I have always believed in nonviolence. I was a conscientious objector during the Vietnam conflict, and I now want to use technology only for life-affirming applications. Building weapons is not something I can contribute to." He quit that job after a few short years, describing his experience as "traumatic as hell."

During this period, Barry became close with Claire, a single woman who is dyslexic. Claire had two sons, ages three and five. The older boy was also dyslexic. Barry had never been around children and was surprised to discover that he got along very well with kids. He found that teaching children was emotionally very satisfying.

Barry also helped Claire with her college courses. Statistics was particularly challenging for Claire due to her dyslexia. One day she was struggling to comprehend the logic of a problem and when she suddenly caught on, she felt an overwhelming feeling of joy. This experience was a turning point for Barry. He became fascinated with the connection between our emotional and learning selves. It was a fascination that would lead to his life's work.

In 1990, Barry stumbled on an opportunity to take a position as a visiting scientist with an educational research organization. Even though this position would yield very little income, Barry figured this might be the perfect environment to test his theories about the relationship between emotions and learning. He put himself on a one-year sabbatical and founded MicroMuse, an unfunded, nonprofit, on-line educational community for children. Eight years later, he is still on that sabbatical.

By all accounts, MicroMuse is an outstanding success. MUSE stands for "Multi-User Simulation Environment." The award-winning program provides informal science education, including the use of computer animations and virtual communities. Participants adopt different personas or characters and enter imaginary worlds of science and adventure. About 1,000 children participate in the programs each year. Homeschoolers are a strong presence in this on-line community. On line, Barry is known as Moulton. He can be found collaborating with young people and adults who share his interest in puzzles, creative problem solving, invention, and science. The MUSE program is designed and maintained by volunteers, including many children. The children learn not only how to program, but also how to do other creative design work, mentoring of other students, and community building.

Barry's MicroMuse—what an extraordinary tour de force! Not only does MicroMuse make a significant contribution to on-line education, it provides Barry with work that incorporates his passions—science, technology, and teaching. It's tempting to envy Barry. So many of us struggle to find work that would let us soar like eagles. How did Barry pull this off? All he did was follow his passions, his interests. That meant quitting the corporate job that was not in alignment with his values and being open to an opportunity that excited him. He did not limit himself to conditioned notions of what a successful career should look like. He followed his heart.

No doubt you are wondering how Barry supports himself as he enters the ninth year of his sabbatical. First, he purchased a condo outright, using savings from his corporate positions. He lives frugally, on about $10,000 a year, primarily from his savings and the income from an occasional small research project. He drives a Honda Civic and cooks simple meals at home. He has no expensive habits or hobbies. For example, Barry has never purchased a computer in his life. With the help of his student volunteers, he salvages older computers, rebuilds them when needed, and gives many of them to schools. His three-bedroom condo looks less like a home than a computer laboratory—a maze of old computers and cables filling almost every inch.

Barry's contributions do not stop with MicroMuse. He has volunteered at the Children's Discovery Space at the Boston Museum of Science in his community every Saturday for years, even when he still had a corporate job. Related to his work with MicroMuse, he conducts E-mail Mentoring, one-on-one exchanges with students that are designed to stimulate the student's imaginative and creative learning processes. After close to ten years of research in this field, Barry concludes,

What works in education (regardless of the medium of communication) are intelligent, caring adults spending lots of quality time with children in a close, one-on-one setting. Technology all by itself isn't the answer. What matters is whether I and others like me bother to pay attention to individual students, to work with them over extended periods of time in cooperative and collaborative learning activities.

When I last spoke with Barry, he was ebullient about a new project. He is in the development phase of a new community outreach program at the University of Massachusetts Lowell. It is his intention to provide Internet computer support, including web site design and e-mail access, for the community, including ethnic groups, civic associations, literary groups, and other community groups. Using his skills to help those truly in need is much more satisfying for him than a corporate career: "I would rather help the 'underserved' than the 'undeserved.'"

Barry continues to follow his heart and discover new passions. He is exploring a second career as a peace activist and on-line journalist. Through a friend, Barry met social activist Phil Berrigan when Phil was in jail and has subsequently written many on-line articles relating to Phil Berrigan's encounters with our legal system. Barry studies and ponders the issues related to violence in our society. Based on the last ten years of Barry's life, I think we will be impressed to see what Barry accomplishes in the next ten.

> The recurring theme in Barry's life is his ability to open himself up to new opportunities. When he quit his last corporate job, he let go of the cultural trappings of success. His experience of success is tied to his level of personal satisfaction, which for him, is inextricably bound with helping those in need in ways that make good use of his skills, preferences, and interests. His life integrates selfless and self-satisfying action. Doing for others and pleasing himself are one and the same.

Home is Where the Heart Is—Jef and Lorraine Murray

Six years ago, Jef and Lorraine Murray's lifestyle was typical of so-called "yuppies." This early thirty-something couple had professional jobs, a single family home, and plans to build a second home on the Florida coast. This is a story of a couple whose lives have been completely transformed. Well, a few externals remain the same—they live in the same home in a community outside of Atlanta, Georgia, and they both work at the same jobs. But that's just a surface view. They simply are not the same people they were six years ago.

Six years ago, Jef and Lorraine felt trapped in their jobs. Jef's work as an engineer was intellectually satisfying, but it was still a grind and often stressful. Lorraine felt much the same way about her job as an editor at a local university. The thought of working for another 30 years until retirement was depressing for both of them.

The Murrays' personal lives during that period did not bring them much pleasure either. They had a few friends but for the most part they kept to themselves. Jef was an electronics junkie; buying the latest and greatest gave him immediate but fleeting highs. The Murrays channeled their discontent into a fantasy of a waterfront cottage in Florida. In 1990, they designed and built their waterfront cottage. It provided an escape from their jobs, and they looked forward to making it their permanent home one day. The debt on their two homes totaled $140,000.

In 1993, Jef and Lorraine read *Your Money or Your Life* by Joe Dominguez and Vicki Robin. This book changed their lives. I'm not talking about a shift in attitudes or priorities; in the Murrays' case, it was a total transformation. As Jef explains,

Without the book and the support of the New Road Map Foundation [the non-profit group founded by Joe Dominguez and Vicki Robin], none of the rest would have followed. I, for one, needed someone to point out the blinding light of the obvious—that all of the stuff I was buying was not bringing me fulfillment, and that I was trying to satisfy a fundamentally spiritual yearning through material consumption.

Fifteen percent of the simplicity study participants indicated that reading one or more books played a critical role in leading them to simplicity. The book *Your Money or Your Life* was mentioned by the participants far more than any other book. This book has inspired thousands of people to incorporate the principles of simplicity in their lives. You can read about the experiences of people who have followed the program out-

> lined in *Your Money or Your Life* in *Getting a Life: Real Lives Trans-formed by Your Money or Your Life* by Jacqueline Blix and David Heitmiller.

What followed were major changes in every aspect of the Murrays' lives. First, they worked through the nine steps to financial independence outlined in *Your Money or Your Life*. By going through these steps, they discovered they did not need to remain employed for another 20 to 30 years after all. They could reach financial independence much sooner. This single insight freed them from the emotional burden of feeling trapped in their jobs. Just knowing that they didn't have to stay in their jobs forever made all the difference in the world. The negative aspects of their jobs have diminished significantly to just one small part of their otherwise very rewarding lives.

As part of the program outlined in *Your Money or Your Life*, Jef and Lorraine figured out what was really valuable in their lives and let the rest go. They kept their home and two cars (but are working up to becoming a one-car family), and let go of expensive entertainment, such as frequent movies at theaters and dining in restaurants. Jef's cravings for the newest electronic gear also lost steam.

During this process, the Murrays started to question their dream of moving to their waterfront cottage some day. They discovered that this dream was not so idyllic after all. They loved it for about a year, but then started to feel burdened by the never-ending maintenance chores. While they cherished the natural beauty surrounding their cottage, they were not too keen on the 30-minute drive it took to get anywhere else—to the church, the library, health food stores, interesting people and activities. Within a few years, their dream bubble burst:

With our cottage, we rationalized the "more is better" impulse by saying we were going to live there some day. When we started really looking at living there, we realized that we were kidding ourselves—we weren't really ever going to do it. Once we saw that clearly, we knew we couldn't keep the house. It's interesting to note that we have categorically kept knowledge of the house a secret, except for close family. We never wanted to be known as the sort of people who would own two houses. This sort of sums up the truth that we were at heart ashamed of the fact that we had two houses, when so many others in this world don't even have one.

Jef and Lorraine had been living in the "if only" mode. *If only we could dump our jobs and move to a charming waterfront cottage in Florida, we would be happy.* They were fortunate that they could test that dream before they actually moved. Sometimes it's difficult to know when our desire for something, such as a waterfront cottage, is a manifestation of what would truly bring us joy, or whether it's a hoax—an escape from what is negative in our present lives. Here's a good rule to follow: Don't make a change if you are wallowing in what is not working in your current life. First, discover and enjoy what is positive in your life right now. An excellent book to help you in this process is *How To Want What You Have*, by Timothy Miller. Then, if you are still inspired to make a change, you might want to consider it.

When Jef first responded to the simplicity survey, their Florida home was on the market. When I checked back with him 18 months later, they had sold it and paid off the mortgage on their Atlanta home. They have reduced their living expenses to approximately $1,700 a month and plan to reach financial independence in two to three years. At that point, they will have a full second half of their lives ahead of them.

The impact of *Your Money or Your Life* on the Murrays' finances was just the beginning; the book's emphasis on examining your values led to other, more profound changes in their lives. Jef had been a spiritual seeker most of his life, primarily studying and experimenting with eastern religions and philosophies. He also loves ritual and for a time, was attracted to neo-pagan beliefs and practices. But after reading *Your Money or Your Life*, Jef dug deeper into his inner self and discovered that something very important was missing from his life— the experience of community.

Then a turning point arrived for Lorraine. Jef was in New York on a business trip when he stopped in at St. Patrick's Cathedral. He decided to light a candle for his deceased father and for Lorraine's parents, who were also deceased. When he came home and told Lorraine this, she experienced an intense "aha" moment. She felt a deep sadness that she had never lit a candle for her parents or even said a prayer for them, even though she was raised Catholic. That moment of insight initiated Lorraine's return to the Catholic Church. Jef was drawn to the ritual and community elements in the Catholic Church and soon converted to Catholicism.

The Murrays' personal lives now overflow with a rich assortment of community and church activities. Both Jef and Lorraine sing in their church choir and enjoy frequent potluck dinners with this group and other friends. Jef joined the speaker's bureau of The New Road Map Foundation. He speaks enthusiastically about the *Your Money or Your Life* program to various community groups, including churches, colleges, business groups, and the local food co-op. For several years now, he and Lorraine have hosted a voluntary simplicity study circle that meets twice a month.

The Murrays participate in other community and church events as the opportunities arise, such as a project of renovating a home for AIDS patients. Lorraine takes communion to people who are unable to get to church. These activities are very satisfying for the Murrays:

We used to be a pretty insular couple who watched a lot of TV and frequented restaurants and theaters. We've instead started trying to give rather than get. This latter emphasis, and the fulfillment it brings, cannot be overemphasized.

Lorraine is also exploring a new dimension of herself, experimenting with creative writing and poetry. Beekeeping, gardening, sewing and wine making are favorites in the Murray household. Quite simply, they have never enjoyed life so much as they do now. While their jobs can still be stressful at times, the Murrays' rich personal and community life makes those stresses far less significant than they were when work was the primary focus in their lives. Jef's personal growth is also evident:

I am a lot less self-conscious than I used to be. Before, I was very concerned about image. As an engineer, I felt I had to portray the image of a scientist, deserving and worthy of respect. Simplicity has allowed me to return to who I was as a child. For example, I studied drama in high school and am now reconnecting with that part of myself when I give talks and host dinners. After Mass on Sundays, I often play with a friend's four-year-old boy while the adults are visiting—we can get pretty silly together. This is something I would never have done before simplicity.

Many simplicity study participants expressed feelings similar to Jef's. They might describe themselves as introverts, but then also mention that their interactions with others have become much more expansive, often more meaningful and enjoyable. While the Murrays' level of community involvement is rare among the simplicity study participants (see *Lessons and Reflections*, below), people report a greater ease in relating to those they do interact with. It makes sense. Simplicity is a tool to live more authentically. When we are authentic in our relationships, there is less disparity between the people we think we are and the people the rest of the world thinks we are. Without that conflict, there is no reason to feel self-conscious.

The Murrays are so immersed in their community they can't imagine moving, ever. Their fantasies of waterfront cottages have been replaced by an appreciation for what they already have:

We can walk to nearly all shopping. There are plenty of job opportunities. A church, library, and music festivals are within walking distance. Cheap and high quality produce is available. Food co-ops and health food stores exist. Intelligent and interesting people with similar interests abound. There are opportunities to get involved in state and national activism with respect to the environment and voluntary simplicity. There is also lots of nature, plus one can garden without losing crops to hurricanes. We never realized how much we enjoy living in Atlanta until we

*speculated about leaving it. We learned that we want to visit the ocean,
but we don't need to own it.*

Jeff's insight that you don't need to own something (like an
oceanfront cottage) to realize its benefits (spending time at
the ocean) is the opposite of what our commercial culture
would have us believe. When we see a beautiful painting in a
gallery or a particularly fine piece of jewelry, our immediate
reaction is to want to possess it. It's not enough to gaze at it,
basking in its beauty. We want to grab it and bring it into our
control. Our appetite to possess can be voracious. In his book,
To Have or To Be?, Erich Fromm explores the negative aspects
of this desire to own, to take dominion over objects that bring
us sensual pleasure. Fromm suggests that the *having* aspects of
our lives can do serious damage to the experience of *being* in
our lives.

Jef believes that putting down roots and becoming involved in
community is a fundamental need we sometimes overlook: "People
want to surround themselves with others of similar values. We really want a tribe of folks around us. We have a deep need for a stable
community in our lives." Jef and Lorraine found that community
and in the process, they found themselves.

A Man of Passion—Andy Rudin

Andy Rudin is a man of passion. Now in his mid-fifties, his three
children are all out of college. He has been self-employed for close to
30 years, working as an energy management consultant for most of
that time. If he and his wife Joyce had pursued the traditional American dream, they would now be enjoying a large, luxurious home in
the suburbs, taking lavish vacations, and playing golf on the weekends. But their story is anything but traditional.

Six years ago, Andy and Joyce were living in an apartment that they had rented for ten years. The apartment complex was deteriorating and it was time to move on. Andy approached this task systematically. He and Joyce made a list of what they wanted, and it didn't look anything like a large home in the suburbs. On the list was a home with a dry basement and a southern-facing roof (to accommodate a solar system), located in an integrated neighborhood near mass transit. And that's just what they found—a twin home (also known as a "duplex" in some parts of the country) in an integrated neighborhood filled with children just outside of Philadelphia.

It is interesting that Andy and his family had lived in an apartment rental for ten years prior to their recent move. With both Andy and Joyce working, they undoubtedly could have afforded to purchase a home, but apparently saw no need to, at least not until the apartment building started to show substantial deterioration. It is not that renting an apartment is nobler than buying a home. However, some people buy a home to prove to the world (and themselves) that they are worthwhile and successful. Choosing to rent instead of buying a home, when you can afford to buy, often indicates that you are looking within for your values. Of course, the reverse is not necessarily true. Your choice to buy a home may well be based on your authentic needs and desires. Still, too many of us buy a home automatically, as a statement of self-worth, without considering whether such a move will truly serve our needs.

In their new neighborhood, Andy's passion for community shines. He and Joyce enjoy sitting on their front porch, talking to the kids playing in the streets, getting to know their names, sharing in their laughter. These relationships touch Andy's spirit and soul:

I like nothing better than running into these kids somewhere outside the neighborhood and have them call me by my name. Just the other day I met up with a six-year-old from the neighborhood, and the boy turned to his friend and said, "This is Andy; he's ok."

Andy also enjoys other neighborhood happenings, including informal rock and roll musical gatherings and the annual flea market, followed by a festive party. He has joined with two neighbors to play background band music for anyone in the neighborhood who wants to play a musical instrument for the good-sized neighborhood crowd. Facilitating a simplicity discussion group at the local library and helping to organize a community improvement association are some of his favorite activities.

Andy is passionate about the experience of community. He does not relate to those in the simplicity movement who focus primarily on living frugally for their own personal benefit. This is not where his heart is. He believes we should focus more on community rather than our individual needs and pleasures. In fact, he believes that we can best fulfill our needs and experience pleasure through community. Similarly, he feels that the emphasis on self-sufficiency within the voluntary simplicity movement is misplaced. He believes that the ideal is not for each family to become self-sufficient but to build a reliance on each other—exchanging services and helping each other out.

No question about it—since the middle of this century we have increasingly reduced the experience of community in America. Not only has there been a dramatic shift to living in the suburbs far away from our work, we tend to hole up in our individual homes as a means of recuperating from our stress-filled, workaholic, physically exhausting lifestyles. When you are living with an energy deficit, in survival mode, you have nothing left for community.

The move to a neighborhood with public transportation also allowed Andy to give up his car. He really detested driving, not so much because of the stress of traffic *per se*, but he grew weary of the road rage that has become all too common today. Joyce still drives her car to work but their favorite choice of transportation is their own feet. They often walk the three and one half miles to and from the local library.

Andy and Joyce have also maximized the benefits of home ownership by converting their lawn to a garden where they grow organic vegetables and flowers. They installed a grid-tied photovoltaic solar system that generates almost enough electric power for their needs, with a second solar system to heat water.

> Andy and Joyce are perfect examples of people whose choice to buy instead of rent makes sense. They are taking full advantage of the benefits of ownership. Few landlords would permit a tenant to install solar systems and rip up the lawn to grow a vegetable garden.

Through Andy's experience in energy management, he developed a passionate interest in technology and efficiency. He has studied the relationship between technology, efficiency, and the utilization of natural resources for 20 years. In the late 1970's, he became aware of studies that argued that the human factor, not the technology factor, is the primary cause of the rapid deterioration of the earth's resources.

Andy was disheartened when he observed a change in the environmental movement during the Reagan era—a change in emphasis from conservation to efficiency. "Let's make the cars (or any other technology) run more efficiently and save the environment," became the new rallying cry. Andy was saddened by this development. He believes that the emphasis on efficiency has encouraged us to neglect the one hope we have to save our earth—that is, humans acting in ways to conserve resources. As Andy explains, "It is not the miles per gallon, but the gallons, that will do us in." In fact, in Andy's view, improved efficiency does just the opposite of what one would think; it actually increases our utilization of technology and natural resources. For example, when a car runs more efficiently, and there- fore costs less to run, we tend to use it more. We may take a job that involves a long commute if we have an efficient, cost-effective auto- mobile. With the old gas guzzler, we might chose to live closer to our work or rely on public transportation. Andy sums it up well: "Every one of us is both a poet and a technician. Efficiency is what the technician hears; simplicity is what the poet hears."

What a refreshing, novel point of view! Who would ever chal- lenge the desirability of improved efficiency of our technology? Ideally, it would be terrific if we did both—decrease our utili- zation of resources and increase the efficiency of our technology. But human nature seems to be wired to defeat such an approach. Our response to greater capacity resulting from increased efficiency is to just want more. Data from the U.S. Energy Information Administration confirms his view: since 1950, America's energy production and consumption levels have steadily risen, notwithstanding any gains in effi- ciency. Andy has written some excellent articles on this topic. If you would like further information about his work in this area, you can contact Andy Rudin at 7217 Oak Avenue, Melrose Park, PA 19027.

Andy's views on the role that efficiency plays in environmental preservation contradict the views of his colleagues. But he contin- ues on, writing articles and studying this area in depth. And as he points out, it is not just the earth that is at stake:

We need to set and accept limits the way the Amish do, partly because less environmental harm would result, but more importantly because of what happens to our spirit. Merely increasing efficiency destroys the spirit and rationalizes increased use of stuff. We can efficiently waste a whole lot of energy and other inherited gifts.

Andy is a man of passion. He is passionate about the need for a renewed sense of community as a way to restore the essence of what it is to be a human on this planet. He is passionate about preserving the earth's diminishing resources. He is passionate about his life.

And he walks his talk, living the life he believes in.

Lessons and Reflections

The people profiled in this chapter are blessed. Not only have they discovered purpose and passion in their lives—an admirable accomplishment in itself—but those passions have led them to seek community, to be deeply connected with others. If we believe that love is a major purpose or lesson in our lives, then people whose paths lead them to be deeply connected with others are blessed. And from a purely selfish point of view, have you noticed that whenever you focus on caring for others, any physical aches and pains or twinges of depression or self-pity seem to evaporate?

The extent of community involvement enjoyed by the people profiled in this chapter is not the norm for the majority of the study participants. The chart in Figure 12-1 provides an overview of the level of community involvement reported by the study participants.

Figure 12-1: Community Involvement by Participants

45%	None, or very infrequent involvement
29%	Occasional involvement, nothing regular
26%	Frequent involvement in community activities

These findings surprised me. I would have guessed that people who live simply would be very active in their communities, but as

you can see, only 26 percent of the participants fall into this cat-
egory. It is interesting to note that many who are not actively involved
expressed some feelings of guilt about their lack of involvement.
Most look forward to a time when they could participate in more
community activities on a regular basis. Typical responses included:

*I am not involved in my community as much as I would like to be. I
live in a very large community that is culturally, economically, and socially diverse. My community is relatively safe, though many surrounding
communities are infested with crime, gangs, ignorance, and violence, which
deeply concerns me. I would love to work with people of all ages, cultures,
and religious affiliations. I suffer from major guilt in this area, because I
have not yet made the effort to participate in my community the way my
intuition tells me I could* (from a woman who lives in the greater Los
Angeles area).

*I am disappointed in myself with reference to my community involve-
ment. I don't do anything. I do think that community involvement is
important, however. I wonder if one reason I don't get involved is that I
don't plan to stay in Winnipeg. In addition, as a bus person and a woman,
I don't like to be out late at night doing things, especially when I have to
walk half a mile from the bus stop to my house. We have no children. I
think that children help to get a person out in the community* (from
Donna Dunn of Winnipeg, Manitoba, Canada).

The ambivalence felt by many participants on this issue is sometimes related to maintaining balance in their lives. Armando Quintero,
a father who recently left his career position to take care of his two
daughters and who has not yet become actively involved in his community (see his story in Chapter Seven, *On the Road to Simplicity: Travelers
in Transition*), talks about the priorities in his life:

Time with family
Time with kids
Care for parents
Care for extended family

How do you survive in this day and age on one income?
How do I fit into this community?

This last question is perhaps the most interesting. I am in a position usually reserved for philanthropists. But I do not have money to give. I have skills, knowledge, and time. So, am I selfish? Am I selfless?

Other participants affirm the sentiment of wanting to focus more on family life than the broader community:

This [community involvement] is one of our goals that we have yet to reach. We both long for a sense of community, but find that it is difficult to fit in after work, family, and us as a couple (from Lisa Tuckett of Everett, Washington*).*

We are not involved that much with community activities—mainly our neighbors and family. We look out for one another, but as far as being a part of civic organizations, we aren't. I want my family to enjoy our lives; outside interests usually mean running around a lot on evenings or weekends. I figure after a hard day at work and school the best thing we can do is enjoy each other and not have to push ourselves. I want my kids to remember being a kid—not a clock watcher (from Stephanie Waldron of Rockport, West Virginia*).*

A threshold question is how to define *community*. Does *community* require participation in structured organizations that serve a common good? What about our interactions with friends and family (now greatly expanded through the use of e-mail)? What about helping a neighbor plant a garden? Do these relationships constitute involvement with community? I believe they do. What I see in the lives of the simplicity study participants is substantial time and energy invested in sharing and caring for family, including extended family, neighbors, and friends. This is community. It may not be the organized community structures that we normally think of, but acts of working together, caring for each other, and sharing our life experiences is clearly evident in the lives of people who live simply.

What about participation in Internet discussion groups and chat rooms? Some online communities have provided enormous support and critical information to people who are suffering or struggling with life's challenges. Recall the story of "Q" (see Chapter Eleven, *Living Well on Very Little: Amazing Stories of Courageous People*) who set up a web site to help fellow sufferers of multiple sclerosis. Joe Judge's (see Chapter Seven, *On the Road to Simplicity: Travelers in Transition*) experience is not uncommon:

I suppose I've developed a community of friends on the web. I chat a lot on the net. Is this volunteer work? I'm in contact with people who are in real personal crisis—family problems, health problems—and need support.

Several themes are revealed in the surveys. First, people who live simply have already ventured off a traditional path, so they are not likely to be drawn to community activities *just because it is the thing to do*. Their participation needs to be personally meaningful to hold any appeal. Far too often, social and political organizations are characterized by a fair amount of conflict and in-fighting as people attempt to further their own agendas, often hidden, even from themselves. Some of the participants feel this way:

I'm not community oriented. When I had to work I was forced to be involved with communities that were irritating or destructive—competitive colleagues, socially dubious enterprises, and friendships based on consumption. "Let's go shopping... Let's meet for dinner at X... Let's go here or there...." (from Joe Judge whose story is told in Chapter Seven, *On the Road to Simplicity: Travelers in Transition)*

No involvement except through prayer. Political activity became too trying and was no different than the practice of law. Yes, my interest changed in that I am more aware of my role in the universe and look at life differently (from an attorney living and working in the south*).

I'm finding collective action to be increasingly frustrating and de-energizing. This is the case because we are still awaiting the emergence of *effective alternative forms of organizing and guiding collective human activities. In my part of the world, whenever people clump together to work toward a common purpose, they invariably default to traditional institutional and organizational forms (corporations, by-laws, boards of directors, committees, hierarchies, politics). Inherent in these very forms are all the shortcomings that are rendering life on earth unsustainable, and all their destructive gambits are played out over and over. We need fundamentally new organizational forms if we're going to achieve fundamentally positive social goals (*from Mark Burch of Brandon, Manitoba, Canada*).*

People who live simply tend to avoid activities and relationships that complicate their lives. If your life is already filled with activities that nourish you, you are not likely to seek additional commitments. On the other hand, if you feel a calling to participate in community groups and activities, you will find ways to open up opportunities for that to happen.

The form of community participation—whether it is structured community groups or friends and family—should be a matter of in-dividual preference. If we force ourselves—or correspondingly feel guilty if we don't—to participate when our hearts are not in it, we do little to contribute to the welfare of others. Consider the artist who does not participate in community activities because he does not enjoy interacting with people on group projects. Should the art-ist feel guilty for not becoming involved? I don't think so. Perhaps that same artist is making an even greater contribution to society by creating inspiring art that brings joy to others who in turn obtain satisfaction from volunteer work. The human community is like a circle—we give to others who give to others who give to others. Ideally we would all give of ourselves in ways that are true and authentic.

The true meaning of community is the experience of sharing and caring for others. Living simply opens up time and energy to do just that.

Chapter Thirteen

Environmental Champions:
A Passionate Love for the Earth

As we have learned from the stories in this book, many people explore simple living as a means to enhance their lives, to experience a greater depth of feeling and sense of peace. They seek to relieve the stress of enervating jobs, to reduce personal debt, and to spend more time with loved ones or on their passions.

However, other people are attracted to this way of life primarily for reasons that are not directly related to their personal needs and desires. These people come to simplicity out of their passionate concern and respect for the earth. They focus on living in ways that minimize the wasteful destruction of the planet's diminishing resources. They also seek to model earth-respectful behavior that will inspire others to live in harmony with the earth.

Even those who seek simplicity for primarily personal reasons often develop a greater respect and appreciation for nature and the planet in the process of simplifying their lives. Eight-two percent of the simplicity study participants take steps to preserve nature's resources.

People describe this affinity for the earth in terms that are reminiscent of religious or spiritual experiences. In fact, many see no distinction, no separation, between their deep respect and love of the earth—including all its life forms—and their spirituality.

Soulmates/Earthmates—Kevin Johnson and Donna Philippe

Six years ago, Kevin Johnson and Donna Philippe met at a *Course in Miracles* spiritual discussion group. They were both coming out of stressful marriages, each with three children. Two of Donna's children were grown, but all three of Kevin's daughters were still young. Kevin provides child support for his daughters who live with their mother.

Kevin and Donna became romantically involved and soon started to live together. Their partnership is enhanced by a strong spiritual bond, their passionate love for the earth, and a loving concern for people. Reflecting on these issues is second nature to them—they spend many hours conversing, thinking, writing, and reading about spiritual matters and ways to live with respect for our planet and its inhabitants. Their insight is reflected in Kevin's words:

Donna and I liken our life on earth as that of "fleas on a dog." Most of the fleas think the dog exists for them, but really the dog is more important because the fleas are dependent upon the dog, not the other way around. The fleas should be grateful to the dog, respectful of her, wishing her well so they can be happy and well too.

There is a definite spiritual quality to Kevin and Donna's love for the natural world. In fact, they view spirituality and living simply, with respect for the earth, as one and the same thing. As Donna explains,

Instead of the beliefs and philosophies of religions, I now see my spiritual life as something more practical that I can do, rather than just something in my head. My spiritual practice and my physical life have become one unified whole, where appreciation for the simple, natural world is everything. What I desire and what I need have become the same. I have found relative peace.

The union of their spirituality and physical lives is evident in the way Kevin and Donna spend their leisure time. Acquiring more things, watching TV, and dining in restaurants hold little appeal for them:

Generally, Donna and I spend evenings talking about what we're into—for example, natural diet and gardening, yoga-stretching and practical, biogenic simple living. We like to walk and write. Sometimes I play the guitar and write folk songs. Often we just hang around the house and don't say anything. We try to create space, quietness, and tranquillity because so much of society is caught up in expanding. We actively try to reduce, which is the total opposite of what's considered normal.... Happiness is a state of mind where living simply allows you to realize that you don't need anything, you don't want anything and yet, you care deeply for all things.

Kevin and Donna's journey to this state of inner peace and knowledge has taken some interesting twists and turns, not to mention a few *false starts*. Soon after they met, they began to explore ways to live more simply and mindfully. Ending a long-term marriage that Donna felt encouraged her to be dependent and weak, she was determined to find freedom and independence in her new life. She realized that reducing her living expenses and the clutter in her life would further that objective. Kevin came from a different place: "I was simply tired of paying the electric bill and supporting greedy corporations who don't care about the earth." He wanted to become as self-sufficient as possible.

As a first step, Kevin moved into Donna's home, a retrofitted 20-foot by 30-foot garage. Kevin appreciates the benefits of such a move: "It is a modest dwelling, very clean, spacious and quite comfortable. Making the change to live in a smaller house was the best thing we've ever done toward simplicity."

For the next phase of their journey, Kevin purchased a few acres in the Ozark mountains in Arkansas, and the two of them took off in a small, used travel trailer to fulfill their dreams. They planned to build a small cabin, purchase food in bulk, and grow vegetables on their land. Much to their dismay and surprise, this experience turned into what they describe as "a total disaster." Because they had no electrical power, they rigged up four extension cords to their neighbor's home, but this was not a practical permanent solution. They filled pickle barrels with water from a stream and carted the barrels back to their home site in their pickup truck. The cost to drill a well was $3,000, a sum of money they did not have. Kevin started to build a 30-foot by 30-foot home, but he had neither the building skills nor the physical conditioning to meet this challenge. Kevin was devastated; he couldn't believe that they had failed. In retrospect he recognizes that, "We took on more than we realized. We saw how unprepared we really were and eventually had to accept the fact that it was almost impossible for displaced urbanites to go back to the land." Their experience was a classic *false start*, but not without value.

As we have seen from the stories in this book, *false starts* are common events in the lives of those who live simply. Even though Kevin and Donna had read many books about living off the land, it was quite another thing to actually try it. There simply is no substitute for learning by doing. If we try something new, if we seek to stretch our skills and knowledge, we risk failure. Don't plan on it, don't expect it, but welcome failure when it happens. It means you are living life with gusto. Learn from it. If nothing else, it will teach you humility.

Kevin and Donna returned home to regroup and decide what to do next. Kevin returned to his job as a draftsman, even though it offered little satisfaction:

Drafting does not stir my heart. It is not something I take a lot of pride in because it still feels as if I am compromising my true convictions about a life of right livelihood, true simplicity, and being connected to the earth. Due to my particular life situation, however, I have opted to continue to work in this capacity in order to achieve my goals.

The income from Kevin's job provides child support and health benefits for his daughters, an important priority in his life. It also provides the resources for building a new life that we will hear about later in this story. And, finally, Kevin can see that his need for this level of income will not continue forever.

Kevin's current work as a draftsman is a classic illustration of the concept of *deferred gratification*, often a critical stepping stone in creating a life of simplicity. In Kevin's case, he continues this work to provide for his daughters and to build an economic base for the life of his dreams. But don't make the mistake of assuming that it is always, or even usually, the lack of money that requires us to defer our gratification in life. Even if you had all the money you needed to indulge every material wish, you may still not be able to create an ideal lifestyle right away. For example, to pursue your right livelihood, you not only have to discover what truly brings you joy—a task that can take years—but it will likely take time to develop a certain skill level to enjoy your chosen work fully. Money, by itself, is woefully inadequate to create a life of inner peace and fulfillment.

Donna had other challenges to face. For the better part of 20 years, she suffered from chronic fatigue syndrome, a debilitating condition that produced symptoms of severe fatigue, flu-type body aches, and headaches. She explored various treatments with no success: "I received no help whatsoever from the thousands of dollars I spent on traditional medical treatment as well as numerous alternative therapies, such as biofeedback, vitamins and mineral supplements, acupuncture, massage, macrobiotic and vegan diets, ozone therapy, and yoga." She was understandably miserable and desperate to heal.

Donna then stumbled on something that changed her life and as she explains, "returned me to a state of excellent, radiant health and vibrant energy." In their readings on simplicity, Kevin and Donna discovered the works of the late Edmond Bordeaux Szekely, a visionary scholar and writer. Mr. Szekely authored *The Essene Way—Biogenic Living*, which describes a way of life based on the principles of the Essene gospels—a quiet, meditative, simple and healthy life connected with the earth. A key element of biogenic living is a diet based primarily on raw foods—sprouts, seeds, fruits, and vegetables. Donna had nothing to lose in trying out this diet. What's more, it wouldn't cost her any money beyond what she would have spent anyway. Within six weeks of changing over to a raw food diet (85 percent raw, 15 percent cooked), Donna was completely well. Within a year, she was eating a 100 percent raw food diet, which she continued for a second year. Since then, she has gradually added more cooked foods to her diet without a return of any symptoms. One thing Donna has learned about the effort to live simply: "It is all about process, growth, and change, rather than finding a permanent solution for any aspect of our lives."

Good health and vibrant energy are key elements in living simply. These assets will facilitate your search for what's important in your life and your efforts to actualize that life. Many of the simplicity study participants reported changes in their health practices as they started to incorporate the principles of simplicity into their lives (see Chapter Fourteen, *The Pierce Simplicity Study: Reflections and Inspiration*). Typical changes include a diet with no or reduced amounts of meat, reduced or no alcohol, and an increase in gentle forms of exercise, such as walking and yoga. Often the participants did not set out to make these changes, but naturally gravitated to them.

With the return of Donna's health, she and Kevin could focus on how to reach their goals of living more in tune with their values. They were fascinated with Edmond Szekely's principles of biogenic living. In addition to nutrition and meditation, biogenic living is enhanced by a dwelling called a Biogenic Ecodesic Living Lighthouse ("BELL"). A key feature of this polygonal structure is its small size; it is designed to eliminate the superfluous space present in more traditional dwellings. The original design had 24 equal sides, providing the advantages of a circular shape, without the disadvantages of circular construction. Double sliding windows form the upper half of each wall. The purpose of this design is explained in the article *Biogenic Dwelling* by Edmond Bordeaux Szekely, published by the International Biogenic Society:

Smallness is one important factor; beauty, the true esthetic beauty of nature, is another. For too long the human dwelling has been an effort to cut ourselves off from nature; to over-protect ourselves from her and create as firm a barrier as possible against the intrusion of nature into our lives.

A home should not be a decorator's showpiece nor a status symbol; just as we are an extension of nature and an integral part of it, so should our dwelling be a natural and harmonious extension of ourselves.

A human dwelling should be an integral part of nature and shall have a maximum of fresh air and light. It should not be wasteful of energy.... It should also satisfy only our real needs and guarantee freedom from all kinds of superfluous expenses, such as large capital investments, mortgage payments, taxes, etc.

The BELL is a life-generating (with its indoor green garden) and human life-sustaining living unit utilizing light, heat, coolness, air, sun, water, and soil for optimal human health, not interfering ecologically with the environment and able to recycle everything...into biodegradable, clean, useful substances....

For information on The International Biogenic Society, see the Resource Guide (Organizations section) at the end of this book.

The aesthetic and functional characteristics of home dwellings are critically important to most people who live simply. The common desire to declutter the excess material baggage in our lives extends to our home structures—people who have more space than they need often feel burdened by that space, not only in terms of maintenance or expenses, but also psychologically. It is almost as if our occupation of that space uses up psychic energy that is then not available for other important aspects of our lives.

Kevin resonates with the concepts of biogenic living on the deepest level of his being. A section from his favorite passage of the above article explains why:

For tens of thousands of years our ancestors lived mostly in simple, peaceful dwellings, surrounded by nature. The DNA in our cells is programmed for a simple and peaceful environment, which we have dramatically, even hectically, transformed into a pandemonium of modern technological living.... Our senses, as well as our phylogenetic subconscious, programmed for a natural environment, revolt against the increasingly complex weight of our artificial, stressful way of life.... Consider the BELL as a refuge, a declaration of independence from the Grand Central Station.

Not surprisingly, as of this writing, Kevin and Donna are building a modified BELL structure on two and a half acres Kevin recently purchased. It will be 20 feet in diameter, 12 feet in height at its peak, with eight equal sides, a wood stove, a cistern for collecting rain water, and it will be wired for AC/DC power. Kevin has already completed construction of an ancillary 10-foot x 12-foot bathhouse and storage structure, complete with sleeping loft. The price of the land was $10,000, which Kevin plans to pay off in another year. He is paying for the materials as he builds; he expects the total cost for building materials to be $9,000.

Kevin still works full-time as a draftsman and spends his evenings and weekends building their home. His commute is an hour each way. However, this grueling schedule does not dampen his enthusiasm for this project—he realizes that it is not a *forever* proposition:

I am very excited about the freedom in this lifestyle. Once the land is paid off, I could choose to work only eight months out of the year. And, I would still be able to save money for retirement and pay child support and health benefits for my children.

As passionate as Kevin and Donna feel about sustainable living, they do not preach to others about it. Their dream is to model a way of life that is sustainable, without sacrificing comfort and beauty. Toward that end they founded the *EarthStar Primal Habitat Project* (www.geocities.com/~newliberty/earthstar), a working model for alternative, earth-friendly simple living.

There are certain characteristics that stand out among the simplicity study participants. For example, as passionate as these people feel about their chosen way of life, they tend to be nonjudgmental of those who do not live as they do. They may feel sad when they witness a lack of concern for the earth, or compassion when they see people who are unhappy, but they are not patronizing toward others. They share their views with those who express interest; yet they have no desire to impose their simplicity values on others. Rather, these people seem to derive their satisfaction from quietly living and modeling a life of simplicity. Their personalities are more akin to St. Francis of Assisi than Joan of Arc. Their attitudes and personalities are in stark contrast to high-profile environmental advocates who choose an aggressive approach to effecting change.

Kevin is seriously concerned about the world he is leaving for his children:

It seems reasonable to me that the world cannot go on at the present rate. With topsoil depletion escalating, drug abuse and health problems mounting, and the widening gap between the rich and the poor, more and more people are experiencing a certain level of unconscious hysteria and deep unhappiness about the American dream not working. What

I'd like to do is create a real alternative lifestyle—another way to live in this world—and hopefully make it a little better by my being here.

Donna and I care deeply about people and are willing servants to a great vision of health, fulfillment, and happiness for all beings. What we see in the world at present—such things as crime, starvation, poverty, frustration, and violence—breaks our hearts. We would love to cut a pathway in consciousness, pave an alternative road for young people to follow—not another belief system or philosophy—but instead, real and practical solutions, through simple living and natural diet, so there can be the experience of paradise and health on this planet.

In talking to Kevin and Donna, it is clear that this couple has embarked on a path of profound, spiritual growth. Kevin explains the evolution of their journey:

First, you begin to live more simply because you want to relieve stress and have more time. Then this other thing happens on a much deeper level. You begin to experience this indescribable sense of how precious the present moment is; it is such a delicious experience. Like feeling the cool rainwater coming out of the cistern and running down my hot and sweaty face and body after a hard day's work. Or when I wake up each morning in the sleeping loft and feel the glorious sun in my eyes.

Donna also believes that living simply has deepened her spirituality and facilitated a shift in consciousness:

My desire to simplify my life led me to the changeover in diet, which in turn has given me a heightened clarity of mind, resulting in significant changes in my thinking about spirituality.... Living more simply has allowed me to live more fully in the present moment, closer to nature, to experience the "eternal now" moment.

The following passage is a portion of Donna's essay entitled, *The Tao of Nobody*. It is a beautiful expression of her experience of the connection between simplicity and spirituality.

Reduce everything. Reduce thinking, reduce effort and struggle, reduce possessions, reduce debt, reduce shelter, reduce eating, reduce consuming, reduce participation in unnecessary concerns of daily life, reduce the seriousness and importance we give to this self...drop something every single day, become smaller, become nothing, no-self. Reduce the some-body as compassionately and non-violently as possible. Allow the some-body to grieve the impermanence and unsatisfactoriness of life, to let its heart break that it cannot find the peace, security and happiness it seeks, that it has no answers for anything in this life and the suffering that it sees all around itself. Allow it to grieve that it cannot escape.

But, at the same time, realize that we are also the divine No-body, the Self beyond the self, the True Identity, the Mind that is permanent, eternal and satisfying. This No-body self is vast and boundless; it is what we call "the peace of God." Finding the balance between these two states of being requires that we honor both as legitimate realities, walking the middle path. To polarize to either the some-body or the No-body exclusively is to experience a lack of peace. These two are manifestations of the same Being and cannot be separated. They are inextricably bound together as One.

Johnny Appleseed aka Tom Kirdas

For the last 27 years, Tom Kirdas, fifty-six, has lived on a 150-acre farm in Ohio. Most of the land is leased out to a farm operator who grows corn and other crops. Home for Tom is a 50-foot x 10-foot mobile home, although with the modifications he has made to it, it looks more like a cabin the woods. When I interviewed Tom on the telephone, he was sitting in a rocking chair on his front porch, watching several blue jays take turns at the bird feeder filled with sunflower seeds, a daily ritual for these jays. Across the country road that borders his property, Tom looks onto a 12-acre virgin forest, the perfect setting for his long, daily walks. He can see the Appalachian foothills in the distance.

Tom is a bit of a mystery and a paradox. He loves his solitude, craves personal freedom, and at the same time, he thrives on human contact:

I moved here to get open horizons, fresh air, and freedom to do my own simple thing in my own simple space. Although I live alone (except for birds and other wild animals), and am sometimes lonely for connections with people of similar values, I far prefer living here to living where there are people everywhere I turn. I love my free, simple, self-designed life.

For many years, Tom tried to balance his love of nature and his need for people involvement by living on the farm and working in town managing group homes for adults with retardation. With a commute of twenty miles, work hours that often extended into the evenings and weekends, extensive community involvement, and the inherent stress of dealing with the bureaucracy of group home institutions, Tom finally decided that a change was in order. He was really burned out. Two years ago, Tom bid good-bye to his stressful career: "I wanted to reconnect with what is real, natural, and vital. This is probably the main reason for simplifying my life—more birds and trees, fewer neurotic, materially obsessed, work-driven people."

Tom quit his job and accepted a 36-hour per week position as a night clerk at a motel fifteen miles from his home. Although the pay is not terrific and there are no employee benefits, he enjoys the people contact enormously. Meeting many people from other states and countries is stimulating. In the two years he has held this job, Tom has looked forward to going to work every evening.

If we were to take a random poll of the public's views on a middle-aged guy with two master's degrees working as a motel desk clerk, what do you think the results would be? The words *success*, *admiration*, and *envy* would not likely be included in the responses. As a society, we need to free ourselves of these limiting restrictions. Tom is an accomplished professional, but he chooses a different life—and a much more satisfying one for him—at this point. Developing expertise in a particular field doesn't mean we should continue on that path forever. Inevitably, at different points in our lives, we will desire various levels of intellectual stimulation, professional challenge, and work activity levels. When we choose a quieter work life of any form, we are not less accomplished, or less of anything. If we make these choices to enhance the quality of our lives, we are living more authentically, rather than letting society dictate what should make us happy and fulfilled.

Tom's job also leaves his days free to soak up the natural beauty that surrounds him. He has no trouble finding things to do with his free time:

I try to meditate a couple of hours every day. I read voraciously. I take care of my yard and garden in the summer. I write poems, letters, and keep a journal. I listen to and make music. I go for long walks and gather litter along nearby country roads regularly. Mostly, I watch the birds at their five feeders and think gratefully about being alive.

Tom's enchantment with nature is inspired by the spiritual nourishment it provides and also by his long lasting commitment to care for the earth. These values were instilled in him by his mother, who considered it her duty to pick up litter and who taught her children to do the same. Tom has been a self-described "litter fanatic" for decades, long before he moved to the farm that he and his siblings inherited from their grandfather: "Honoring the little world where I live, keeping these roads clear of litter, recycling, and living gently on the earth are very important to me." He spends several hours each week gathering litter on nearby country roads. At first he did this on foot, but eventually he switched to using his bicycle to cover more ground. He also maintains a web site to educate people about litter. He believes we can learn a lot about our society by looking at the litter we throw on the roads:

Litter is a barometer of the American lifestyle—we are a throw-away culture. We buy stuff, get bored with it, then throw it out. If we continue this foolish wastefulness, we will force ourselves as a society to live an ascetic life sometime in the near future. Material simplification will become mandatory as our resources near depletion.

According to Tom, litter surveys indicate that approximately 80 percent of the litter in all areas of the country is alcohol-related—primarily beer cans and bottles. He feels strongly about the abuse of nature through littering: "I can imagine myself dropping out of society completely someday, becoming a cross between Diogenes and Johnny Appleseed, walking across this county on its back roads just picking up litter." When you look at Tom's past, this is not inconceivable. In 1977, struggling with depression over a divorce, he decided to take a long walk—a very long walk. He walked from St. Louis, Missouri, to the Oregon coast, all in 89 days. Naturally, he gathered litter all along the way.

As one individual, Tom's actions to eradicate litter are not likely to make a substantial impact on a practical level. However, his example and educational efforts may cause others to think twice about disposing of litter carelessly, and about wasting material products generally. And as Margaret Mead says, "Never doubt that a small group of thoughtful, committed citizens can change the world. Indeed, it's the only thing that ever has." Tom's passion for the earth might inspire others to seek out and embrace their own passions. Even if the people in Tom's life do not see the litter problem as intensely as he, they can't help but admire his fervent commitment to his cause. Perhaps the lesson of Tom's life is less about litter and more about living with passion.

The driving force in Tom's life is his spirituality, which for him is inextricably connected with living simply in nature and caring for the earth. Although he has studied world religions and even obtained a Master of Divinity degree, he unabashedly calls himself a Pantheist, believing that nature is the ultimate context for his spiritual connection. His meditation practices have guided him throughout his adult years:

It was because of my meditation in the early 1970's that I decided to come to our family's farm in Ohio in 1971. I got in touch with the Thoreau, Wordsworth, and Diogenes in myself, and it became a matter of integrity to honor them. In the past 28 years I have alternated between the solitary simple life and a so-called "life" of almost overwhelming community responsibilities. (Simple is better!) Anyway, through the years, when my mind seemed to flap in the wind like a faded, worn out flag, I would somehow eventually remember to return to meditation. Quieting the mind helped bring sanity to the rest and was always available, if I would just release myself to be in that solace. So now that I have made simple living (rather than work-work-work) the central focus of my life, meditation is the hub out of which all the activities of my life emanate. I fancy myself to be a sort of Buddho-Pantheist eco-monk whose spiritual order and monastic community is Nature Herself. My "sitting" has evolved into a rough form of Zazen (though I'm sure a Zen master would slap me soundly for my sloppiness!—I often open my eyes to watch the birds at their feeders, even look through binoculars as I meditate, or I'll watch the trees sway in the wind). To be perfectly honest, I need meditation right now for a deeper authentication of my life-choice—so that I don't feel guilty about it, or anxious, or all alone.

Again, we see a cross-over between spirituality, simplicity, and concern for the earth. For Tom, like Donna Philippe and Kevin Johnson, these three aspects are experientially one and the same. Tom cannot separate his spirituality from his life of simple living, or his concern for the earth. See *Lessons and Reflections* below and Chapter Fourteen, *The Pierce Simplicity Study: Reflections and Inspiration*, for further discussion of this process.

Tom's journey of simplicity has not been free of doubts and fears. Sometimes he panics about money, especially when large unexpected expenses surface—the furnace blows up or the car needs major repair work. Once for a five-month period, he took a part-time job in a group home to supplement the meager income from his motel clerk job. Eventually he realized he didn't really need the income from a second job; it was just his conditioned fear rising up, demanding to be heard:

I harbor a strong Taoist notion that letting things be is the best cure for security anxiety. I truly do trust the benevolence of the universe. Nature is my foremost guru, and I try to be receptive to her cycles. My personal experience is that I have always had (and thus believe I will always have) everything I really need.

However, Tom's life is not perfect. He misses being a part of an on-going community. While he does meet interesting people in his motel job, those relationships are fleeting. One thing that means a great deal to him is the men's group he has attended twice monthly for the last five years: "We are six mutually caring and very diverse guys, a tremendous support group." He often spends Sundays with a close woman friend. But still, ideally, he would like more involvement with people. He ponders the possibility of volunteering as a teacher's aide at a small school six miles from his farm. It's a matter of balancing his desire for freedom with his need to be of service to others, not an easy task for someone who tends to overcommit himself. Living mindfully and simply is like operating the tiller on a sailboat. Arriving at a desired destination may require innumerable subtle changes of direction. Trying to remain flexible, Tom walks a determined but sometimes meandering path.

Living on the Edge—Dawn Griffin

Dawn Griffin grew up in a middle class family with parents who had no particular love of the earth or affinity for simplicity. And yet, inexplicably, Dawn matured into a young woman whose driving force in her life is a passionate love for the planet and all its creatures. She appears to have been born with deep feelings for nature, as though biologically wired to feel a strong attachment to the earth. Even as a small child, Dawn would sit for long periods staring at a flower or other natural beauty.

Today at age forty-two, Dawn's love for the earth has not abated. "As a young adult," she says, "I dreamed of saving the world." She reflects on her emotional intensity during those years, recalling her self-righteous, angry, and arrogant attitudes. When she was thirty-five, she went back to college to obtain a degree in environmental policy and planning, desiring to balance that emotional intensity with knowledge. As she matured, Dawn developed more compassion and tolerance. Now she focuses on the more realistic goal of making a contribution to the betterment of the planet.

During the last 15 years, Dawn has struggled to find work that is both personally meaningful and economically sufficient to support her. She describes her true vocations as that of "writer, poet, dreamer, and seeker of truth." She has found an impressive array of opportunities to fulfill her experience of *right livelihood*, including: "Working for a socially responsible investment firm, helping to create a framework for a nonprofit organization to search for health and human potential breakthroughs, working as the office manager for an environmental education organization, owning and operating my own food delivery business (using a bicycle), working as an assistant editor on a scientific reference book on California's endangered species, writing and producing a video on creating positive alternatives for the future, conducting market research on grid-tied rooftop photovoltaic solar systems, and working as a director of communications for a nonprofit organization dealing with managing growth issues."

Unfortunately, many of Dawn's most fulfilling work projects have netted little or no financial compensation. Still, she doesn't give up. She continually strives to find work that is personally meaningful rather than resign herself to a mainstream job that would produce more income but leave her soul feeling dry. As she sees it, "If we are going to be on this planet, we should be engaged fully." For Dawn, this does not mean working all week in a job that has no meaning, waiting for the weekend to live one's life. Ideally, her work would meet at least three criteria: (1) it should reflect the person she is, a communicator, (2) it should fulfill her purpose in life, contributing to the betterment of the world, and (3) the time commitment would involve approximately 20 hours a week. Dawn considers a 20-hour work week "a much more manageable schedule for people wanting a deeper sense of community and time for personal creativity and renewal."

Have you ever thought about how many hours would fill your ideal work week? This is largely an individual matter, determined in part by your energy level and interests. For example, I want to spend time each day to exercise, meditate, and prepare nutritious meals. By the time I add in a few errands and the usual tasks of daily living, like bathing and doing the dishes, I might work four to five hours each week day and another five or six hours over the weekend on my writing projects. My work week adds up to about 30 hours. And that's with a low-maintenance condo and no children to care for. I rarely do anything "productive" in the evenings, preferring to spend time visiting with my husband, reading, and sharing occasional dinners with friends.

If Dawn's pursuit of her right livelihood requires that she struggle to provide for her basic material necessities, then so be it. She acknowledges, "It is true that I live on the edge, but I always manage to get by." For example, at the time Dawn responded to the survey, she was living in a large studio apartment over a barn, which she shares with her boyfriend. The only heat is from a wood-burning stove, and there is no indoor toilet. However, it is in a beautiful location in the mountains outside of Boulder, Colorado, allowing Dawn to enjoy her favorite outdoor activities—walking, hiking, biking, river running, and camping. She confesses that, "I need little other than a connection to the natural world to make me happy." She doesn't own a car—she travels by bike, walking, bus, and rides with friends—

and has very little furniture or other stuff, allowing her to live lightly. She also recognizes that her choice not to have children has enabled her to live an unpredictable lifestyle with marginal financial security. She is truly a free spirit, living on the edge, being true to the values that are most important to her.

Dawn's sense of inner peace, with a lifestyle that is definitely low on the material accumulation scale, is enhanced by her spirituality. In addition to both sitting and walking meditation, she engages in what she calls "attention to kindness" as a spiritual practice—that is, "reflecting on each action to decide whether it is the most conscious thing to do." She also spends time in prayer, emphasizing gratitude rather than wanting. Yoga, for the "centering and clarifying state of mind it brings," and writing poetry round out her spiritual practice.

Dawn's strong interest in community is a reflection of her love for the earth and its inhabitants. She sees a real connection between the need for community and preserving the earth. She believes that people's core unhappiness leads to the destruction of the environment. She takes this lesson to heart:

One of the ways I feel I can contribute to a better world is to be a more consciously loving being because I believe that when people feel loved, a lot of their needs for other things naturally fall away. If people are at peace in themselves they don't want to harm others, including the environment.

Dawn is excited about the potential of building healthy communities. She lived in a community setting for five years, and while the experience was far from ideal, she feels that this way of life can be transformational, benefiting individuals and society alike:

A return to a deeper and more meaningful sense of community would address many of the issues we face today, such as pollution and stress from excessive commuting, violence and gang problems with today's youth, financial stresses with trying to keep up with the Joneses, relationship strains due to lack of renewal time and quality time together, and isolation of the elderly.

Dawn dreams of living in a cohousing or intentional community at some point in the future. Again, the economic necessities in life present obstacles. In this instance, she does not have the resources to make the initial financial investment that is required in many cohousing communities. Still, she does not give up her dreams.

The appeal of a full community life for those who live simply is mixed. As discussed in Chapter Twelve, *Community: Are We Our Brothers' Keepers?* many simplicity study participants say that they would like to become more involved in community but haven't done so yet. Dawn sees the value of community in terms of preserving the environment and alleviating social ills. Others who are active in their communities feel that their actions are an expression of their spiritual beliefs and religious faith. Once again, we see the blending of spirituality, simplicity and love for the earth. See *Lessons and Reflections* below and Chapter Fourteen, *The Pierce Simplicity Study: Reflections and Inspiration*, for further thoughts on this topic.

Dawn has lived simply all her adult life. Her motivation is two-fold. Her deep love of the earth is the paramount force in her life. Her desire to express herself as a communicator is also a high priority. She has paid a price to live her life in tune with her values, and that price is a materially comfortable life. For Dawn, she wouldn't have it any other way. It is not that she aspires to be an altruistic person who foregoes her own material needs and wants; rather, she derives the most personal satisfaction from living in harmony with the earth and contributing to the well-being of others.

Still, Dawn experiences the life she is called to live as an intense struggle: "The benefits are enormous in line with the commitment to live consciously, but it will take you to the mat time and again in the process." Dawn's level of commitment to her values is inspiring. Her experiences should reassure and encourage others who walk a similar path; you are not alone.

Lessons and Reflections

Is caring for the earth an essential aspect of simple living? Is it possible to embrace the principles of simplicity without a deep concern for preserving the earth's resources? How many people are motivated to live simply primarily because of environmental concerns?

These and related questions have been actively debated and discussed in simplicity discussion groups. For the vast majority of the simplicity study participants, living in ways that respect the earth is a vital element of simple living. The chart in Figure 13-1 provides an overview of the level of interest and concern for the earth among the study participants:

Figure 13-1: Participants' Interest in Earth Concerns

45%	Strong interest in the earth and its resources (belief that concern for the earth is an essential element of simple living)
37%	Moderate interest in the earth (typically including recycling, reusing products and avoiding the purchase of new products)
18%	Little or no interest in the earth and its resources

Caring for the earth illustrates the principle that *simple living* is not the same thing as *easy living*. Sometimes, it is not simpler to live simply. For example, if you live in a community that does not provide curbside recycling, it is more time consuming to take your recyclable trash to a center than to simply toss it into the garbage. Simplicity is often a paradox. Buying frozen pizzas and burritos could be viewed as a way to simplify food preparation, perhaps giving you more time for higher quality leisure. However, frozen foods, with their increased energy requirements and packaging, are more harmful to the environment. Living simply is a balancing act. We balance our personal needs and desires with those of the environment and other people. The key is to live consciously. Do not make choices out of a sense of deprivation; those decisions will backfire on you. But do be mindful of the choices you make. When the opportunity arises to honor the earth and other life forms without feeling deprived, you will find yourself naturally gravitating to those actions.

Many participants who feel that honoring the earth is an essential element of simple living did not approach simplicity with this belief. Often they were motivated by other reasons: stress from too much work, too much debt, or a general feeling of dissatisfaction in life. Later they came to feel that earth issues were vital in their lives. Whether we are motivated to live simply by a love for the earth or such concerns are a by-product of our lifestyle, caring for the earth is an essential element of simplicity for most people.

Indeed, as we have seen in many stories in this book, the experiences of simplicity, spirituality and love for the earth become intertwined, making it difficult to determine where one ends and the others start. This process can take many forms.

Here is a typical scenario: I may start to simplify my life because of stress or lack of fulfillment with my work. I reduce my work hours or change jobs and reduce my living expenses accordingly. Now that I am not so stressed out, I start to reflect more during my day; perhaps I start writing in a journal.

I begin to get a glimpse of another level of my existence, something that goes beyond my five senses. As I live with this deepening experience for a while, my heart opens up more and I start noticing that I become more empathetic with those who are in pain or are deprived of the basic necessities of life. I start to feel that we are all connected—all peoples, the plants, the animals—in a way that is beyond my rational comprehension. My slower, more contemplative lifestyle leads to more mindfulness and I start noticing the natural beauty all around me. My senses are sharpened. I delight in every day moments of doing simple things—feeling the warm water run through my hair in the shower, relishing the crisp autumn air on a morning's walk, tasting the delicious sweetness in a bite of fresh pineapple.

The barriers between me and the rest of the world begin to dissolve. I feel closer to people and to everything else in my life. Plants and animals delight me as they never have before. I feel more fully awake. Time stands still.

The experiences of simplicity, spirituality, and love for the earth are inextricably related. One leads to another, which leads to the next. As Anne Fong Ma, a study participant from San Francisco, California, related,

I am not very involved with my community or societal/global issues, although I recently attended a seminar of likeminded people, "St. Francis, Simple Living and You." It was very interesting to see so many environmentalists at this church-sponsored event. I guess in a lot of ways simplicity, spirituality and environmentalism go hand in hand in hand. I do feel in myself a greater sense of urgency regarding the need to respect the earth and each other as fellow human beings.

Likewise, Karen Skowron, a study participant from Victoria, British Columbia, Canada, feels that developing a concern for the environment is a natural outgrowth of living simply:

Concern for the environment is a given when one simplifies because when we return to basics we really do have/make time to "smell the roses." We come to an understanding of all this entails—in short, we realize those "roses" must be preserved. I am moving toward the purchase of more and more organic items (have always gardened organically), my interest in heritage plants is expanding (I experiment with them), recycling is automatic, and reusing is part of the tapestry of my day (at present I am turning old clothes into a nine patch Amish quilt pattern). Most importantly, I have found over the last decade when I have truly focused on simplifying that this journey of self (for that, really, is what simplifying is) results in a deeper and deeper appreciation of this body, this world, and of course I want to take the very best care of them both!

I see these three experiences—simplicity, spirituality, and concern for the earth—as overlapping circles in the journey of life. It doesn't matter at what point we enter the cycle. They all lead to one another. Eventually, they become one.

Chapter Fourteen

The Pierce Simplicity Study:
Reflections and Inspiration

As I mentioned in the Preface, my journey to simplicity acceler-ated in 1995. I immersed myself in the subject, reading over 60 books and numerous articles relating to voluntary simplicity. But the books did not answer my questions. I found myself wanting to hear directly from those who had actually tried it. I wanted to know what prompted and guided them on their journeys. What challenges did they face? Did their peers accept them? Did they feel deprived of material comforts? What benefits do they see from simplicity?

I kept digging. I participated in on-line discussion groups related to voluntary simplicity. I started asking friends and acquaintances questions about their lives. It was my curiosity, my desire to really understand simplicity in our modern world, that led me to start my research project, *The Pierce Simplicity Study*. I set up a web site for the project (http://www.mbay.net/~pierce). I included a survey form (see the Appendix for the survey text) on the web site, inviting all who had experimented with simplifying their lives to respond. The web site also included simplicity-related book reviews, information on newsletters and magazines, and links to related sites.

I received 211 survey responses from people in 40 states and eight other countries. The vast majority of the responses came in through the web site. Some responded to the survey after hearing about the study in various magazine and newspaper articles. No effort was made to select a representative sample of the population or to solicit certain age groups, income levels, educational levels, occupational profiles, or racial and ethnic groups.

Of course, the fact that the simplicity study was publicized primarily through the Internet influenced the types of people who responded. For example, most of the respondents have access to a computer and the Internet. Some people responded by accessing the Internet at their local libraries. A few sent in handwritten and typed responses after requesting a copy of the survey through regular mail.

Most of the questions on the survey were designed to elicit open-ended responses on all aspects of living simply in today's world. Since responding to the survey required a certain comfort level with writing, people who do not have basic writing skills, or who do not like to write, are not well represented in this study.

In addition to gathering and analyzing the data from the survey responses and from subsequent correspondence with the participants, I conducted in-depth interviews, either in person or by telephone, with 40 of the participants.

My intention with this research was not to produce data that could be extrapolated to the population at large, or even to the segment of the population who have adopted lifestyles of simplicity. Rather, it was an exploratory survey. I wanted to hear the real life stories of those who had experimented with simplifying their lives. And I wanted to share with you, the reader of this book, the joys and heartaches of those who have walked the simpler path. I believe we can learn volumes from each other's experiences. Learning by watching others is often more pleasant and effective than trying to absorb abstract concepts on a purely intellectual level. As Susan Libby, a study participant, said, "Telling our stories gives others hope. The simplification movement is not a cultural whim—it's the beginning of a cultural transformation and healing."

It should be noted that the stories and summary data included in this book relate to what was happening in the lives of the study participants at the time they responded to the survey (1996-1998). In some instances, people have made significant changes in their lives since that time.

Who are the Simplicity Study Participants?

The 211 people who participated in *The Pierce Simplicity Study* represent a wide range of ages, income levels, occupations, educational backgrounds, and geographic locations. The chart in Figure 14-1 sets forth the basic demographic information on the participants:

Figure 14-1: Summary Demographics on Participants

Gender:	70%	Female
	30%	Male
Age:	14%	Twenties
	37%	Thirties
	32%	Forties
	14%	Fifties
	3%	Sixties
Marital Status:	64%	Married or in a long term relationship
	36%	Single
Children:	61%	No children living at home
	39%	One or more children at home
Household Income:	8%	Less than $10,000
	19%	$10,000 – $25,000
	39%	$26,000 – $50,000
	16%	$51,000 – $75,000
	7%	$76,000 – $100,000
	11%	Over $100,000

Continued...

Educational	8%	High School Graduate
Level:	19%	Some College
	19%	Undergraduate Degree
	54%	Postgraduate Work

Geographic	17%	Rural area
Location:	15%	Small town (under 20,000 pop.)
	22%	Suburban or bedroom community (less than 100,000 pop.)
	18%	Medium sized urban area (100,000 to 500,000 pop.)
	28%	Large city (over 500,000 pop.)

Over 95 percent of the survey respondents described themselves as Caucasian (ethnic/racial identification was an optional question on the survey). A surprisingly high number of participants (73 percent) have at least a college degree; 54 percent have undertaken postgraduate work. I suspect that the format of the survey—requiring the respondent to write out detailed answers to open-ended questions about the important issues in life—naturally appealed to people who are thinkers and writers, resulting in an unusually large percentage of highly educated participants.

The income distribution of the participants is not consistent with the higher income levels often associated with people who have college and postgraduate degrees. Two-thirds of the participants (66 percent) live in families with household incomes of $50,000 or less. Clearly, many of the participants have chosen to earn less income than what their skills and backgrounds might enable them to earn.

Another interesting demographic factor relates to the participants' ages. Over half (51 percent) of the participants are younger than forty years old. Again, this may or may not be representative of the simplicity population at large. Since the survey was distributed primarily through the Internet, it would obviously come to the attention of people for whom computers are an integral part of their lives. It is well known that younger people tend to have a greater skill and comfort level with computers than older people. Still, the participation of people under the age of forty does argue against the notion that voluntary simplicity is primarily a movement of middle-aged, former professionals who have downscaled their lives.

Note also that only 32 percent of the participants live in rural areas or small towns. Voluntary simplicity is not primarily a back-to-the-land movement. It is also practiced in large cities, medium sized urban areas, and suburbs—indeed, wherever people live.

The results of the simplicity study that relate to subjects covered in previous chapters are discussed in the respective chapters. Other themes were revealed in the survey data and are discussed below.

Leisure Time

When we talk about reducing our work hours, of finding balance in our lives, what exactly are we looking for? What do we want to do with this time that is freed up when we say "no" to exhausting jobs with long hours and stressful commutes? How do people who live simply spend their time?

At the top of their time wish list is more time and energy to enjoy family and close friends, a subject discussed in more detail below. Another major focus in the lives of the participants is their spiritual and religious lives (also discussed below). It is interesting to note that the preferred leisure activities of the participants tend to be informal, unstructured, and oftentimes solitary activities. For example, reading, gardening, and walking are popular forms of leisure for the participants. Playing musical instruments and making things by hand, such as carpentry work or embroidery, were also frequently mentioned. Mark Burch, a study participant from Brandon, Manitoba in Canada, describes the various activities other than work that fill his life:

I'm very interested in continuing to develop my practice of T'ai-chi, meditation, reading and writing, and building/nurturing relationships with my family and friends. I also volunteer time to community activities, mostly through teaching T'ai-chi and through various roles I play in my church. In summer, my partner and I enjoy spending time outdoors, walking, hiking, meditative sitting outdoors, occasional day trips into the bush.

As you can gather, these activities are very inexpensive, but allow for almost infinite variations and scope for development. There is always something new to read, something new to learn in the practice of martial arts and meditation, some new path to walk, some new way to practice love and nurturing. It's a very rich life, but not costly. I feel wonderful about it. Liberated, focused, grateful and free.

Watching Television

There is a question on the survey (see the Appendix for the survey text) that asks the participants about the *stuff* in their lives. The original version of the survey form did not ask about television specifically. However, in responding to this question about the *stuff* in their lives, many participants volunteered information about their feelings and practices of watching television. Because of the volume of unsolicited data on this topic, I revised the survey form to ask the participants how many hours of TV they watched each week. I then went back to those participants who had not answered that question originally to get their response on this point. I was able to get responses from 190 of the 211 participants. The chart in Figure 14-2 provides an overview of their TV watching habits:

Figure 14-2: TV-Watching Habits of Participants

27%	Watched no TV
26%	Watched TV less than five hours a week
24%	Watched TV between six and ten hours a week
23%	Watched TV over ten hours a week

Some of the participants view watching TV as having a substantial negative impact on their mental and spiritual health. As one participant said,

Not to beat a dead horse, but I think getting rid of the TV had a tremendous effect on us here. We occasionally see a program at my in-laws' house, and we are amazed at the garbage that is broadcast. Once we stopped filling our minds with ridiculous plots, less than admirable characters, and other mindless drivel, our mental capacity (and spiritual health) improved exponentially.

The number of TV-watching hours by the study participants is far less than the national average. Why is this so? I believe that in some cases, we watch TV compulsively, as a salve to take away the stress and emotional pain of our so-called normal lives. When we force ourselves to work in competitive, stressful work environments that deplete us physically and emotionally, we come home seeking comfort, much as a toddler reaches for her security blanket. As adults, our security blanket is the television. We want to be spoon fed entertainment; we want to be distracted in ways that require little mental effort. In contrast, when we simplify and create lives of inner peace and fulfillment, we seemingly remove the need for that special salve, for our television blanket. At that point, we can watch television for positive reasons, selecting shows that enrich us, or not at all. The overall result is often fewer hours of watching television.

Television is like other forms of technology. We can use it to enhance our lives or we can abuse it. Some people avoid television altogether because they feel they have little control over the impact it has on them. That is the case for Beth Heins, whose story is told in Chapter Nine, *Starting Out Simply: Generation X Takes a U-Turn*:

I have never owned my own TV and when I moved out here [from the East Coast], I thought I'd experiment with not having one at all. I love it! That's partly because I'm incapable of ignoring the TV if it's on. There's

no such thing as background television for me; I'm riveted, no matter what's on. So I avoid it as much as I can.

For people who feel riveted to TV when it is on, living without television can be a liberating experience. Others are able to watch TV shows selectively and do not feel in danger of being sucked into activities that do not serve them well. A common preference among the study participants is to use the television to watch rented videos.

Personally, watching television has never appealed to me, even though I grew up as the daughter of a man who enjoyed a long and successful career in TV management. (My husband thinks my aversion to TV stems from teenage rebellion that just won't die.) I believe my lack of interest in TV stems in part from a desire to control the amount and type of information and stimulation that flows into my brain. In our society, we are constantly bombarded with information and entertainment. It can be overwhelming! Surfing the Internet can be equally overwhelming, although the surfer has a bit more choice in what he or she takes in, assuming it does not become addictive.

An essential element of a simple life is time spent in quiet reflection on a regular basis. Watching many hours of television, just as working many hours, can take us away from those quiet, peaceful moments of our lives.

Health

Eating nutritious foods is a priority for the study participants. A surprising 32 percent of them eat a vegetarian or vegan diet. Some make this choice for health reasons. Others cite environmental and animal cruelty issues as the primary motivating factor. Another 51 percent eat some (moderate or little) meat but still focus on fresh produce and unprocessed foods. Only 17 percent of the participants eat what might be viewed as a typical American diet, high in animal products and processed foods.

Exercising purposefully for the sake of maintaining health is rare among the study participants. While walking is a popular activity, it is done primarily for the purpose of transportation, the physical pleasure of moving the body, or the pure enjoyment of being in nature. Many participants feel that exercise is a natural part of their lives. Generally, they do not create workout routines or allocate special times to exercise. A few are passionate about specific outdoor activities such as hiking, running, and canoeing.

Some of the participants mentioned that they take a proactive role in maintaining good health practices in part because they do not carry health insurance. While health insurance was not a question on the survey, a few participants volunteered strong opinions about why they did not carry this insurance coverage. Cost was a major factor for most but not all of those who go without health insurance. A few indicated that their low opinion of the health care system in the United States influenced their decision. Others take a modified approach, purchasing a policy that covers catastrophic illness only and paying for their routine medical care themselves. Some families set up a specific savings plan to cover their out-of-pocket medical expenses.

Relationships

The survey responses are filled with testimonials of enhanced relationships with family and friends. Precious, priceless moments of giving and sharing. Marjan Wazeka (whose story appears in Chapter Ten, *Having Enough: Living Simply with Financial Freedom*) appreciates the deepening of her relationships with family and close friends that has evolved from simplifying her life:

All of the serious relationships with family and close friends have become stronger and deeper. I speculate that this is because my attention to the meaning of life, which precipitated my voluntary simplicity, logically brought me to devote more life energy to relationships. By dumping those activities that seemed of low value, I've had both more time and a heightened sense of the value of maintaining strong connections with other people.

Armando Quintero (whose story is included in Chapter Seven, *On the Road to Simplicity: Travelers in Transition*) shares a heartfelt family experience:

Recently, one of my cousins called and asked if I would photograph my Aunt and Uncle's 50th wedding anniversary party. If I had still been working my full-time job, it would have been nearly impossible for me to do this. As it turned out, not only did I photograph the celebration, I took portraits of all my relatives who attended the celebration. I was able to create a one-day family album of my large extended family—several hundred pictures that to me (and my relatives) are priceless. Simplifying has not meant that we are living "less." In fact we feel richer. I feel like I can put my arms around the experiences and time that are of great importance to us.

However, some relationships do not fare so well during the transition to simplicity. It is not uncommon for some friendships to fall away; the ones that remain tend to be stronger. This was true for Kathleen Tierney, a study participant:

I am no longer close with women who work full-time, have huge new homes, wear the latest fashions, drive several new vehicles, have their kids in daycare, and complain they have no time or money. I seek out women who enjoy raising their families, gardening, browsing at rummage sales, sewing and crafting, baking from scratch, etc. I have always liked older women because they are not so materialistic as many of my contemporaries and they have values closer to mine.

Grace Brinton, another participant, talks about how challenging it can be to form friendships with those who are still caught up in consumption and speed:

If we have had one disappointment (for lack of a better word) with our decision to simplify, it has been that we still find it hard to develop good relationships with people. We may have simplified, but others are still so busy and overcommitted. We know that we value time with people more than accumulating more stuff, but they are still super busy buying for their children. We have found that people we know talk about simplifying, but when it comes down to making the hard choices and actually letting go of things and activities, they don't seem to be able to do it. So we have a lot more time, but still find it hard to get together with people because they are so busy every night. It is unbelievable.

In some cases, one person in a marriage will be interested in simplifying when the other is not. This understandably leads to strain and conflict. However, like any other marital conflict, often the strain can be ameliorated by patience and understanding on both sides. Meredith Harmon, a study participant, describes her evolving relationship with her husband on this subject:

I drive a 12-year-old car, wear mostly garage-sale clothes, and generally try to avoid excessive consumerism. My husband loves cars and other big-ticket items. This led to serious conflict in the past, but we've now learned to peacefully co-exist; he has scaled down his wants quite a bit, and I've become less judgmental of his habits. I've realized that even though he's more materialistic than I am, he's still far less preoccupied with things than most Americans.

My husband and I continue to learn from each other, although I think he's probably changed more than I have. Things are about to get even more interesting, because we're expecting our first child in October. I'm pretty much a tofu girl, and my hubby is still a McDonald's boy.... I really have no idea what that kid is going to end up eating!

When we bear in mind that simplicity is not about deprivation, trying to force one partner in a relationship to live more simply makes no sense. It is contrary to the spirit and purpose of simplicity. A better approach is for the partner who has a greater interest in simplicity to propose small changes gradually over a period of time. Often the reluctant partner will find those changes more rewarding than he or she expected.

And in the process of simplifying, often a couple will take a new look—in some cases the first, real look—at the values they each have. Christine Pokorny, a study participant from Chicago, talks about how simplicity helped her and her husband clarify their individual and shared values:

My husband is very supportive of my simplicity efforts. After I got involved with it (largely to reduce my own stress), he found simplicity to be very valuable to him, too, to reduce his stress and help clarify his own values. I think it has strengthened our marriage, because it helped us look very closely at what exactly our independent values were, and what values we wanted to share together in our marriage. Now we're both on the same path together. Most folks take values for granted, and rarely look at how they affect their marriage until there is a big crisis.

Many participants feel somewhat isolated in their journey to simplicity. They long for the support of kindred souls. The degree of support and/or criticism for their simplicity lifestyle varies from very supportive to hostile. The chart in Figure 14-3 details the level of support from family, friends, acquaintances, and colleagues, as reported by the participants:

Figure 14-3: Level of Support Reported by the Participants

40%	Mixed reactions, some supportive, others don't understand
34%	People are generally supportive
26%	People are generally disapproving, often thinking the participant is nuts!

As noted above, the most common reaction from friends and family is mixed. Often others see some value to living simply, but cannot imagine making those choices themselves. As one study participant explained,

My friends generally enjoy the simplicity of our home and informality of our entertainment style, but most of them still see the adoption of simplicity as a sacrificial process rather than a pathway to something much more positive in a qualitative sense. Almost everyone remains essentially hypnotized by the more-is-better mantra of consumerism. They find the paradox of "less-is-more" intellectually fascinating but not really a strategy for organizing their daily affairs.

If you choose a lifestyle outside the mainstream, you will likely encounter resistance. Many of the study participants have sought support for their lifestyle choices through simplicity circles and discussion groups. A summary of simplicity circle programs is provided in the Resource Guide at the end of this book.

Spirituality and Religion

Spirituality, as with simplicity, is not easily defined. For some people, spirituality is tied to an organized religion with participation in religious services and related church activities. Others prefer a more solitary path, focusing on spiritual practices such as meditation, spiritual reading, journal writing, and yoga. Still others combine some aspects of both traditional religions and nontraditional spiritual practices, such as meditation circle groups or the silent prayer meetings of the Quaker tradition. And then there are those who say that they have no interest in anything spiritual or religious, but who resonate with the concepts of personal fulfillment, introspection, emotional development, and inner growth. In my view, the differences between these various experiences are primarily semantic.

Among those who feel that spirituality and religion are personally meaningful, there appears to be common threads in their beliefs. One is a sense of a higher being—either God, or a god or gods, or a higher life force—outside of ourselves, beyond our rational comprehension. Another underlying belief that permeates most spiritual traditions is that we are somehow connected to each other in a manner that, again, is beyond the realm of our five senses. It is this feeling of connection that propels us to look outside ourselves and develop true compassion and love for others.

So, what does all this have to do with simple living? What exactly is the connection between spirituality and simplicity? These questions were an integral part of the research undertaken in *The Pierce Simplicity Study*. The survey included the following questions relating to spirituality:

Describe your participation in religious and/or spiritual practices and experiences. Do you engage in any activities such as prayer, church services, meditation, yoga, journal writing, or spiritually related reading? Do these practices/experiences represent changes resulting from your efforts to simplify? If so, please describe.

Approximately 70 percent of the survey participants indicated that their religious or spiritual practices and experiences are a high priority in their lives. In fact, the vast majority reported that living simply had enhanced their spirituality if, for no other reason, by giving them more time to participate in spiritual and religious practices. A few reported that their actual spiritual practices had lessened. They explained that their prior yearning for spirituality seemed to be connected with an emptiness or stress they felt in their lives. With simplicity, they feel less of a need to engage in spiritual or religious practices.

Many study participants believe there is a strong relationship between spirituality and simplicity. Indeed, some feel that it is impossible to separate the two experiences. It is not always clear which comes first, but simplicity appears to reinforce spirituality and vice versa. Here are some representative statements from the participants:

◆ *Living this way has brought me closer to realizing that each moment is a spiritual, divine moment. I can't separate it out from anything else I do* (from Jenna Duran, whose story is told in Chapter Five, *Urban or Rural Simplicity: Choosing a Nurturing Milieu*).

♦ *I think that my previously simple lifestyle was good preparation for active spiritual practice, and may have had something to do with putting me in a receptive frame of mind* (from Blake Wellington, whose story is told in Chapter Twelve, *Community: Are We Our Brothers' Keepers?*).

♦ *I see these inner-growth/spiritual reachings as the cause, not the consequence, of my turning to a simpler lifestyle* (from Elissa Wurf of Poultney, Vermont, a self-described former atheist who had no spiritual life five years before responding to the survey, and who has since developed a regular meditation practice, affirmed a commitment to Judaism, and reads volumes of spiritually-related books).

♦ *My spiritual life has been completely transformed. I have partici-pated in formal religious services off and on, but the foundation of my beliefs has been enriched by a lot of reading and a growing recognition of the role the universe or God plays in everyday life. I have started to see the miraculous in the ordinary, and am develop-ing a rock-solid faith that there is a path we are supposed to be on. If we stop fighting and start believing, we will get to the place(s) we are supposed to be. Letting go and having faith are the toughest, but most rewarding lessons I have learned* (from Deborah Lawrence of Indianapolis, Indiana).

♦ *I'm not real sure what happened first, but I think there was a spiritual surrender that opened the door to simplification. There followed three years of emptying out on all levels and another three years of "filling up," mostly spiritually. Life has become a joyful adventure—a conscious adventure. It's not without its struggles, but I see it all differently* (from Susan Libby of Warren, Pennsyl-vania).

Living simply in and of itself can be viewed as a spiritual act with deep meaning. Mark Burch, a study participant, explains how this works for him:

The practice of simple living has become, for me, an essential expres-sion of my spirituality. It both helps to "clear my mental deck" for a calm, silent, attentive practice of the things which seem to build my spiritual awareness, as well as being an expression of the fruits of that awareness. Living simply is, when you really think about it, a very radical and very public proclamation about just exactly what a person believes about the source of meaning and goodness in human life. It is at the same time a gentle reproach to consumerism, materialism, selfishness, competition, etc., and a very quiet affirmation of nonmaterial, interpersonal, ecological and community-based values. To me, that's pretty spiritual—and much more spiritual than worrying about whether or not one is obeying can-non laws.

Something rather magical happens when we start simplifying our lives. Without really trying, many people develop a greater aware-ness of a spiritual self, a sense of their own souls, and a sense of a connection to a spiritual presence larger than themselves. It all makes perfect sense. When you declutter your life of unneeded material possessions, unwanted social commitments, and excessive work re-lated stress, you create a space within yourself for some quiet, for an opportunity for reflection. Solitude and contemplation have long been the gateway to a spiritual life.

But spiritual awareness involves more than just having the time to think. Developing this awareness requires a certain frame of mind—a mind that openly seeks knowledge of the inner life. When we live simply, our relationship to the material side of life changes. Rather than being consumed by materialism, we choose to surround ourselves with only those material possessions we truly need or genu-inely cherish. Inevitably, this is less than what our North American culture would have us believe is necessary for the "good life." As a result of reducing the role of materialism in our lives, a door opens to the nonmaterial facets of life—relationships, pursuit of artistic and intellectual endeavors, and spirituality.

I share the belief of many of the study participants that we are all somehow connected on a spiritual level. In my view, it is one of life's great mysteries. My efforts to live simply are a reflection of that be-lief. I want to take only what I need, not because my taking less will necessarily provide greater resources to the truly poor, but out of honor and respect for the people who really do not have enough. This sentiment naturally flows from my belief that we are all one in some mysterious way.

Mindfulness

Many of the participants talk about mindfulness. They feel that simplicity is about living mindfully and consciously. Some of them believe that it is through the practice of daily, mindful living that we come to experience our spiritual selves. Mindful living is developed through the conscious awareness and appreciation of the tasks we do each day, of the people with whom we interact, and of the natural beauty that surrounds us. Mark Burch, a study participant, expresses what mindfulness means to him:

I think the conscious development of mindfulness is the essential core of a positive practice of simple living. I do this through meditation, martial arts, gardening and mindful living, but there are many other ways. I think mindfulness names an essentially different "paradigm of being" from the one represented by consumerist, market-driven lifestyles. Put simply: To the degree that we cultivate the capacity to enter deeply into the experience of the moment, we also cultivate the experience of joy, plenitude and well-being in our lives. This requires few things, but the capacity to know and enjoy them with profound intensity. It is a process, finally, of cultivating oneself and one's relationships with others, including God. Mainstream society consists of the exact opposite—ever briefer and more superficial encounters with ever larger quantities of goods, services, and people. There is no pleasure or contact, only the giddy adrenaline-fueled whirl of changing experience without substance, touch without intimacy, information without meaning, company without community.

Living simply and mindfully seems to create a consciousness shift in how we view time. We tend to lose any sense of time being scarce—that feeling there is never enough of this precious resource—and focus more on living in the present without worrying about what else we could or should be doing right now. Katy DeBra, a study participant from Long Island, New York, describes how simplicity has affected her experience of time:

Simplifying has led me to give myself a break, to live more presently and in the moment, thereby allowing myself the chance to gain greater satisfaction from every little thing I do. I feel more purposeful yet am losing the need to be doing something all the time. I no longer feel I have to read every magazine I get in case I miss some life-changing article, or make to-do lists all the time, in case I forget something. I am no longer so afraid of the prospect of doing nothing. I am more interested in listening to others and less interested in getting in my two cents.

Relationship to Nature

Closely associated with a spiritual life are the participants' experiences of nature. When we slow down the pace of our lives, we seem automatically to gravitate to natural beauty. We notice natural beauty in ways and in places we never looked before. It can happen anywhere, as described by Sarah Hagan, a study participant from Cambridge, Massachusetts:

Longing for more of the natural world was one of the first things that stirred thoughts of voluntary simplicity/financial independence in me. I was working in a 40-story office building in 1993 and it had been a stressful, hectic day. I was running to deliver a file to another office when I looked up. In front of me was a conference room with the door ajar and through that door I could see the most stunning, vibrant sunset through floor-to-ceiling windows. I literally stopped moving and stared through that doorway until, looking around to make sure no one saw where I was going, I went into the room and closed the door. The experience reminded me of the medieval monks who prayed in cells that were plain on three walls and painted with a beautiful, inspirational spiritual scene on the fourth wall. I felt like that conference room was temporarily transformed into a spiritual space that evening, and I remember so clearly thinking, "What is really important here: that this folder is delivered or that I can experience nature?"

The amount of time spent in nature by the simplicity study participants is set forth in the chart in Figure 14-4.

Figure 14-4: Time Spent in Nature by Participants	
37%	Little or no time spent in nature
33%	Moderate time spent in nature, such as trips to neighborhood parks and summer camping trips
30%	Extensive time spent in nature, such as living in a rural environment, regular walks or hikes away from traffic and buildings, frequent camping, canoeing, birding

Reducing our dependence and attachment to material possessions seems to open a door, a passageway to an intimate relationship with nature, leading us to experience the majesty and awe of the world we live in. About ten years ago, Terri Reed sold her house in a northeastern city, quit her job and took to the road in her truck, taking little other than a tent to sleep in and her dog, Bella, for companionship. Almost three years later, Terri settled down in an abode she describes as "a small bungalow in the forest, under a dozen pine trees that are at least 200 years old." She cannot imagine going back to a life in the city:

When I visit the northeast, I feel like a Martian, an alien from another planet. My bungalow in the forest is sort of like a continuation of my wonderful travels, which I dearly enjoyed. Life was wonderfully simple during my years of living on the road and being resourceful. During my travels, I got in tune with the earth, this planet we all live on. I remember laying in my tent, straining to hear the wind, wondering if it might storm or rain, and marveling about how the air currents move, ocean tides change, the earth's rotation angle changes constantly, and seeing the moon and stars all in place like they taught us in fourth grade, and here I am, a speck of life in all this majesty.

It's an awesome experience to shed everything—a job, a house, friends, family—and to make each day fun without TV, malls, commercialism, etc. I suppose during those years of simplicity, I just decided that less was more.

Nature's ecstasy is not limited to those who enjoy a camping lifestyle. Sally Armstrong, whose story is told in Chapter Six, *Work We Can Live With: A Balancing Act*, describes her attraction to nature's splendor:

My vacations are usually in nature. I just spent a week on the coast of Maine watching the ocean and the moon change. Being nearer to the stars, having all the windows open day and night to feel almost as if we were outside. I've never been much for overnight camping, but being close to nature has grown since I left the corporate world. I remember the awe I felt when I first found myself living a simpler life, watching the change of light at sunset, hearing the birds and animals, seeing the seasons change. Life became much more living for me.

Housing

Our home is our castle—or is it? Sometimes, it is our prison. It can hold us hostage to a job we may not enjoy. It can steal our zest for life by presenting us with a long list of chores to be done each weekend. But our home can also be a refuge, a source of comfort and joy, and a friend. So, obviously, the trick is avoiding the former and creating the latter.

The simplicity study participants displayed considerable enthusiasm about their homes. They talked about cozy, light-filled rooms, and spaces that are just right and not too big. Some of them had downsized from larger homes. Only two who had moved into smaller quarters expressed any regrets. The chart in Figure 14-5 provides a breakdown of the size of residences of the participants who answered this question (Note: some respondents referred to square footage; others mentioned the number of bedrooms):

Figure 14-5: Size of Participants' Homes	
60%	Fewer than two bedrooms or less than 1,300 square feet
21%	Three bedrooms or 1,400 to 2,000 square feet
19%	More than 2,000 square feet or four or more bedrooms

Since 1950, the size of the average home being built in the United States has roughly doubled to the current average size of approximately 2,200 feet. During these last fifty years, homes have not only grown larger, but they have also taken on more of a showpiece quality, featuring massive formal rooms with soaring ceilings, large expanses of glass, and marble entryways. Some of the formal rooms in these homes are rarely used. How many times have you attended a party in a home where the living and dining rooms remain empty while the crowd hangs out in the more comfortable, more inviting kitchen and family rooms? Sarah Susanka, well-known architect of residential homes and author of *The Not So Big House*, presents an effective case against building large homes for display, offering instead a vision of homes with aesthetically pleasing rooms that are used everyday and that are not too big.

Eighty-one percent of the study participants live in homes that are smaller than the national average. While their choices may be motivated primarily by economics, it is interesting to note that when this group talks of their hopes and dreams, living in a larger home is rarely mentioned.

The majority of the study participants (62 percent) own their homes, or as some of them related, they and their lenders own their homes. Of those who rent, a few mentioned that they are saving to buy a home, but many of the renters expressed a genuine content- ment with renting, citing the savings of money and labor required for maintenance, insurance, and property taxes.

Transportation

For many of us, finding the right home and the right job are the major infrastructure decisions of our lives. If we are pleased with our choices in these two areas, then life makes sense. But we often neglect to connect the dots between the two. We don't pay much attention to the third major infrastructure decision of our lives— how we are going to transport ourselves to and from our home and work, and to other places we might frequent. Often, transportation to and from work is an afterthought, viewed as a necessary but un- pleasant aspect of modern life.

In fact, the need to transport our bodies from one place to an- other has major implications for the quality of our lives. For example, if we commute an hour each way to our jobs, that is ten hours a week that we spend in transit. Those are ten hours you might use for other activities, such as a morning walk, meditation or prayer, or a leisurely breakfast with your spouse or children.

More often than not, commuting is not high quality time. Driv- ing in heavy traffic is physically restrictive and mentally draining, no matter how entertaining the books on tape or music you have play- ing in the background. Even if your commute takes you on quiet, peaceful, scenic roads, you are driving at times when your mind is often on something other than the landscape. You are thinking about what lies ahead in your work day, or decompressing from your day's efforts.

Even if you commute by public transportation, a long commute will often drain you. Traveling is not inherently stressful, but there is quite a difference between a Sunday afternoon ride in the country and traveling at the beginning or end of a long work day.

In America, it is not uncommon for families to live in suburbs far away from their jobs. These days, with property values skyrocketing, many people are commuting as much as 100 miles a day to enjoy this home in the suburbs. We say we do this because we want a nice home (affordable only in the suburbs) in a safe neighborhood. However, a growing number of people are questioning these assumptions. Let's say the price of an 1,800-square-foot home in the suburbs is roughly equivalent to that of a 1,400-square-foot home in a city neighborhood that is closer to our jobs and other events we might want to attend. The home in the suburbs comes with a 45-minute drive to work, in contrast to the 15-minute bus ride you could take from the city home. Is that home in the suburbs really more affordable? Perhaps the city home would allow you to go from a two-car to a one-car family, resulting in significant savings each year. And what value do you place on the additional wear and tear on your body and psyche each week?

But, you say, we need the larger home. We have two children and we need the space. Again, we need to question these assumptions. How is it that American families in the 1950's lived in homes half the size they live in now and reported a higher level of happiness than they do today? Also, consider the time and energy savings of living in a smaller home in a city neighborhood. You will likely have a smaller lot than you would in the suburbs, resulting in less time and expense for yard maintenance. If you are a parent, you will spend less time chauffeuring your children to events. There will be more opportunities for your older children to walk, bicycle, or take a bus to their friends' homes and other activities.

I do not doubt that suburban life may be ideal for some families. Rural living is the best choice for others. The point here is to consider the total package—home, work, *and* transportation—before choosing the individual elements of your life's infrastructure.

In general, the simplicity study participants considered the issue of transportation as an important factor when choosing the location

of their home and place of work. Limiting the time they spend driving or riding in an automobile is a high priority, not only to save
wear and tear on the body, mind, and pocketbook, but also because
of the environmental harm caused by driving automobiles. In contrast to the negative aspects of commuting by car, the participants
stressed the benefits of walking or riding a bicycle to get from place
to place. Steve Cullinan, a study participant from Albuquerque, New
Mexico, walks the three miles between his home and his work:

*My walk to and from work (six miles a day) is my primary form of
exercise. This is also my commute, so I no longer have to pay for parking,
buy as much gas for my car, maintain it as often or find time to exercise
after work. This has truly been a simplifying factor in my life.*

The number of cars in the participants' households is summa-
rized in the chart in Figure 14-6.

Figure 14-6: Number of Cars in Participants' Households

60%	One car per adult
24%	One car for two adults
12%	No cars
4%	More than one car per adult

Those in the study who live auto-free seem to thrive on that choice
(see the stories of Melissa Reid in Chapter Nine, *Starting Out Simply:
Generation X Takes a U-Turn*, and "Q" in Chapter Eleven, *Living Well
on Very Little: Amazing Stories of Courageous People*). While the majority
of the participants (60 percent) follow the typical pattern in America
of owning one car per adult in the family, it is significant that 36
percent of the families are either auto-free or share a car. Learning
to live well with fewer cars is an important step in conserving the
diminishing resources of the earth.

Self-Sufficiency

One of the issues explored in the simplicity study is the subject of self-sufficiency—the act of meeting your material needs directly yourself or within your own family, rather than depending on outside goods and services. This is a frequent and sometimes provocative topic within simple living circles. Are people who live simply isolationists? Is it somehow more desirable or admirable if we make our own clothes, for example, rather than buy them in a store? Is the point of doing things yourself to save money, or is there some greater purpose served? What about bartering or exchanging goods and services with others in our community? At the time of this writing, concerns about potential disruptions of life as we know it as a result of the so-called Y2K problem place even greater emphasis on these questions.

The simplicity study participants had plenty to say about these matters. They commented on the types of activities they either did themselves or hired others to do, such as cutting their own (or members of their family) hair, growing their own food, repairing appliances and automobiles, maintaining and cleaning their homes, landscaping and gardening, and building or remodeling their homes. The chart in Figure 14-7 provides an overview of the level of self-sufficiency versus dependence on others reported by the participants:

Figure 14-7: Level of Self-Sufficiency by Participants

41%	Little or no self-sufficiency
36%	Moderate level of self-sufficiency
23%	High level of self-sufficiency

In interpreting the level of self-sufficiency by the participants, I classified bartering and sharing of goods and services within the community as a form of self-sufficiency rather than a form of dependence on others. For example, one participant's daughter babysits for her piano teacher in exchange for piano lessons. Another homesteading participant (Jenna Duran, who is profiled in Chapter Five, *Urban or Rural Simplicity: Choosing a Nurturing Milieu*) exchanged maple syrup and tomatoes for her midwife's services. I made a distinction between paying for goods and services with money (dependence on outside goods) or with goods or labor of our own (self-sufficiency).

The people who are self-sufficient to some degree were motivated in part to save money. They would rather clean their own homes or repair their automobiles than pay for those services. But there were non-monetary motivating factors as well. Some participants felt a reassuring sense of security from being able to take care of their own needs. Chandra Bennett, a woman who works full-time as an administrator, and also gardens, bakes bread, and sews clothes for her family, explains what these activities mean to her:

Doing stuff for yourself does cycle energy back into your being. The result goes beyond satisfaction, which is a self-centered feeling, to a real sense of security. Doing for myself, no matter how time-consuming the task might be, means to me that I can handle almost any situation or disaster. I have no fear about the future. If we return to the Dark Ages, I know I can live well as a modern day caveman if need be. So the sense of security, of serenity in the face of the unknown future, is the best result of doing for yourself no matter how much time is spent on the task.

Eliminating the *middle men* in life can be wonderfully simple. I may choose to do more for myself not because I am averse to being dependent on others, but from my desire to live more simply. If I can fix my own car, I don't need to call for an appointment, make arrangements to drop off and pick up the car, and earn the income to pay for the labor. In my experience, doing my own housecleaning simplifies my life in that I don't need to hire and supervise someone, coordinate with that person when I am out of town, and have someone in my home when I am trying to write.

When you simplify you tend to do more for yourself, if for no other reason than to conserve money. As a result, you experience life more directly, cooking your own food rather than dining out, walking or bicycling instead of driving, or repairing something yourself. These experiences bring you closer to your essence and to the earth. In other words, there are fewer layers between your essential self and the experiences of your life.

John Burroughs, in his classic essay, *What Life Means to Me*, published in 1906, expresses this phenomenon beautifully:

Many persons know the luxury of a skin bath—a plunge in the pool or the wave unhampered by clothing. That is the simple life—direct and immediate contact with things, life with the false wrappings torn away—the fine house, the fine equipage, the expensive habits, all cut off. How free one feels, how good the elements taste, how close one gets to them, how they fit one's body and one's soul! To see the fire that warms you, or better yet, to cut the wood that feeds the fire that warms you; to see the spring where the water bubbles up that slakes your thirst, and to dip your pail into it...to be in direct and personal contact with the sources of your material life; to want no extras, no shields; to find the universal elements enough; to find the air and the water exhilarating; to be refreshed by a morning walk, or an evening saunter...to be thrilled by the stars at night; to be elated over a bird's nest, or over a wild flower in spring—these are some of the rewards of the simple life.

The Stuff in our Lives

Our relationship to material possessions is a powerful one. Many writers have explored this relationship—living with less stuff, getting great buys for your stuff, organizing your stuff, decluttering your stuff (see the Books section of the Resource Guide at the end of this book). It is a popular topic in simple living circles. The full impact of this relationship is beyond the scope of this book, but the following serves as a basic primer on the relationship between simplicity and the stuff in our lives:

♦ Deprivation is not part of the simplicity experience.

♦ The key is balance. Your material possessions should support and empower you to live an authentic life, a life that values meaningful work, quality relationships, respect for the earth, and spiritual and/or inner growth. Either too much or too little will complicate your life and draw away time and energy from living these values. Most of us find that we have too much stuff in our lives and gradually pare down the volume.

♦ Aesthetics in our daily lives—being surrounded by beauty, both man-made and earthly beauty—is an important priority for most of us. Witness the appeal of the bestselling book, *Simple Abundance*, by Sarah Ban Breathnach. The marriage of simplicity and man-made beauty is nothing new. For example, the Arts and Crafts movement of the early twentieth century promoted simple, high quality *and beautiful* furnishings and accessories.

♦ Simplicity often results in a greater love for material possessions (this is not a typo!). If your possessions truly support an authentic life of your highest values, you will naturally come to respect and care for those possessions. With fewer possessions and greater mindfulness in your daily life, you learn to appreciate and cherish what you have.

♦ Material objects appear to have a spirit of their own. Perhaps it is the human and spiritual energy that went into creating the item. When we honor and respect that spirit, we naturally do not want to waste these material resources. This leads to our desire to pass on those items we do not need or refrain from acquiring them in the first place.

♦ *How much is enough* is entirely a subjective inquiry. What seems a burden to one person may be an aesthetic enhancement to another. It is a very personal choice. Good questions to ask yourself as you contemplate acquiring or keeping a material possession are: "Will the presence of (fill in the blank) enhance my life in ways that are truly satisfying to me?" and "What is the impact of my consumption patterns on others and on the environment?"

A sense of deprivation and sacrifice will eat away at you and not let you live the life of peace and fulfillment you want to live. It is important to distinguish *deprivation* from *deferred gratification*. Sometimes we put off getting a material object we desire in order to have more freedom and peace of mind now. The key is not to give anything up unless it is based on a decision to go for something better, such as the time and freedom to do work that we love or the satisfaction of giving to others. Richard Gregg, author of the essay, *The Value of Voluntary Simplicity* (see the Books section of the Resource Guide at the end of this book), shared with Mahatma Gandhi his frustration about his desire to keep so many books. Gandhi responded, "Then don't give them up. As long as you derive inner help and comfort from anything, you should keep it."

Many of the simplicity study participants report a feeling of liberation when they let go of those material possessions they do not need or genuinely cherish (see, for example, the story of Brent and Ellen Farrow in Chapter Five, *Urban or Rural Simplicity: Choosing a Nurturing Milieu*). Melissa Reid, whose story is told in Chapter Nine, *Starting Out Simply: Generation X Takes a U-Turn*, shares her positive experiences of living with less:

I continue to pare away a little at a time to see what I can really do without. How did Thoreau put it? "A man is rich in proportion to the number of things which he can afford to let alone." I believe that. The less I have, the calmer and richer I feel. Every year I go through my possessions and either sell or give away what I'm not using, and I guess I'm not quite done yet, as I still manage to find a little every year.

Living lightly on a material basis can translate into an emotional and spiritual lightness of being. Mark Burch describes his experience:

I have removed a great deal of extraneous "stuff" from the decoration of my home, which has lent it a certain quality of Zen-like minimalism. I find that my decoration preferences are moving more and more away from human-made objects and toward living things (like plants), or natural objects, like rocks or wood. I've found that as I simplify my physical surroundings, I experience an ever-increasing inward lightness of being. There is a clearness, a spiritual quality about the emptiness of space, the ambience created by plants, the lovely textures and colours you can find in some rocks, with a tastefully placed painting or shard of stained glass as an accent. That's what I think human artifacts should be—accents that complement nature.

Our minds can optimally handle only so much stimulation, a finite number of *things* to attend to. If we reduce the load of material possessions in our lives, we make more room for the nonmaterial rewards in life, such as relationships, spirituality, passions, hobbies, and meaningful work.

Since this is such a subjective area unique to each person and family, there are no set guidelines for determining how much (and of what) is enough. John Stott, of Madison, Wisconsin, carries in his wallet his *Purchase Manifesto*, a typed card of criteria he refers to when considering a purchase:

Aesthetic/appeal
Versatility/functionality
Earth friendly
Well made/repairable – Is there a warranty?
Value - would a used version be just as good or better?
Consider substitutions
Do I really need this?

Many of the study participants buy used cars, clothing, furniture, and appliances. They do this not only to save money but also out of respect for the earth's diminishing resources. They do not feel they are sacrificing quality one bit. Quality and aesthetics are not exclusively the province of brand new merchandise; in fact, the reverse can often be true.

I found two books to be especially helpful for making choices about material possessions in my life. In his book *How to Want What You Have: Discovering the Magic and Grandeur of Ordinary Existence*, Timothy Miller talks about our innate desires to always want more. Miller not only validates a part of me that I sometimes want to ignore, he also prescribes an effective treatment—developing *compassion, attention*, and *gratitude* in your daily life—to deal with those insatiable desires.

To Have or To Be?, by Erich Fromm, is an inspiring treatise about the distinct experiences of *having* and *being* in the world. I learned an invaluable lesson from this book: I do not need to own something to experience its pleasures. I am fortunate to live in a beautiful town, graced with old-world style architecture and wondrous gardens. I walk everywhere—to the post office, bank, library, bookstore, grocery store, photocopying shop, and several stage theaters, all of which are within a six-block radius of my home. My husband and I live in a rather plain condominium compared to some of the incredibly charming cottages and homes in our town. Rather than feel sorry for myself for not being able to afford to live in one of those charming cottages, I focus on the beauty that surrounds me. When I walk around town, my eyes feast on the beautiful gardens and architecture—sometimes my heart skips a beat. I often feel a twinge of guilt for receiving the gift of this beauty without any effort (money or labor) on my part. I also enjoy three-mile walks along the ocean almost daily. All of this beauty in my life is not exactly free—property values in my town are very high because of it—but I don't need to *own* the gardens, the charming cottages, or the ocean to experience their beauty. It's a revolutionary concept to me—I don't need to possess these things in order to enjoy them!

Developing a new relationship with the stuff in our lives is not an intellectual exercise. We cannot just wake up one day and decide to feel differently. We need to evolve organically in this area. We need to experiment with having more or less stuff in our lives, and then observe our reactions. It is best to take your time and be patient. Sometimes a change in our relationship to material possessions will trigger other changes in our lives. Here is what happened for Tabitha Metreger, a study participant:

The change in my life did not involve a decision to stop doing everything I did before; it was a decision to stop and think about something before I did it. I just can't stress enough how liberating it is. I was living my life, as most people do, not realizing how complicated my life was and how much anxiety it caused me. It wasn't until I began to give away many of my possessions and stopped buying new ones that I realized happiness cannot be found in material items. I never would have said I was searching for happiness through commodities, but that's what I was doing. Our lives are centered around consumerism—not religion, community, or family. And everyone wants to be happy. Thankfully, I finally realized I was just chasing my tail. Not only does consumerism not make us happy, but it actually causes us unhappiness. I had to break my consuming habits before I realized this, however. Now I am working at getting my life centered on the things that do really matter—my spirituality, my family, and the community.

Parting Words

People often ask me what are the five or ten things they can do to simplify their lives. "Gee, whiz," I want to say, "I don't have a clue." Well, if you were one of my younger sisters or a close friend (for whom I have unlimited reservoirs of advice), I would have plenty of suggestions. But remember: Simplicity is an inside job, and it will find a unique expression for each person. To live simply, we must answer the callings from within. We must pay attention to those rumblings. First we must hear them.

So, if I were to tell you how to simplify your life, I would advise you first to quiet your life. I would suggest that you carve out moments of reflection for yourself on a regular basis. Out of this experience of systematic reflection, your life of simplicity will become clear to you. If you were to insist that I be a little more specific, lend you a hand, give you just a smidgen of guidance, I suppose I would offer you this:

A Prescription for a Simple Life

1. Write in a journal daily, or almost daily.
2. Take three to four months off every few years and go live in some very different place, preferably a foreign country.
3. Limit your work (outside of the home) to 30 hours a week, 20 if you are a parent.
4. Don't let any material thing come into your home unless you absolutely love it and want to keep it for the rest of your life or until it is beyond repair.
5. Spend at least an hour a week in a natural setting, away from crowds of people, traffic, and buildings. Three to four hours of nature time each week is even better.
6. Live in a home with only those rooms that you or someone in your family use every day.
7. Select a home and place of work no more than 30 minutes away from each other.
8. Do whatever you need to do to connect with a sense of spirit in your life, whether it be prayer, religious services, meditation, spiritually-related reading, or walking in nature.
9. Seek the support of others who want to simplify their lives. Join or start a simplicity circle if you enjoy group interaction.
10. Practice saying no. Say no to those things that don't bring you inner peace and fulfillment, whether it be more things, more career responsibility, or more social activities.

I offer you my warmest wishes on your journey to simplicity!

APPENDIX

Text of Simplicity Survey

A. WORK LIFE. Describe the nature of your work life and how you feel about your work. How many hours do you work each week? If you made changes in your work as part of your efforts to simplify your life, describe how you feel about the changes.

B. HOME. Describe your current your home or apartment. Do you own or rent? Location? Size? Cost/Expenses? Style/aesthetic factors? Did you change your residence as part of your efforts to simplify your life? If so, how do you feel about the changes?

C. YOUR STUFF. Describe in general terms your needs, wants and current use of appliances, furnishings, clothes, entertainment toys, etc.? Do you own a TV? If so, how many hours per week do you watch TV? Have you made significant changes in these areas as an effort to simplify your life?

D. NON-WORK TIME. Describe in general how you spend your non-work time. Do your leisure activities represent major changes as a result of simplifying your life?

E. RELATIONSHIPS. Have your relationships with family and close friends changed in significant ways since you made changes to simplify your life? If you have children, what has been the impact of simplification on their lives and your experience of raising them? Please describe.

F. ENVIRONMENTAL ISSUES. Describe your interest, if any, in environmental issues, including any practices you engage in to preserve the earth's resources. Has any of this changed since you started to simplify your life? Please describe.

G.   COMMUNITY.   Describe in general terms your involvement with community and/or concern for societal/global issues. Has your interest changed at all as a result of your efforts to simplify your life? If so, how so?

H.   HEALTH. Describe your activities in the following areas and indicate whether these activities represent a major change in your life as part of your efforts to simplify:
  1. Your eating patterns (are you a vegetarian?)
  2. Your exercise habits (what exercise, if any, do you regularly engage in?)
  3. Other health enhancing practices (any alternative, holistic or preventive health practices?)

I. SPIRITUALITY/INNER GROWTH/RELIGION. Describe your participation in religious and/or spiritual practices and experiences. Do you engage in any activities such as prayer, church services, meditation, yoga, journal writing, or spiritually related reading? Do these practices/experiences represent changes resulting from your efforts to simplify? If so, please describe.

J. NATURE. Do you spend time in nature? If so, what do you do and how often? Has this changed at all since you started to simplify?

K. SELF-RELIANCE. Have you altered your dependence on outside goods and services for your daily living needs, such as repairs, cleaning, gardening, clothes, grooming? Please describe.

L. TRANSPORTATION. What type of transportation do you use to get around? Do you walk, bicycle, or use public transportation regularly? How many cars per adult (18 years or older) are in your household? Is your current transportation means related to your efforts to simplify? If so, how so?

M. MONEY. Have your income and expenses changed in a major way (other than already described above) since you made the move to simplify your life? Please explain.

N. MOTIVATION/ATTITUDES.

1. What were the primary events or influences that motivated you to make changes to simplify your life?
2. With respect to your life prior to making changes toward simplification, what did you like and not like about that life? Do you miss it? Any part of it?
3. What do your friends and family think of the changes you have made?

O. ABOUT YOU. Please state the following information:

1. Your age:
2. Your gender: M or F
3. Your race or ethnic identification (optional):
4. Your marital (or cohabitation) status:
5. The number and ages of children living with you:
6. Your occupation:
7. Your total household annual income:
   a. Under $10,000
   b. $10,000 to $25,000
   c. $25,000 to $50,000
   d. $50,000 to $75,000
   e. $75,000 to $100,000
   f. Over $100,000
8. Your total number of years of formal education (including grammar school, high school, college, post graduate):

9. Type of area where you live:
   a. Rural area
   b. Small town (under 20,000 pop.)
   c. Suburban or bedroom community (less than 100,000 pop.)
   d. Medium sized urban area (100,000 to 500,000 pop.)
   e. Large city (over 500,000 pop.)
10. Your religion, if any:

P. OTHER INFORMATION. Please share any other experiences, thoughts or feelings that have been significant in your process of simplifying your life.

Q. SOURCE. How did you hear about this survey?

Resource Guide

The following resources will broaden your understanding and study of simplicity. While this list is far from exhaustive, it includes some of the better writings and resources in this area. If you discover that a book is out of print, do not despair. Your local public library may have it. If it does not, ask your librarian if they participate in an "inter-library loan program." If so, they may be able to borrow the book from another library for you.

Books (alphabetically, by author's last name)

Andrews, Cecile. *The Circle of Simplicity: Return to the Good Life*. New York: Harper Collins, 1997. In this book, Cecile Andrews explores themes integral to simplicity, such as finding your passion, living authentically, connecting with community, and spirituality. As the foremost leader in the development of voluntary simplicity study circles, Andrews discusses the significance of a study circle as a learning tool, a form of democracy in action, and a way to experience community with others.

Aslett, Don. *Clutter's Last Stand: It's Time to De-Junk Your Life*. Cincinatti: Writer's Digest Books, 1984. Writing with a touch of Dave Barry type humor, Don Aslett discusses our stuff—why we buy it, why we hoard it well beyond its pleasurable or useful life, and how to let go of it. In addition to all the obvious tangible items like clothes, furnishings, books, and office paraphernalia, he also delves into mental clutter, such as money (tracking it, investing it, and managing it), people, and activities that complicate your life.

Bender, Sue. *Plain & Simple: A Woman's Journey to the Amish*. New York: Harper, 1989. In this book, Sue Bender describes her experiences of living with the Amish. She is impressed with how the

Amish live mindfully, viewing their daily work as inherently valuable. Bender reveals the Amish lifestyle of living in a community in which they help each other out with medical and other needs, thereby reducing the need for outside support.

Bennett, Hal Zina and Susan J. Sparrow. *Follow Your Bliss*. Ukiah, CA: Tenacity Press, 1997. This book is an excellent companion for your journey to simplicity. The authors show us how to first discover, and then follow, our bliss through the exploration of our inner selves. With this self-knowledge, we can then embark on our life paths, creating work and relationships that bring inner peace and fulfillment.

Blix, Jacqueline and David Heitmiller. *Getting a Life: Strategies for Simple Living Based on the Revolutionary Program for Financial Freedom from Your Money or Your Life* (revised edition). New York: Viking Penguin, 1999. This book is a sequel to *Your Money or Your Life*, often referred to as the bible of simple living. The authors share the inspiring stories of people (including their own) who have used the nine-step program in *Your Money or Your Life* to live with greater financial intelligence, financial integrity, and in some cases, financial independence.

Burch, Mark. *Simplicity: Notes, Stories and Exercises for Developing Unimaginable Wealth*. Gabriola Island, B.C.: New Society Publishers, 1995. In this beautifully written book, Mark Burch discusses the spiritual nature of voluntary simplicity, mindfulness, direct personal involvement in our everyday living, ecological issues such as reducing waste and consumption, sustainable development, and a more equitable distribution of the world's wealth and resources.

Campbell, Jeff. *Clutter Control: Putting Your Home on a Diet*. New York: Dell Publishing, 1992. This book discusses all the "stuff" in our lives. Jeff Campbell touches on some of the psychological aspects of our relationship to our things and suggests ways of managing our lives and our stuff to reduce the negative impact of too much clutter.

Cloninger, Claire. *A Place Called Simplicity*. Eugene, OR: Harvest House, 1993. Claire Cloninger is a lyricist, public speaker and writer who writes this inspirational book from a strong, Christian perspective. She describes her own story of moving from Mobile, Alabama to a log cabin in a rural area overlooking the Alabama river (Juniper Landing) and also provides many, thoughtful ideas for traveling on the path to a place called simplicity.

Cox, Connie and Cris Evatt. *30 Days to a Simpler Life*. New York: The Penguin Group, 1998. This book is an excellent resource for simplifying your physical environment. The authors offer guidance on organizing your living spaces, your office, your wardrobe, photos, books, magazines—all the "stuff" in our lives. Travel, financial planning, and leisure are also covered.

Dacyczn, Amy. *The Complete Tightwad Gazette: Promoting Thrift as a Viable Alternative Lifestyle*. New York: Random House, 1999. This publication consolidates material from the author's former newsletter and books. Amy Dacyczn presents detailed, practical, and thoroughly researched ideas for ways to live frugally. This book would be particularly useful for people who are living close to the land, enjoy working with their hands and are parents.

Dappen, Andy. *Shattering the Two-Income Myth: Daily Secrets for Living Well on One Income*. Mountlake Terrace, WA: Brier Books, 1997. This excellent book provides a thoughtful summary of why and how we evolved into a two-income society, as well as practical advice on how to live on one income. Andy Dappen offers many good suggestions for maintaining a life of quality while keeping costs down.

Dominguez, Joe and Vicki Robin. *Your Money or Your Life: Transforming Your Relationship with Money and Achieving Financial Independence*. New York: Viking Penguin, 1992. In this bestseller, often referred to as the "bible" of the voluntary simplicity movement, the authors present a nine-step program to reach financial independence. The premise of the book is that we can live a higher quality of life with less materialistic trappings and help save the earth at the same time. The book provides a good blend of philosophical and practical advice on why and how to accomplish this. A revised edition is scheduled to be released in the fall of 1999.

Durning, Alan. *How Much is Enough?: The Consumer Society and the Future of the Earth*. New York: W.W. Norton, 1992. In this book, Alan Durning provides a comprehensive overview of the consumer society—how we got to where we are, the damage done to the earth by the consumer class, and the striking lack of fulfillment resulting from the consumer way of life. He asserts that true fulfillment comes from the nonmaterial aspects of life, such as relationships, work and leisure. This book is both scholarly and easy to read!

Elgin, Duane. *Awakening Earth: Exploring the Evolution of Human Culture and Consciousness*. New York: William Morrow, 1993. With this visionary, hopeful, and insightful text, Elgin has produced a brilliant, intellectual perspective of where we are, how we got here, and what we can do to improve the odds that we will avoid ecological collapse and social anarchy.

————. *Voluntary Simplicity: Toward a Way of Life that is Outwardly Simple, Inwardly Rich* (revised edition). New York: William Morrow, 1993. First published in 1981, this classic text was the forerunner of the many books and articles on simplicity published later in the decade and in the 1990's. The book evolved from a study completed by the author while working as a social scientist for SRI International. Duane Elgin considers the implications of voluntary simplicity from both the individual and societal or global points of view. The tone of the book is philosophical. It is an excellent overall review of voluntary simplicity.

Fogler, Michael. *Un-Jobbing: The Adult Liberation Handbook* (revised edition). Lexington, KY: Free Choice Press, 1999. Michael Fogler, a freelance musician and peace activist, discusses the benefits of living a home-based, freelance-work lifestyle rather than working in a single, full-time, career-oriented job. He challenges our cultural conditioning that a career position is necessary and desirable.

Fromm, Erich. *To Have or To Be?* New York: Harper, 1976. This is a thought-provoking, insightful book written by the well-known psychoanalyst and author of *The Art of Loving*. Erich Fromm explores the differences between the *having* mode, based on our relationship to things, and the *being* mode, based on our relationship to people. He discusses how the material abundance realized through the industrial revolution led us to an erroneous assumption that the satisfaction of material pleasures would bring us happiness.

Gregg, Richard. *The Value of Voluntary Simplicity*. Pendle Hill, 1936. This 31-page essay was written by the then Acting Director of Pendle Hill, a Quaker Center for Religious and Social Study. The essay is a clear and surprisingly contemporary view of why simplicity is needed and what its benefits are. Richard Gregg's comments about the ever-present desire for more stuff, the lack of time (even with all our technology), and keeping up with the Joneses are just as relevant today as they were in 1936. He takes a philosophical look at society and talks about why simplicity is so desperately needed, considering such issues as the competition and greed in our capitalistic economy and the need for spirituality. He is credited with coining the term, *voluntary simplicity*. This publication is out of print, but you should be able to get it through your library's inter-library loan program. It is worth the effort.

Johnson, Kevin and Donna Philippe. *Primal Conscious Living: Voluntary Creative Simplicity and the Biogenic Ecodesic Living Lighthouse*. Clinton, LA: L. Kevin Johnson and Donna Philippe, 1999. This 103-page, spiral handbook features practical information on biogenic living (including the Biogenic Ecodesic Living Lighthouse) and the authors' first person account of their journey to simplicity. For ordering information, contact Kevin Johnson at 4402

Gilead Road, Clinton, LA 70722 or the authors' web site, *EarthStar Primal Habitat Project* [www.geocities.com/~newliberty/earthstar].

Levering, Frank and Wanda Urbanska. *Simple Living: One Couple's Search for a Better Life* New York: Viking Penguin, 1992. This is a delightful book written by a married couple about their adventures in living simply. The authors take you on their journey from their life as struggling writers in Los Angeles to becoming working partners in an orchard business in Virginia owned by Frank's parents.

Lindbergh, Anne Morrow. *Gift From the Sea* (reissued edition). New York: Vintage Books, 1991. In this poetic rumination of her life and the values of simplicity, Anne Morrow Lindbergh describes the fast paced, crazy-making lives people were living at the middle of the twentieth century. She yearns to simplify her own life and writes beautifully about the values of simple living. Her language is exquisite, her metaphors captivating.

Long, Charles. *How to Survive Without a Salary: Learning to Live the Conserver Lifestyle* (revised edition). Toronto: Warwick Publishing, 1996. This book is about the conserver lifestyle, reducing expenses, saving, and earning casual income. It is not about surviving without income; it's about surviving without a salaried job. The emphasis is on earning casual income to meet monetary needs that have been reduced to a minimum.

Longacre, Doris Janzen. *Living More with Less*. Scottdale, PA: Herald Press, 1980. The theme of this book centers on the finite nature of the earth's resources and the need for the *haves* of this world to reduce their consumption of resources so that the *have-nots* have a shot at obtaining the basic necessities of life.

Luhrs, Janet. *The Simple Living Guide: A Sourcebook for Less Stressful, More Joyful Living*. New York: Broadway Books, 1997. This guide provides a comprehensive summary plus resources on various aspects of simple living, drawing on material gleaned from the author's newsletter, *Simple Living: The Journal of Voluntary Simplicity*. Topics include time, money, inner simplicity, work, simple pleasures and romance, virtues, families, holidays, cooking and nutrition, health and exercise, housing, clutter, gardening and travel.

Mate, Ferenc. *A Reasonable Life: Toward a Simpler, Secure, More Humane Existence*. Pflugerville, TX: Albatross Publishing, 1993. This book reveals a compelling, witty, radical and passionate diatribe on the state of American society, with corresponding suggestions on how to turn our world back right-side-up. In many ways, Ferenc Mate prescribes an utopian dream, but at the same time leaves the reader with no satisfactory explanations of why his visions could not, or should not, be realized. Mate has an uncanny ability to cut to the chase and tell the truth about the sad, loss of quality in our lives. He explores the loss of the life no longer common— relaxed, free, unencumbered childhood experiences, real community in country and village settings, a sense of security and self-reliance, and living in harmony with the earth. This book is truly inspirational, bordering on the revolutionary.

Meadows, Donella H., Dennis L. Meadows, and Jorgen Randers. *Beyond the Limits: Confronting Global Collapse, Envisioning A Sustainable Future*. Post Mills, VT: Chelsea Green Publishing, 1992. This scholarly book is a sequel to the international bestseller, *Limits to Growth*, published in 1972. The authors use a systems analysis approach to review the sustainability issues of population and capital growth, planetary sources for materials and energy, and the planet's ability to recycle or absorb the pollutants we create. The basic message is that if we continue on our current growth and use patterns, we are headed for a global collapse. However, the authors assure us that this result is not at all inevitable and suggest ways to turn our world around to provide a sustainable, sufficient lifestyle for all the world's inhabitants.

Miller, Ph.D., Timothy. *How to Want What You Have: Discovering the Magic and Grandeur of Ordinary Existence*. New York: Avon, 1996.

This is a powerful book written by a clinical psychologist. Miller contends that it is human nature to always want more; it is in our genetic makeup. But, alas, studies show that there is no connection between material wealth and happiness. In this book, Miller offers an alternative path to happiness, based on principles that have strong spiritual elements, namely, compassion, attention and gratitude.

Nearing, Scott and Helen. *The Good Life: Helen and Scott Nearing's Sixty Years of Self-Sufficient Living*. New York: Schocken Books, 1990. This one-volume book combines the authors' earlier books, *Living the Good Life* and *Continuing the Good Life*. The Nearings describe their experience of living a homesteading lifestyle in rural Vermont, complete with detailed descriptions of the work involved in providing food and shelter. The Nearings also promote the value of spending substantial leisure time engaged in reading, music, and conversation.

Postman, Neil. *Technopoly: The Surrender of Culture to Technology*. New York: Alfred A. Knopf, 1992. Postman defines *technopoly* as the cultural state of mind that assumes technology is always positive and of value. The book challenges that mind set, suggesting that we must be much more vigilant in our love affair with technology. It is really a lesson on mindfulness. Postman also contends that our culture is suffering from information glut—information appears indiscriminately, directed at no one in particular, in enormous volume, and at high speeds—that is disconnected from theory, meaning, or purpose.

Rechtschaffen, MD, Stephan. *Timeshifting: Creating More Time to Enjoy Your Life*. New York: Doubleday, 1996. This fascinating book explores the experience of time in our lives. Rechtschaffen focuses on the common experience of never having enough time and provides thought-provoking and insightful ways to view time differently, thereby creating and expanding time as we experience it. The core lessons to be learned from this book center on living mindfully in the present.

Robbins, John. *Diet for a New America: How Your Food Choices Affect Your Health, Happiness and the Future of Life on Earth* (reprint edition). Tiburon, CA: H. J. Kramer, 1998. Originally published in 1987, this book is an illuminating, fact-filled expose on the impact of America's meat and dairy agribusiness on our health and the well-being of the earth and its creatures. In addition to considerable discussion on the negative impact of animal products on our health, Robbins explains the connection between the meat and dairy industries and other themes common to the simple living philosophy, such as the unequal distribution of the earth's resources and environmental harm caused by producing animal products for mass consumption.

Robinson, Jo and Jean Coppock Staeheli. *Unplug the Christmas Machine: A Complete Guide to Putting Love and Joy Back into the Season* (revised edition). New York: William Morrow, 1991. This popular book is a classic on how to create a more meaningful holiday, focusing on deeply satisfying spiritual and family experiences rather than the shallow pleasures of materialism.

Schor, Juliet. *The Overspent American: Upscaling, Downshifting, and the New Consumer*. New York: Basic Books, 1998. Schor explores America's relationship with its spending patterns—why and how we spend and consume. She focuses on the psychological motivations for our spending, specifically our desire to keep up with the Joneses. She also discusses her recent research on people who have chosen to work less and spend less.

———. *The Overworked American: The Unexpected Decline of Leisure*. New York: BasicBooks, 1991. Schor presents an excellent discussion of the evolution of the American culture of work and consumerism, the work-and-spend treadmill. Schor's research shows that even though we have doubled our productivity in the last 50 years, we do not have more leisure in our lives. In fact, we have increased our workload by approximately one month per year. Schor presents compelling arguments for restructuring our work and spending lives to provide for less work, less spending, and more time for living.

Schumacher, E.F. *Small is Beautiful: Economics as if People Mattered*. New York: Harper, 1989 First published in 1973, this is a classic text written by a visionary British economist who exposes the damaging and short-sighted aspects of Western economies, specifically the desire for ever increasing growth without concern for non-renewable sources of energy. The book includes commentary and practical suggestions for solving world-wide problems of inequality of wealth and poverty in developing countries.

Shi, David E. *The Simple Life: Plain Living and High Thinking in American Culture*. New York: Oxford University Press, 1985. David Shi, a scholar and researcher of intellectual history, has written this comprehensive historical review of the various simplicity movements starting with the 17th century. What emerges is a cyclical pattern of periods of excess materialism followed by a return to simple living. Shi observes that Americans remain ambivalent about the values of simple living—espousing its virtues, but continuing to become enmeshed in the consumer culture.

Sinetar, Marsha. *Do What You Love, The Money Will Follow: Discovering Your Right Livelihood* New York: Paulist Press, 1987. In this inspirational best seller, Marsha Sinetar contends that it is possible to do work that you enjoy while also providing for your material needs. Sinetar explores the concept of right livelihood and describes the various paths some people have taken to realize their own versions of deeply satisfying work.

———. *Ordinary People as Monks and Mystics: Lifestyles for Self-discovery*. New York: Paulist Press, 1986. In this author's first book, Marsha Sinetar discusses the experiences of people who have explored their inner selves as part of the process of becoming whole, of becoming, in Abraham Maslow's words, a self-actualizing person. While the focus of the book is not voluntary simplicity, most of the study participants featured in this book are living simply.

St. James, Elaine. *Inner Simplicity: 100 Ways to Regain Peace and Nourish Your Soul*. New York: Hyperion, 1995. This book, the second in a series of bestselling books on simple living, focuses on our inner lives, offering inspiration for developing and nurturing our inner and spiritual selves. Like the style of the author's first book, *Simplify Your Life*, it is presented in the format of short, concise sections and is very easy to read.

————. *Living the Simple Life: a Guide to Scaling Down and Enjoying More*. New York: Hyperion, 1996. This book is a nice blend of the practical and the more spiritual or inner aspects of simple living which were presented in the author's first two books, *Simplify Your Life* and *Inner Simplicity*.

Susanka, Sarah. *The Not So Big House: A Blueprint for the Way We Really Live*. Newtown, CT: The Taunton Press, 1998. This book promotes the idea that what we need are informal homes that are not so big, where each room is used everyday. The author's web site [www.notsobighouse.com] contains information on simplicity and sustainability as they relate to shelter.

Thoreau, Henry David. *Walden*. Boston: Beacon Press, 1998. This new edition of Thoreau's classic, with an introduction by Bill McKibben, reveals the author's experience of living on Walden Pond for two years in the nineteenth century. Still relevant for today's world, Thoreau's writings are inspiring, providing a depth of meaning to the quest for simplicity.

Web Sites

Awakening Earth [www.awakeningearth.org] is a web site directed by author, speaker, and social entrepreneur Duane Elgin. This site provides resources in four major areas: indicators of global consciousness change, voluntary simplicity, media activism, and the evolution of human culture and consciousness.

Frugal Living Resources [www.igc.apc.org/frugal/frugal.html] provides a wide range of informational resources on frugal living and voluntary simplicity, including discussion lists, practical tips, and information on related books, newsletters and articles.

Growing Without Schooling [www.holtgws.com] is a comprehensive web site on homeschooling by John Holt of Holt Associates. This web site provides information on homeschooling books, the magazine *Growing Without Schooling*, and links to related sites.

Ithaca Hours Online [www.lightlink.com/hours/ithacahours] provides information on the local currency system serving Tompkins County, New York, a list of other communities using local currency systems, and a starter kit for setting up a new local currency system.

Intentional Communities Web Site [www.ic.org] is a comprehensive web site offering information and a directory of intentional communities (an inclusive term for ecovillages, cohousing, residential land trusts, communes, student co-ops, urban housing cooperatives and other housing projects). Also included are links to related sites.

Living Gently [www.islandnet.com/~see/living.htm] is a web site featuring articles from *Living Gently Magazine* promoting a voluntary simple and frugal lifestyle that enhances personal satisfaction and reduces environmental impacts.

The Simple Living Network [www.simpleliving.net] provides tools and examples for those who are serious about learning to live a more conscious, simple, healthy and restorative lifestyle. Their web site includes a free quarterly Newsletter, chat rooms, discussion message boards, a database of voluntary simplicity study groups and circles, links to other web sites and almost 3000 resource pages.

The Simplicity Resource Guide [www.gallagherpress.com/pierce] was created and is maintained by Linda Breen Pierce, the author of this book. It provides summaries of books, newsletters, organizations, and links to related sites on the topics of voluntary simplicity and simple living.

Additional web sites are included in the sections that follow.

Simplicity Study Circles

Andrews, Cecile. *The Circle of Simplicity: Return to the Good Life*. New York: Harper Collins, 1997. This book includes a guide to forming your own simplicity study circle, based on ten (at a minimum) weekly meetings of six to eight people. A summary of the book is included under the *Books* section above.

Burch, Mark. *Simplicity Study Circles: A Step-by-Step Guide* (New Society Publishers, 1997). The author of *Simplicity: Notes, Stories and Exercises for Developing Unimaginable Wealth* offers a guided tour of a study circle program based on ten meetings featuring different aspects of voluntary simplicity. Copies of the guide can be ordered from New Society Publishers, P.O. Box 189, Gabriola Island, B.C., Canada VOR IXO. (250) 247-9737. [www.newsociety.com].

Northwest Earth Institute offers instruction for an eight-session discussion course on voluntary simplicity. There are affiliated, regional groups that also offer these courses. For further information, contact Northwest Earth Institute at 921 SW Morrison, Suite 532, Portland, OR, 91205. (503) 227-2807.

Your Money or Your Life: A Study Guide for Groups (New Road Map Foundation). This guide is designed for groups to begin implementing the first five steps described in the book, *Your Money or Your Life*, by Joe Dominguez and Vicki Robin. These steps focus on tracking the money that is coming into, and going out of, your life, evaluating the exchange of life energy for money, and determining whether the expenditure of your life energy is in alignment with your life values and purpose. Available from *The Simple Living Network* (see Web Sites above).

Your Money or Your Life: A Study Guide for Contemporary Christians (New Road Map Foundation). This guide is a variation of the study guide for groups discussed above. It integrates Biblical teachings about money with the nine steps to transforming your relationship with money and achieving financial independence discussed in the book, *Your Money or Your Life*, by Joe Dominguez and Vicki Robin. Available from *The Simple Living Network* (see Web Sites above).

Your Money or Your Life: A Study Guide for Money and Spirit (New Road Map Foundation). This guide is similar to the other study guides published by The New Road Map Foundation (see above), with an emphasis on spiritual and philosophical readings from many traditions. Available from *The Simple Living Network* (see Web Sites above).

Workshops, Seminars and Educational Resources

Voluntary Simplicity Workshops by Mark Burch. Mark Burch is a writer, lecturer, and facilitator of workshops on voluntary simplicity. His workshops explore the relationship between voluntary simplicity and personal growth, mindfulness, healthy families and communities, and environmental sustainability. You can contact Mark Burch at P.O. Box 22071, Brandon, Manitoba, Canada R7A 6Y9. (204) 727-7253. E-mail: mburch@mb.sympatico.ca.

The Institute for Deep Ecology [www.deep-ecology.org] offers a series of training programs in deep ecology, described by the Institute in part as "a philosophy based on our sacred relationship with all beings." At the training, participants discover practices to help alter unsustainable patterns of thinking and acting. P.O. Box 1050, Occidental, CA 95465. (707) 874-2347. E-mail: ide@igc.org.

Newsletters and Magazines

The Accidental Entrepreneur is a newsletter devoted to the needs of the "accidental entrepreneur," defined as "one who has been fired, retired, laid off, reduced-in-force, downsized, rightsized, outsourced, bought out or fed up with corporate life." A wide range of topics relating to self-employment for corporate refugees is covered, including practical tips and motivational resources. 3421 Alcott Street, Denver, CO 80211. (303) 433-0345. E-mail: sknkwrks@ix.netcom.com.

The Caretaker Gazette [www.angelfire.com/wa/caretaker] is a newsletter dedicated to matching property owners who need caretakers with people who are interested in exchanging caretaking duties for free rent. P.O. Box 5887, Carefree, AZ 85377-5887. (480) 488-1970. E-mail: caretaker@uswest.net.

Changing Course [www.changingcourse.com] is a newsletter that provides creative alternatives to the 9-to-5 world, practical "how-to" advice and inspiration to help you live a simpler, more balanced life working at what you love. To subscribe, contact Making Waves, 137 Barrett Street, Northampton, MA 01060. (800) 267-6388. E-mail: info@changingcourse.com.

Simple Living: The Journal of Voluntary Simplicity [www.simpleliving.com] is a newsletter featuring tips on simple living, letters from readers who share their experiences, book reviews and more. 4509 Interlake Ave N, Box 149, Seattle, WA 98103. (206) 464-4800.

Yes! A Journal of Positive Futures [www.futurenet.org] features hopeful reports from the United States and around the world on efforts made toward integrating the self, nature, and community life in a responsible way. It is a project of the *Positive Futures Network*. P.O. Box 10818, Bainbridge Island, WA 98110-0818.
(800) 937-4451 (US) or (206) 842-0216.
E-mail: yes@futurenet.org.

Organizations

Center for a New American Dream [www.newdream.org] is a not-for-profit membership-based organization that helps individuals and institutions reduce and shift consumption to enhance quality of life and protect the environment. 6930 Carroll Avenue, Suite 900, Takoma Park, MD 20912. (301) 891-3683.
E-mail: newdream@newdream.org.

E.F. Schumacher Society [www.schumachersociety.org] is an educational, non-profit organization named after the author of *Small is Beautiful: Economics as if People Mattered.* The Society sponsors an annual lecture series and provides other resources designed to further Schumacher's vision of environmental sustainability and human-scale communities. 140 Jug End Road, Great Barrington, MA 01230. (413) 528-1737. E-mail: efssociety@aol.com.

International Biogenic Society is an organization that publishes the works of the late Edmond Bordeaux Szekely, a visionary scholar who wrote about living simply in nature (biogenic living), based on the principles of the Essene Gospel. The Society also conducts workshops in Canada. P.O. Box 849, Nelson, B.C., Canada V1L 6A5.

The New Road Map Foundation [www.newroadmap.org] is a not-for-profit, all volunteer organization that provides numerous resources, including books, audio tapes, study guides and pamphlets, relating to financial integrity, simple living, and preserving the earth's resources. P.O. Box 15981, Seattle, WA 98115. (206) 527-0437.

Seeds of Simplicity [www.slnet.com/cip/seeds] is a national, nonprofit membership organization helping to mainstream and symbolize the simplicity issue as a household word in America, especially through The Simplicity Circles Project. P.O. Box 9955, Glendale, CA 91226.(877) UNSTUFF [867-8833]. E-mail: seedsofsim@aol.com.

Index